BEYOND REAGAN

BEYOND REAGAN

The New Landscape
of American Politics

JERRY HAGSTROM

W·W·NORTON & COMPANY NEW YORK·LONDON

The text of this book is composed in Baskerville Alternate,
with display type set in Baskerville.
Composition and Manufacturing by the Haddon Craftsmen, Inc.

First Edition

Library of Congress Cataloging-in-Publication Data
Hagstrom, Jerry.
Beyond Reagan.
Includes indexes.
1. United States—Politics and government—1981-
2. Economic forecasting—United States. 3. United
States—Economic conditions—1981- . 4. Reagan,
Ronald. I. Title.
JK261.H32 1988 973.927 87-28133

ISBN 0-393-02521-7

W. W. Norton & Company, Inc., 500 Fifth Avenue, New York, N.Y. 10110
W. W. Norton & Company, Ltd., 37 Great Russell Street, London WC1B 3NU
1 2 3 4 5 6 7 8 9 0

FOR MY PARENTS

Contents

Foreword

Beyond Reagan grew out of a continuing fascination with the many and different places of the United States and how they are changing, yet staying the same, during our fast-paced age. The book reflects many travels throughout the United States during the past ten years for this and other writing projects. In writing it, I am especially indebted to Robert Guskind, my fellow contributing editor of *National Journal* and my coauthor on many articles.

To give historical perspective to the Reagan years, I have relied upon regional writings by syndicated columnist Neal R. Peirce, with whom I wrote *The Book of America: Inside Fifty States Today*, and his coauthors on previous books, Michael Barone and John Keefe. Peter C. Choharis was the principal researcher and reporter. I also wish to acknowledge the contributions of John Fox Sullivan, publisher, and Richard S. Frank, editor, of *National Journal*, and those of my colleagues at the magazine, whose writings have become part of my own thoughts: James A. Barnes, Ron Brownstein, Timothy B. Clark, Richard E. Cohen, Richard Corrigan, Dick Kirschten, Julie Kosterlitz, W. John Moore, David Morrison, Larry Mosher, Jonathan Rauch, William Schneider, Burt Solomon, Rochelle L. Stanfield, Carol F. Steinbach, and Bruce Stokes. Substantial contributions were also made by John DeFigueieredo, Joe Lipscomb, Steven Hamberg, and Ben Currie. I also wish to acknowledge several friends who had faith in this project during the many months of writing and traveling that led to its birth: Scott Pannick, Steve Rabin, Sandra Solomon, Laurence Ratier-Coutrot, and Christopher Lehfeldt, Patricia Keefer, and Roan Conrad.

Introduction

The question is simple: "Are we better off than we were eight years ago?"

It's tougher to answer than Ronald Reagan's question in 1980, when he asked American voters to think hard about Jimmy Carter's four years of record inflation, hostages in Iran, and poor relations with Congress.

For every great Reagan success, there is a terrible failure. Inflation went down, but at the cost of a major recession and a stock market crash. Millions of service jobs were created, but manufacturing, energy, and agriculture suffered. Interest rates plummeted, but the federal deficit skyrocketed and the nation lost out in world trade. Individual incomes went up, but the incomes of families with children declined. Wage differences between men and women and between minorities and whites decreased, but mostly, it appeared, because the wages of white men went down. The rich got richer—not a bad thing in itself if it increases the country's investment pool—but the average American seemed to just hang on. The ranks of the poor swelled from 29 million to 33 million (close to 15 percent of the population), the highest level since the 1960s.

But in our continent-sized country, "the national numbers," as economists call them, hide the truth of millions of people's lives. Life under Reagan varied dramatically from one part of the United States to another, from the federally funded defense plants of southern California to the over-abundant farm fields of Kansas and the shut-down oil rigs of Texas and Colorado, from the decaying factories of Chicago and Detroit to still-growing Atlanta and worse-off Appalachia, from the takeover-minded investment banks of New York City to the new-born high-tech firms of Boston.

This book examines how each of the seven regions from Reagan's own Pacific Coast to New England has fared during the Reagan era, how some politicians helped Reagan achieve his goals and how others fought hard to keep his most radical proposals from being enacted.

The story of the eighties quickly becomes the saga of the states and regions themselves rather than of the president's policies. The Reagan era does not end up, after all, as one man's crusade to change the country. It is, in fact, shocking to discover how ghostlike the president appears in many sections of the country, how detached and remote he really has been from the problems of individual industries and regional pain.

Freed or forced by the absence of the federal helping hand, each region's long-term strengths and weaknesses reasserted themselves. California continued on its road to domination of American political and cultural life while the rest of the Pacific states were left to natural resources, tourism, and the scramble for leftover defense money. The energy-rich Mountain states went through a depression that may be surpassed only by the farm foreclosures and low oil prices that make the Plains states from the Dakotas and Minnesota to Texas a com-modity culture resembling the Third World.

The manufacturing states of the Great Lakes were the hardest hit by international competition, but even worse, their nascent high-tech and service jobs added up to a lower standard of living than they had in their industrial past. Down South, the cities which had been behind their northern sisters since the Civil War continued to grow and diversify, but poor rural areas suffered terribly as commodity prices fell and low-wage plants moved to take advantage of cheaper labor over-seas.

Oddly enough for a president whose western backers had always hated the eastern liberal establishment, the Mid-Atlantic power corri-dor from New York to Washington, D.C., proved it is still the most diversified, wealthy, and stable region of the country. Even New York City, which nearly went into formal bankruptcy proceedings in the seventies, recovered. New England, transformed from above-average unemployment in the seventies, emerged as the economic miracle of the eighties. But its coolest, wisest heads knew that the high-tech boom was one of the region's periodic spurts of inventiveness, that the new industries might soon be lost to other regions and overseas competitors, and that it was financed more by defense spending than most New Englanders were willing to admit.

THE END OF IDEOLOGY

The time frame for the Reagan revolution actually begins two years before his election, on June 2, 1978, when the people of California, fed up with inflation-induced tax increases and constantly growing government, went to the polls and voted overwhelmingly for the Proposition 13 tax cut. The citizen-initiated Proposition 13, which rolled back property taxes to one percent of home values, started a tax revolt around the country and paved the way for Ronald Reagan's election to the presidency and for a Republican-controlled Senate for the first time since 1954.

After this entire decade of conservative political domination, it is clear that the Reagan revolution is almost totally limited to the economy. A New Right of Darwinian social thinkers, foreign-policy hawks, and religious conservatives assured Reagan the Republican nomination in 1980 and then drafted a party platform more conservative than any in modern times. The Republicans proclaimed they were the majority party according to public opinion and vowed to elect officials who reflected those numbers. But the revolution was not to be.

Eight years later, abortion was still legal, prayer was not back in the public schools, and there were no tuition tax credits. One could even find a few liberal advances in laws helping divorced women gain access to their ex-husbands' pensions and other laws allowing states to deduct child-support payments from an absent parent's paycheck; while many people considered such laws "pro-family," they certainly allowed the state to interfere with the old patriarchal view of the world.

To make matters worse for the social conservatives, 1980 may have been the peak of their appeal. As the Reagan era advanced, the postwar baby-boom generation, raised in an era of liberalizing social values, affluence, and television, was becoming a larger and larger percentage of the voting-age population. Lee Atwater, a Reagan strategist and Vice-President Bush's presidential campaign manager for 1988, told me that future Republican coalitions would have to be built on a combination of business-minded conservatives and baby-boom libertarians—people who oppose government intervention in both the economy and personal life—rather than the 1980 Reagan coalition of country-club, Main Street conservatives and populists—people who support a government role both in the economy and in restoring traditional social values.

There have been cutbacks in many federal domestic spending programs, and minorities have charged that Reagan has been uninterested in enforcing the civil rights laws. But almost all programs remained in place, ready to be infused with new funds (if the country could afford to supply them). Liberal advocates for the poor and the minorities were horrified by the Reagan years, but ideologues in conservative think tanks, who could not imagine a more supportive or popular president ever holding office, were perhaps even more upset. "We have now realized that rearranging existing spending, let alone cutting it, is extremely difficult to do," said Stuart M. Butler, the domestic-policy analyst at the Heritage Foundation, which has been promoting conservative ideas since 1973. Only one hope remained for the conservatives: that Reagan's court appointees would one day reverse the liberal trends that have dominated U.S. law since the 1950s. And that possibility was reduced by the Senate's rejection of Supreme Court nominee Robert H. Bork in 1987.

In politics, the conservatives also gained less than they expected. While the American people gave Reagan extraordinary majorities in both 1980 and 1984 and favored his tax cuts, they also insisted that their Congress save them from the most radical proposals to cut government programs and restore conservative social mores. The voters further brought home the point by voting Democratic far more often than the Reaganites expected, considering the president's popularity. In 1987, the Republicans held only 8 more Senate seats and 34 more House seats than they had in 1977. In the historic 100th Congress, there were 54 Democrats to 46 Republicans in the U.S.

Senate, and 258 Democrats to 177 Republicans in the U.S. House of Representatives.

The Republicans did better in the states, gaining 12 governorships since 1977, but they were among the party's least ideological, most pragmatic leaders, often as willing as Democrats to use the wheels of government to improve their people's economic lot. And in 1987 Democrats still held 26 governor's mansions to the Republicans' 24.

Ultimately, instead of realignment, the Reagan years brought "dealignment." Politicians of either party can get elected in any state now, but usually on the basis of leadership qualities, not ideology.

A Free Economy?

On the economic front, the eighties do belong to Reagan. Tax cuts, tax reform, and a defense buildup were what the conservative president wanted, and that's what he got. As he promised, Reagan kept government from interfering with business or technological advancement even when foreign companies grew increasingly powerful. Corporation after corporation fell to hostile takeovers, but Reagan declined to use either antitrust laws or Oval Office jawboning to stop them. Oil prices fell dramatically due to the breakdown of the Organization of Petroleum Exporting Countries, but the president opposed an oil import fee even though some economists argued it was vital for "energy security." An international grain glut caused prices to plummet, but Reagan tried to get the government out of agriculture—a move that was stopped by both Democratic and Republican members of Congress. More than two million manufacturing jobs vanished during Reagan's watch, but the administration preferred to focus attention on the 12 million new service-sector jobs. That the service jobs didn't pay as well didn't matter to the Reaganites. In a competitive world, a Commerce Department official argued, "It's nice for the guy who has [a high-paying, industrial job], but it's not going to do his company or his country any good."

Reagan's pure free market face had a blemish: defense spending. The administration's historic peacetime defense buildup performed like a backhanded tool of industrial planning. Reagan's commitment to rearming the country overwhelmed his desire for a balanced budget,

fed the national debt, caused stark economic differences among regions, and skewed educational and scientific investment toward the
military rather than commercial production.

Whether they admitted it or not, defense spending turned the
Reaganites into Keynesian, pump-priming economic activists. The
defense budget played a role in reversing the 1982–83 recession just
as surely as the New Deal and World War II federal spending under
Franklin Roosevelt relieved economic distress. The administration's
strategic decision to emphasize high-tech weapons over soldiers rejig-
gled the map of military America. As weapons procurement and
research rose from 38 percent of Pentagon spending in 1980 to 49
percent in 1985, the beneficiaries were not the poor, base-laden southern states (whose representatives in Washington reflexively supported
defense spending), but the nation's traditional and newly emerging
industrial giants: California, Texas, New York, Pennsylvania, Florida,
Virginia, Ohio, Illinois, Massachusetts, and New Jersey. Together,
these 10 states swallowed up nearly 60 percent of Reagan-era defense
spending.

Prosperity followed the Pentagon dollar. Reagan's own California,
peppered with both munitions plants and bases and a recipient of
defense spending more than double any other state, flourished during
his presidency. The trail of defense dollars also led to the only bright
spots in otherwise troubled states such as Texas, Arizona, and New
Mexico, where defense plants stabilized some areas but left other
sections helpless to combat their basic oil, mineral, and agricultural
depression.

Defense spending became so important that governors and even a
few mayors who once lobbied for housing aid for the poor and money
to pave streets began chasing Pentagon money. Given the cutbacks
in domestic programs and the huge defense stakes, their reasoning was
logical. The Reagan administration's defense requests called for
spending an additional $864 billion on personnel and operations and
maintenance by 1990 and a staggering $1 trillion to build aircraft,
ships, tanks, missiles, and other weapons and research projects. Even
after Congress made substantial cuts, the money was still worth fighting for. "It is the last really big barrel of pork that's out there,"
Representative Thomas J. Downey (D.-New York) told me. "And it's
all federal money."

Defense lobbying was only the least of the governors' new jobs. In the absence of federal initiative, the states had to intervene in their economies to cope with unemployment, encourage innovation, promote their own products, look for foreign investment, and try to figure out how to compete with their neighbors and other countries. Governors who had once devoted their energies to thinking up new social programs and getting them through the legislatures spent the eighties focused on one goal: jobs. They chased "smokestacks" and new high-tech ventures, crusaded for better school systems, and became regulars on the investment and product-promotion circuit in Japan and Europe. A few governors, notably South Dakota's populist Republican, William J. Janklow, expressed disgust at the sight of U.S. governors begging foreigners for investment. Others viewed their new role as the unwelcome necessity of the Reaganite (and earlier Nixonian) "New Federalism" that attempted to dump responsibilities on the states and return decision-making to levels of government closer to the people. Some, especially those from agricultural and oil-producing states, testified in Washington that they could not possibly handle international problems on their own. But most recognized that education, the key to the information and high-tech age, had always been a state and local responsibility, and began the greatest effort at educational innovation since the Sputnik era. Some of the greatest educational advances were in the South, but they were limited as always by the South's poverty compared to other regions.

Post-Reagan America

This regional portrait of successes and failures would please a president devoted to "keeping government off our backs." Over the long run, he would reason, inefficiencies will be driven out of the economy, and every region will succeed. Meanwhile, we are being protected from communism. But is this "morning in America" that Reagan claimed to deliver in his 1984 re-election campaign really enough?

Too large a geographic chunk of the country has suffered for Reagan's policies to be considered a success. Disturbing questions—both national and regional—remain about America's basic future. What action should the U.S. government take, if any, to stop the hemorrhaging of manufacturing? How can world trade in agricultural products be revived? Should there be a national energy policy that stabilizes U.S. oil prices? Does the United States, as a nation, care about the wage levels of its workers? What does free trade mean today, with more trading partners and competitors? Should there be any limits on the export of technology if it is destined to compete with the United States? Is there any further action the United States should take to relieve the debt burden in Latin America and enable those countries to import U.S. products once again?

On their best days, the Reaganites started the debate on these long-term issues and opposed knee-jerk Democratic actions toward trade protectionism; on their worst days, they showed a callous disregard for the workers and farmers whose middle-class status has been the backbone of this society since World War II.

The U.S. economy is now too tied to the rest of the world to predict whether Reagan's economic policies will prove successful over the years to come. Early in the eighties, the Democrats contended that the combination of increased defense spending and tax cuts would lead to immediate economic problems. They did not count on the economic role of defense spending, or the strong dollar, which brought billions in foreign investment to this country. As the Reagan years drew to a close, the Democrats were charging that the enormous federal debt and foreign claims on U.S. assets—stocks, bonds, and other investments—would be the country's downfall while the administration claimed a lower dollar and other policies had laid the foundation for a decade of national prosperity and growth.

As the post-Reagan political era is upon us, any judgment on the success or failure of the economic performance under Reagan suddenly seems secondary to whether the president's policies have laid a firm foundation for the times to come. The nineties promise both greater world competition from the low-wage, newly industrialized countries such as South Korea and Brazil and greater pressure at home to help the huge postwar baby-boom generation achieve at least some of the well being their upbringing has led them to expect. One of the greatest accomplishments of the American economy from the late sixties onward has been the creation of jobs (however low paying) for almost all of the 76 million people born between 1946 and 1964. In the coming years, America desperately needs economic growth as the baby boomers try to move up the job ladder, buy family sized houses, educate their children, and care for their aging parents.

Sociologists have made much of the experiences which separate this generation from their parents: postwar affluence and education, television, the space age, the Vietnam War, the civil rights movement, and sexual liberation. Baby boomers are not a solid bloc (they split their votes fairly evenly between Reagan and his competitors and are the audience for both *Rambo* and *Platoon*), but they do live differently from previous generations: women work outside the home, men help raise children, and the races mix much more easily and equally.

Polls show that, despite economic problems, baby boomers consider themselves happier than their parents because they have been freed from old-fashioned regimentation. Baby boomers have so far reacted with relative calm to their worst economic problem, the fantastic rise in the cost of housing because houses and apartments were not built fast enough as they entered adulthood. Women's wages, borrowing from parents, and some downgrading of housing quality have "solved the problem." But keeping the baby boomers satisfied will prove tougher as two-income couples begin to age and reconsider their exhausting life styles.

If the United States does not prove capable of maintaining a middle-class life style for the majority of its citizens, the social fabric and all the advances of the last quarter-century could be torn apart. Whites could be pitted against blacks, men against women, the old against the young, and region against region. If that happens, many Americans might look upon the Reagan years as the last good times and mutter wistfully "If only he were here." But if they do, they must remember whose policies got us to this point.

BEYOND REAGAN

THE
PACIFIC STATES:
Westward to the Future?

The age of the Pacific begins, mysteriously and unfathomable
in its meaning to our own future.

—Frederick Jackson Turner, 1914

Sunset Boulevard starts deep in the canyon of the old pueblo of
Los Angeles and ends 17 miles later at Malibu Beach on the
Pacific Ocean. Sunset lacks the skyscrapers and classical beauty of
New York's Fifth Avenue, but along this single winding, hilly path,
America's mass culture flickers by in jarring juxtaposition: the sta-
dium built for the Dodgers after 1957 when Los Angeles lured them
from Brooklyn; Hollywood's Sunset Strip, home of entertainment
conglomerates such as Motown Records (which moved from Detroit
after Diana Ross and the Supremes hit it big); the turreted Chateau
Marmont in whose bungalow comedian John Belushi died while
mainlining heroin and cocaine; and Spago, the eighties' movie-star
restaurant in which Kirk Douglas and Johnny Carson eat mussel
pizzas while overlooking the neon signs of Budget Rent-a-Car and
Tower Records.

Just beyond Spago, Sunset jerks to the left and descends into the
cool, green lushness of Beverly Hills and twists past old mansions
reminiscent of the setting for *Sunset Boulevard*, the classic 1950 tale of

the movie industry's obsession with youth. Next, the fabled boulevard passes through the University of California at Los Angeles and across the San Diego Freeway before heading into Pacific Palisades, the adulthood home of Ronald and Nancy Reagan. Up the coast to the right is the Getty Museum, now the richest in the world, and, to the left, Santa Monica, home of Reagan's ideological nemes¬s, actress Jane Fonda and her husband, Assemblyman Tom Hayden. Straight ahead, the biggest ocean of them all beckons.

Only a little more than seventy years after Turner wrote, one can only wonder whether the great historian could have imagined such a long string of national cultural images emanating from the West Coast. California's beauty and climate attracted so many people that since 1964 it has been the most populous state in the union. The motion-picture industry's decision to locate on the sunny West Coast and the development of its child, television, gave California the power to define modern culture. As the production center for the most easily transmitted entertainment and information programming yet invented, California has become the broadcaster of cultural values to the nation and the world. To know Boston, New York, Washington, and Chicago today, but not to know Los Angeles, is not to know America.

The presidency of Ronald Reagan has confirmed California's status as the political and cultural leader of the nation. Perceived by the eastern elite as the most ideological president since Franklin Delano Roosevelt, Reagan has instead taken the movie industry's genius for mass marketing and Californized the presidency. Reagan was not the first president to possess consummate media skills; Roosevelt derived much of his popularity from his fireside radio chats, and John F. Kennedy shined in debates and press conferences. But Roosevelt's and Kennedy's appearances seemed like incidental extensions of their political prowess; Reagan was the first president for whom communication came first and foremost. From the beginning of Reagan's political career, his most trusted advisers included highly sophisticated, mainstream public relations and political consultants such as Michael Deaver. The P.R. men were well aware that public-opinion polls showed the general public to be more liberal than the president's stated positions on issues from abortion to the environment. They knew that, like a movie meant for a mass audience, a popular president had to remain close to mass opinion.

There was no greater proof of this than Reagan's relationship to the New Right, which had been crucial to his 1980 Republican nomination. Reagan's rhetoric indicated a real commitment to conservative goals, but as the administration reached its last years, conservative leaders stood in frustration as they saw their goals of banning abortion, restoring school prayer, balancing the budget, and boosting military power soft-pedaled in favor of sex-education campaigns to counter AIDS, compromises on the deficit, and peace talks with the Soviets. Whenever Reagan began to appear too conservative for middle-class taste, the more mainstream first lady was on hand to urge arms-control talks with the Soviets, or to say that she didn't know how she would feel about abortion if she or her daughter were raped.

Public relations and political calculation were not the only strengths of the Reagan administration; his White House was well organized, and he had real legislative victories in cutting taxes, increasing the defense budget, holding back domestic spending, and aiding the Nicaraguan Contras. But staged events and mastery of the media were its heart and soul. The Iran-Contra revelations of Reagan's questionable control of foreign policy brought to mind the line from the musical *Evita:* "Statesmanship is more than entertaining peasants." The public's sadness rather than anger at the Iran-Contra affair, however, showed just how desperate Americans had been for strong leadership and how willing they were to accept the appearance of leadership if the reality were not available. Reagan's extraordinary popularity can only be judged, in fact, against the competition: the unpopular, preachy Jimmy Carter and the dull Walter Mondale.

Reagan's professional performances on television and radio set a new standard for all future-thinking politicians. "I don't advocate that we change our philosophy," said Tony Coelho, the California congressman whose success as chairman of the Democratic Congressional Campaign Committee led his peers to elect him majority whip of the U.S. House of Representatives in 1987. "All I advocate is that we market our philosophy better."

Media politics is only the most visible of the Pacific messages for the post-Reagan era. California's citizen-initiated Proposition 13 tax revolt started the new conservative age two years before Reagan was elected, and the state's experience has much to tell us about the future of social programs around the country. California's agricultural, defense, and high-tech industries lead the nation, and the Golden State's growing worries over the free-trade "Age of the Pacific" reveal the fragility of America's economy today. The other far-flung Pacific states—Washington, Oregon, Alaska, and Hawaii—pale in significance with California, but they too are all at the forefront of social change and produce national leaders. The followers of one of their senators, the late Washington Democrat, Henry Jackson, had great influence over foreign policy making under Reagan.

It is sad that the American people are still crawling toward an understanding of all these West Coast trends. The eastern-based political and cultural establishment has been so shocked or overwhelmed by West Coast ways that our best minds and scholars still prefer to write laments for the past rather than explain the present. The West—and southern California especially—is hard to study. To the first-time visitor who rents a car at Los Angeles International Airport and tries to negotiate the incredible array of freeways (or, even worse, takes a cab to a hotel in Pasadena and finds the fare is $70), L.A. is far more intimidating than New York. And for many years, the important political and cultural trends in the West seemed so derivative, so déclassé, they hardly warranted attention. To many Americans (and perhaps especially to ivory-tower scholars), California may be alluring, but it is also personally threatening. In its distance from American and European cultural capitals, in its headlong, fearless plunge into unknown social territory, in its deepening ties to Japan, China, and other Pacific nations, California represents everything we hope and fear we may become. "Has California gone off the brink?" asks the American from Boston, Toledo, or Atlanta. "Or am I simply too dull and tradition-ridden to join in the new age?"

The price of this fear is much too high to indulge in it. As long as we do not understand this region as we do our Puritan origins in New England, the financial power of Wall Street, and the troubled history of the South, we will wander in a new kind of wilderness. The historians, political scientists, reporters, and members of Congress on the Boston–New York–Washington axis who do not know the West should be rounded up by charter jet, flown to Los Angeles, rented cars, and not let home until they get a tan. By then, they should have an idea of America's future as well as its past.

REAGAN REDUX:
THE SOUL OF THE SOUTHERN CALIFORNIAN

Ronald and Nancy Reagan are the perfect representatives of the
southern California culture that has grown up to dominate the United
States today: midwestern roots (he from rural, religious, northern
Illinois, she from the Chicago suburbs to which her actress mother had
moved from New York after marrying a doctor), early hardship, up-
by-the-bootstraps success, movie-star good looks, sun-induced skin
cancer, and signs of fearsome superficiality. And within Ronald Reagan's career as governor and president can also be found the factors
that make southern California the dominant force in our politics
today: the movies; weak-party, strong-personality politics; and the
frontier ethic.

The Movies: It now seems inevitable that the American motion-picture industry would become the world's greatest source of mass entertainment and that these techniques would play such a key role in
world politics. Politicians and artists alike realized that the movies
would be able to reach millions in a way the theater never had. When
Lenin saw his first movie, he supposedly said, "The cinema must and
shall become the foremost cultural weapon of the proletariat." But in
Europe, many production facilities were destroyed or bankrupted in
World War I, and the film industry developed as a highbrow, somewhat pretentious avant-garde art form. In the entrepreneurial, capitalist United States, the movies started as, and remained, mass entertainment.

The populist nature of movies was reinforced by the cross-country
train trips New York theater people had to make to work in the
fledgling industry. William Churchill deMille (*"Ten Commandments"*
Cecil's brother), who traveled west for the first time in 1914, later
recalled that he was unprepared for the variety of the United States.
"I watched the changing scenes go by," deMille recalled, "cities,
towns, villages, then scattered farms, and finally little settlements and
ranches with miles of desert around them . . . our job was to find stories
which would reach them all; an appeal to any special class of people
no matter how large would still fail to reach enough people. What did

they have in common? Only the emotions. Their ideas on most matters were different, even their gods were different; but love, hate, fear, ambition—these were basically the same in all of them." It was a cultural lesson that would one day assure Ronald Reagan's election to the presidency.

The movies' growing power also prepared the way for the Reagan presidency. As Americans got richer and wanted to lead middle-class lives, they looked toward the movies and the stars as accessible role models. Any American who grew up during the past 50 years has movies and television shows he or she remembers for their profound impact. In their quest for commercially popular themes, Hollywood producers often came upon the theme of individualism, especially in cowboy epics. The many cowboy and adventure films, in turn, re-emphasized the theme beyond historical fact. As Otto Friedrich, author of *City of Nets: A Portrait of Hollywood in the 1940s* (Harper & Row, 1986), noted, Hollywood was "an imaginary city," but "it was the dream factory of the '40s that created much of what Americans today regard as reality."

Producing mass entertainment also meant that almost every movie had to have mass appeal and offend no one. Thus early Hollywood glorified conventional morality. An obsession with respectability also made truth a rare commodity in early Hollywood. Most of the studio heads were immigrant Jews who were insecure in their knowledge of the United States and terrified about offending the American ticket-buying public, which they perceived to be very puritanical. Worried by a few sex and drug scandals in Hollywood's early years, movie moguls such as Louis B. Mayer allowed conservative gossip columnists Hedda Hopper and Louella Parsons and the Catholic Legion of Decency to set behavior standards for both the films and the people who made them. Through the forties, this meant married people slept in twin beds, sinners were always punished, and patriotism was rewarded.

At the center of this imagery was—and is—the star. Stars are actors and actresses, but they also have public images in their own right, partly real and partly manufactured. The movie-goers went to see a story, but the personal image of a John Wayne, Katharine Hepburn, or Clark Gable was at least half the attraction. Stars occupied a curious position in the thirties and forties, when the big Hollywood studios had them under ironclad contract. The heads of the big studios treated actors like children—treasured children to be sure—but children whose finances, careers, marriages, and love affairs had to be watched over, controlled to the greatest extent possible, and, occasionally tidied up. The most secure stars often chafed under this system, but the one thing that management thought stars could not handle was authority. In 1919 when David Wark Griffith, Charles Chaplin, Douglas Fairbanks, and Mary Pickford formed United Artists, a company owned and controlled by stars and directors, Richard Rowland, the head of Metro, remarked, "So the lunatics have taken charge of the asylum."

Reagan never became a big, big movie or television star, but his relationship with the studio reveals much about how he would preside over the White House and the country. Unlike bigger personalities such as James Cagney, Bette Davis, Olivia de Havilland, Humphrey Bogart, and Errol Flynn who resisted studio control over their choice of roles and directors, Reagan worked "harmoniously with the most irascible of Hollywood bosses, Jack Warner," noted Garry Wills in *Reagan's America: Innocents at Home* (Doubleday, 1987). Reagan also was the consummate performer; he never minded taking direction and never expressed a desire to become a director himself. The only thing he seemed to object to was going on location, because it involved night shooting and overtime and kept him from his regular exercise routine.

In the 1950s, when the future president shifted from motion pictures to hosting "General Electric Theater" and to a side job of delivering an inspirational, pro-capitalist, pro-American speech at hundreds of GE plants and local chambers of commerce, Reagan not only cooperated, he gloried in the role, according to Wills. Later, as a political candidate, Reagan was so willing to take direction that political consultant Stuart Spencer said, "I don't think we ever had a candidate more easy to work with. It wasn't really a very democratic operation. It was a benevolent dictatorship." As governor and president, Reagan was proud of his delegation of duties, at least until the Iran-Contra affair revealed the limitations of such a lack of interest in management.

But Hollywood's biggest effect on Reagan's presidential style may have been its easy mixture of reality and fantasy. In Reagan's day,

Hollywood was turned into a small town more moral than any in Iowa or Minnesota. Sex scandals surfaced occasionally, titillating the public, but everyone concerned was dedicated to portraying these as aberrations of the "true" Hollywood. Projecting this idealized image became a way of life. Friedrich asked himself whether the hundreds of Hollywood biographies and autobiographies on which he based his book were true. "Well, perhaps partly true," he replied. "Remember that Hollywood people lived and still live in a world of fantasy, and they are accustomed to making things up, to fibbing and exaggerating, and to believing all their own fibs and exaggerations. . . . the celebrities who sign these concoctions no longer remember very well what really happened long ago." Ronald and Nancy Reagan participated in the usual number of these inventions, so it's easy to see why Reagan could find it difficult to "remember" details about the Iran-Contra affair and still take the questions about it in stride.

Personality Politics: The skills Reagan gained from his careers in radio, movies, and television would not have been enough for an actor to launch a political career, however. Nor would he have been successful in a state like Pennsylvania, Minnesota, or New York in which parties are still powerful and candidates are expected to be born in the state. Reagan benefited from the tremendous migration to California and the weak-party, personality oriented politics that grew out of the early-twentieth-century Progressive reform movement in southern California.

Today we usually think of northern California as the liberal end of the state. But southern California Progressives led the movement to reform the state's politics at the turn of the century. The reason was ethnic background. At the time of the Gold Rush, northern California attracted two divergent groups: the Yankee capitalists who built the Southern Pacific railroad, and European workers, mostly Roman Catholics from Ireland and Southern Europe. This produced class politics similar to older eastern U.S. cities. As southern California slowly moved from ranching to diversified agriculture and commerce in the late nineteenth century, it attracted Midwestern, native-born Protestants. They were small-town, small-business Republicans, distrustful of Jews and labor unions, but imbued with the midwestern-based Progressive movement's idea of "reforming" society. Both their ideology and their aspirations of making a decent living, if not a fortune, in sunny, undeveloped southern California, put them in direct competition with the northern California railroad owners, who hoped to extend their control to the southland. Southern California Progressives opposed the political machines that were dominated by the railroads and ruled California with an iron hand. In 1910, southern Californians voted overwhelmingly for Hiram Johnson, who, as governor, secured passage of the direct primary, the nonpartisan election, the initiative, the referendum, and the recall.

These changes not only cleaned up California politics, they paved the way for California's national leadership role. Because of California's size and the boldness of some of the initiatives, its popular measures soon got national publicity and were copied in other states. Then in the postwar era, California-like suburbs sprang up across the country, and their residents adopted nonpartisan politics in order to avoid the corruption of big-city party machines. Television changed the way people received information, better-educated voters refused to take direction from party leaders, and the primary replaced the more directly manipulated caucus as the main form of nominating candidates for high office. By the 1980s, every serious candidate for the Senate or the governor's office employed a pollster and a commerical filmmaker, and many candidates for big-city mayor's offices, the U.S. House of Representatives, and even some state legislatures were regularly employing consultants.

To bring order into its partyless chaos, California gave birth to the campaign management firm; scientific polling techniques and political radio and television commercials were added to the bundle of tricks. Despite all his radio, movie, and television experience, Reagan's gubernatorial career was not launched until the consulting firm of Spencer and Roberts turned him into a "citizen candidate" and two clinical psychologists of the Behavior Sciences Corporation of Reseda, California, ameliorated the candidate's tendency toward gross errors by "unifying" his message into well-rehearsed attacks on the big government, welfare handouts, and high taxes that blunted the initiative, imagination, and energy of private enterprise.

The Frontier Ethic: Reagan's message grew out of the frontier ethic which still dominates southern California. Los Angeles and the rest of southern California are still young and still far from settled. By the time the United States had won the territory from Mexico and had admitted California to the union in 1850, San Francisco was already an established city. Southern California, by contrast, was still, historian Kevin Starr has written, semiarid, Hispanic "rancho" territory.

Although Los Angeles is the now the second-largest city in the United States, the region retains the frontier fervor for growth and development, and land, not industry, is the guiding force of wealth creation. The Los Angeles–Orange County–San Diego metropolitan area is still constantly expanding north toward Santa Barbara and Ventura County and east into the deserts of Riverside and San Bernardino counties.

But despite the state's vast wealth and economic growth, the California business community knows that in many ways it is still in the minor leagues compared with New York and Chicago. It is the headquarters of only 38 *Fortune* 566 companies, compared with 66 in New York and 50 in Illinois. California is the top state in venture-capital activity but home to only 6 of the 50 largest banks and 3 of the top 50 insurance companies. California industrialists still must fly to New York to arrange major mergers and sell corporate stocks and bonds. Even in show business, Californians are sometimes still unsure of themselves; in 1986, the *Los Angeles Times Magazine* reported that "the big advertising accounts, such as the major department stores, only hire models with New York and European experience."

The depth of Los Angeles's collective spirit could be seen in the 1984 Olympic Games, according to John D. Kramer, a Los Angeles native who headed the failed attempt to bring a 1992 World's Fair to Chicago. Public-opinion polls showed that 90 percent of southern Californians believed the games would not be worth the effort and costs involved, Kramer noted, but Los Angeles mayor Tom Bradley and the business community were so unified the games went forward.

The resiliency of these frontier attitudes may have been surprising to people who believed that the frontier era ended when all the free land was distributed. But the historian Turner, who believed that the gift of free land and the opportunity it provided separated American democracy from European forms of government, wrote that "he would be a rash prophet who would assert that the expansive character of the American people" would cease when the free land was gone.

"Movement has been its dominant fact, and unless this training has no effect upon a people, the American intellect will continually demand a wider field for its exercise." In no part of the country is Turner's prediction more true than in southern California. L.A. may be the capital of hedonistic living in the United States, but it is not decadent. One reason may be its origins; modern Los Angeles was created out of an earthquake-prone desert as a land deal, and the city is so constantly fearful of fires, floods, and threats to its water supply that some psychologists believe a very understandable anxiety contributes to its nervous dynamism. Whatever the cause, Los Angeles is one of the most dynamic and audacious cities on the face of the earth today.

For good or evil, the politics that come out of this and any other frontier will always emphasize individual initiative and the possibility of success. As Turner wrote, "Democracy born of free land, strong in selfishness and individualism, intolerant of administrative experience and education, and pressing individual liberty beyond its proper bounds has its dangers as well as its benefits." California is too big a state for this to be the only theme, of course; the fear of communism has played a major role in helping the Republicans while cleaning up the environment and improving the lot of California's minorities, especially blacks and Hispanics, have been rallying cries for the Democrats.

But the frontier is dominant, as California politicians in all parts of the state know. Speaking of a Democratic presidential candidate who could win the state (none has since Lyndon Johnson), Representative Nancy Pelosi of San Francisco, a former finance chairwoman of the Democratic Senatorial Campaign Committee and daughter of a Baltimore mayor, said, "There is a market for somebody who wants to talk about being a real Democrat and care about the poor, but it can't be an approach that is pessimistic. It has to be shot through with hope. The frontier experience is different from the eastern immigrant experience. There is this enormous sense of optimism that abounds."

Pelosi could have been speaking about most of the United States today. Most of this country remains a frontier of one sort or another. In the oldest parts of the country, suburbs are constantly expanding and new land is being developed for houses and businesses. In rural areas, agriculture has been mechanizing for generations, and the political byword has been industrial diversification. Even in the oldest cities, the movement of middle-class people into architecturally interesting poor neighborhoods was known as "urban pioneering" until it caught on to the point of being called "gentrification." In Franklin Delano Roosevelt's day, this expansion of the frontier was an integral part of the New Deal; that the Democrats seem to have forgotten this in their preoccupation with civil rights and redistribution of wealth is central to their downfall not only in the West but in other growing parts of the United States as well.

Politics California Style:
The Case of Alan Cranston

The little-heralded power of the Democratic party in California proves that liberals can survive and even prosper in the era of Ronald Reagan's conservatism and media politics. At the state level, Democrats have controlled both houses of the California legislature since 1970, and even in the last years of the Reagan era they hold all the statewide elected offices below one Senate seat and governor. Democrat Edmund G. (Jerry) Brown, Jr., held the governorship for eight years through 1982 when he lost a race for the U.S. Senate to then-mayor of San Diego, Pete Wilson; the same year Republican George Deukmejian beat Democratic Los Angeles mayor Tom Bradley. A majority of California House members are Democrats, and Democratic senator Alan Cranston won re-election to a fourth term in 1986. The origins of California's Democratic sentiments lie deep in the class politics of San Francisco, the public works projects of the agricultural Central Valley and the Progressives of the south, many of whom began to vote Democratic as the Republican party became increasingly conservative.

The successful 1986 re-election of Cranston, California's senior senator and a Democrat, illustrates both how tough campaigning gets today and what it takes to win. First elected in 1968, Cranston has a distinguished record in the Senate both as a liberal pushing environmental protection, veterans' benefits, the nuclear freeze and for helping every California cause from the B-1 bomber to vineyards to real estate. Cranston started the 1986 race with two significant drawbacks, however: he had run unsuccessfully for the Democratic presidential nomination in 1984, and he often looked pale, thin, and old.

A lesser politician might have stepped aside, but Cranston put himself in the hands of two skilled media consultants, former Kennedy speechwriter Robert Shrum and his partner, David K. Doak, and pollster Patrick H. Caddell. Cranston's consulting team immediately found that their senator faced not only a Republican party determined to capture the Senate seat, but also an electorate that was poorly acquainted with the candidate's record. Even worse, perhaps, Democratic fatcats had decided Cranston was over the hill and were reluctant to give him money.

To impress the voters and fundraisers, Cranston's early ads depicted him as a thoughtful, highly regarded, and influential legislator, who was vigorous and active at age 72. "Always ahead of the pack," said an announcer, as a jogger's feet and legs moved across the screen. "Sometimes it's lonely to be out in front, but that's where he's been. . . . Like us, he's a step ahead." As the narration concluded, Cranston jogged, smiling, towards the camera in a blue running suit, his nearly bald head covered by a blue hat. Another early ad employed breathtaking Ansel Adams photographs of California's coastline, mountains, and wilderness, as the announcer quoted Adams calling Cranston "a great leader who transcends party politics for causes of human importance." The production values—quick-change cinematic techniques, vivid color, and expensive 35-millimeter film (rather than videotape), were appropriate to a senator from the home state of the motion-picture industry.

The Republicans, after an ideological primary battle, chose Representative Ed Zschau, a 46-year-old entrepreneur from Silicon Valley south of San Francisco who was probably the most liberal Republican in the California House delegation. Zschau's relative youth offered the strongest challenge to Cranston, and the campaigners wanted to take full advantage of it; his early television ads pictured the congressman as an entrepreneur whose drive placed him at the top of the business world. In one spot, Zschau strolled the Stanford University campus where he once taught business administration. "Alan Cranston believes in more government," says Zschau. "I put my faith in individual endeavor." In another, Zschau sat in a park with children and led them in a sing-along while the announcer described his commitment to environmental protection.

Cranston's consultants decided, however, that the key to winning the race was to "define Zschau when he was at his most vulnerable—before he could paint his own image," Doak said. Cranston aired a series of spots during the summer attacking Zschau as vacillating on the issues and lacking in substance. One of the later Cranston ads, featuring two photos of Zschau, one facing left and the other right, asked viewers to "compare two candidates. . . . One says clean up toxic waste. The other voted against it." The announcer concluded: "Funny thing is, both candidates are named Ed Zschau." Later spots added a replica of Zschau's logo spinning across the screen, introducing them as "flip-flop updates."

Zschau first responded with positive ads further detailing his position on issues from the deficit to agriculture, but as election day neared he began running spots attacking Cranston as a big-spending liberal opposed to the death penalty and weak in his support of laws against drugs and prosecution of terrorists. Zschau, himself, vanished from the airwaves.

In later Zschau ads, produced to look like local television news updates, an "anchorman" announced a "U.S. Senate campaign update" and told viewers that "in Washington, despite an overwhelming vote to impose the death penalty for drug pushers who willfully murder, California Senator Alan Cranston voted no. That vote shouldn't come as a surprise to Californians—Cranston also voted against a death penalty for terrorists and hijackers who murder."

Not to be outdone, a Cranston ad claimed that Zschau was anti-environment because he had accepted $250,000 from "individuals and corporations guilty of toxic pollution." But the Cranston team aired its most controversial salvo, a kind of rock video based on the movie *American Graffiti*, which had featured the disc jockey Wolfman Jack. "And now for the greatest hits of that song and dance man, Ed Zschau," announced a disk jockey identified as Jack Wolfman while rock groups sang and song titles rolled and jumped across the screen: "How Many Times Can A Man Change His Mind? . . . Caught In A Dump Cuz I Took Too Much Money Baby . . . I'd Send the Bucks to Nicaragua . . . Do the Zschau Bop Flip-Flop." As this summary of anti-Zschau campaign themes finished, the announcer said, the "flip-flops" were available for a limited time only because "on November 4 the Ed Zschau song and dance comes to an end."

It did, although by only 118,162 out of 6,973,558 million votes cast. Liberal Californians were incensed by both the financial cost of the campaign ($17 million between the two candidates) and the acrimony in the ads. Such anger fails to reflect the reality of modern politics, indeed the whole of how we live today. The joke in political circles is that a California campaign rally consists of two people gathered in front of a television set. Consultants produce negative commercials because polls the next day show that they have a stronger effect on voters.

A case can be made that the Cranston campaign was almost a failure; a pollster who was tracking the candidates' standing day by day said that Cranston was declining daily as the election neared. In another few days, Zschau might have won. But he didn't, and Alan Cranston proved that a Democrat can play the media game just as well as a Republican. The Cranston strategy will be a hard model to avoid.

COELHO AND COMPANY:
CALIFORNIA DEMOCRATS IN THE HOUSE

It is six days before the 1986 midterm election, and Representative Tony Coelho is "campaigning" in Atwater, California, for re-election to his House seat representing the agricultural Central Valley.

At the Atwater Chamber of Commerce, the five-term Democratic incumbent is greeted more like a reigning monarch bringing news from on high than a candidate for office. There is no mention of any opponent. Constituents quietly ask Coelho's opinion of the tax bill, the future of the Central Valley's agriculture, and the likelihood of federal funding to improve housing for servicemen at Castle Air Force. A man Coelho later identifies as a John Bircher waves a pamphlet on U.S. military preparedness and then asks, "What actions have you taken to cut taxes and reduce government?"

"Quite a few," Coelho responds, and the audience looks relieved as their leader quickly moves on to discuss a real political battle which he says would make all their goals easier: his quest to become majority whip of the House of Representatives. "For the first time in 200 years, someone from California would be in the [House] leadership," Coelho says with a smile. "And I will treat the northeast with the same sensitivity and respect they've shown for California for the last 200 years." Perhaps sensing the provincial nature of his joke, he quickly adds that actually "Californians will treat the people from the northeast okay."

Coelho was re-elected with 72 percent of the vote, and later was elected House majority whip, overcoming northeastern and southern Democrats' arguments that House leaders should come from regions where their party appears strongest in membership and ideology. Credited with aggressive leadership of the Democratic Congressional Campaign Committee, modernizing the committee's direct-mail fundraising, and creating the Harriman Media Center (a production facility used by party candidates at all levels), Coelho won the whip's post even though he had served only eight years and ranked only 115th in seniority.

Coelho's easy re-election and ascension to the House leadership are not mere exceptions to the dominance of Republicans in California politics. Twenty-seven of the 45 California House members elected in 1986 were Democrats, and many of this majority are young (6 are under 45) and poised for power in the future. As California's population grows and its number of House seats increases (probably by 4 following the 1990 reapportionment), the potential for more California power in the House is great. If the House of Representatives stays in Democratic hands, it may well be run by Californians. "We're the next Texas," said Coelho, referring to the long succession of Texans who have dominated Congress for much of the post–World War II era.

Within the House of Representatives, the 27 California Democrats are rising to power through a combination of growing seniority, intellectual leadership, and national fundraising ability. Seniority, so far, is the least important. Because many California House Democrats were elected in the 1970s, the delegation as a whole falls only midway in seniority, the traditional measure of power. Only three Californians—all blacks, incidentally—head full House committees: Augustus F. Hawkins, Julian C. Dixon, and Ronald V. Dellums. Three are next in line to take over committees. But California Democrats have also accumulated 21 subcommittee chairmanships and two California House members also chair select committees, which can hold hearings but do not have the power to send legislation to the floor of the House.

Several Californians have already proven able to push their legislative agendas through both intellectual and political leadership. Among the Californians noted for their expertise: Barbara Boxer and Mel Levine on defense; George Miller and Richard H. Lehman on the environment and water issues; Henry Waxman and Fortney H. (Pete) Stark on health care; Robert T. Matsui on taxes; Norman Mineta on air safety; Vic Fazio, Leon Panetta, and Miller on the budget. Waxman, in particular, has become well known for his legislative tenacity, persisting for six years before winning passage of a bill extending Medicaid coverage to poor women during pregnancy.

Waxman, Levine, and Howard L. Berman, who all represent affluent districts on the west side of Los Angeles, have joined together with other southern California politicians in an informal alliance that some political analysts have called the modern-day equivalent of a political machine. Though they dispense no patronage or pork-barrel projects, their fundraising ability and unity have allowed them to develop an independent national power base. "We are just close friends who work together in an alliance and care deeply about a series of issues," said Levine, a description that was echoed almost verbatim by Waxman in another interview. "Generally," continued Levine, "we share a very strong commitment to a traditional social agenda, and the survival of the state of Israel. We believe the whole is greater than the sum of its parts."

No one disputes the legislative abilities of the west L.A. trio, but the core of their enterprise is fundraising within the entertainment industry and the wealthy, liberal Jewish communities that lie within their districts. "People come to California to raise money," Waxman said. "It's a political fact of life. I've never thought there was a political side to things and a legislative side. It's part of the same fabric."

There is no doubt that California House members will use their power to defend the motion-picture industry and Jewish causes when necessary, but Levine contended that "to an exceptional degree California donors are interested simply in electing people who share their philosophical views. It is not strings-attached money. The donors don't expect a return."

The California House delegation has produced great power brokers in the past; Phil Burton and B. F. Sisk were two of the biggest names in the House during their tenure. But the present generation has managed not only to position a larger number in current and potential leadership positions, but also to make unprecedented progress in getting the Democrats in the delegation to work together. The California Democrats had been noted for their lack of unity, which had logical roots in the state's physical size, the conflict between northern and southern California, and the differing political traditions of the state's regions.

In the last few years, the California House Democrats have learned how to walk a fine line between their ideological questioning of defense spending and the delivery of defense contracts to California companies. They voted unanimously in the 99th Congress to decrease the budget for research on the Strategic Defense Initiative, for example. But their general approach, once a defense system has been approved is to deliver as much of the contracting as possible to the state.

The other pet state issue for the California Democrats is the environment. They managed to halt the Reagan administration's plans for oil drilling off the state's northern and central coasts, although a four-year moratorium on drilling was rejected by Congress. Representatives from water-rich northern California and parched southern California remain divided over federal projects and policies to deliver more water to southern California and other arid sections of the country. But these issues have become less important as environmental questioning and federal budget constraints have reduced the number of pork-barrel projects that come under serious consideration.

The California Democratic House members appear ever ready to promote the state; they protested publicly when the Reagan White House served French wine. But California House Democrats do not promote a regional consciousness the same way southerners do. The delegation's other priorities—in issues of environment, health, immigration, jobs, trade, and fair treatment of AIDS victims—reflect many California Democratic members' primary view of themselves as "national" Democrats and natural leaders of that agenda.

No aspect of the California Democrats' record is more unusual, however, than their united liberal posture on the most controversial foreign policy and social issues of the day. California Democratic House members, according to the delegation's records, have voted unanimously in favor of pro-choice measures on abortion, for sanctions to curb trade with South Africa, against school prayer, and against aid to the Nicaraguan Contras. No other Democratic delegation from a large state has such a unanimous liberal voting record on these issues. The California Democrats view these positions as being in line with "the majority of Americans," said Don Edwards, the head of the Democrats' organization. But the California members may also feel freer than Democrats from other regions to take these positions because of the safety of their seats and the generally recognized liberal social climate of their state.

The Democrats' new-found unity has not extended to general bipartisan cooperation on California issues, however. One reason is the ideological chasm that separates the two parties. Most California Republicans are as conservative as the Democrats are liberal. But the divisiveness is deepened by the 1981 reapportionment plan that was once described as "modern art" by the man who drew it, the late Phil Burton, representative from San Francisco. Before Burton went to work on recarving California, there were 22 Democrats and 21 Republicans in the delegation. By the time Burton was finished redrawing the maps to protect Democratic seats, several safe Republican districts vanished and the Democratic delegation grew to 28 members (a total that has only fallen by 1 since). "California Republicans and Democrats have been suffering the scars of the reapportionment wars since the very beginning of the decade," said Vic Fazio.

Burton's district lines are so intricate that all California members— both Democratic and Republican—now hold seats that are difficult for the opposition party to challenge. In 1986, all California members who sought re-election won; only 3 candidates received less than 60 percent of the vote and 25 won by 70 to 80 percent. But California Republicans contend that the Burton plan is gerrymandering and have repeatedly sued to have it declared invalid. A 1986 U.S. Supreme Court decision that reserved the right of the courts to review political gerrymandering has given renewed hope to the Republicans.

The westerners' claim to their place in the Democratic sun means competition for other regions, however. "There's basically a hostility to California in the House," Coelho said. "People keep moving west and the delegation keeps getting bigger and bigger. Other delegations are used to having influence and suddenly they're losing it."

AMERICA'S SOCIAL LABORATORY: PROPOSITION 13 AND BEYOND

Like Luther and Calvin, who believed their bishops had misinterpreted the scripture, businessmen Howard Jarvis and Paul Gann believed in 1978 that their governor and legislators had breached Californians' pact on proper government spending. And like those founders of Protestantism, Jarvis and Gann found others waiting to be led. Californians were incensed at their property-tax bills, which were skyrocketing, not because the voters had decided to give their cities and counties more money, but because inflation and the baby-boom demand for housing were driving up the values of their homes. The voters quickly jumped on Proposition 13's simple, straightforward provisions to reduce property taxes to one percent of market value based on 1975 assessments (later changed to 1979) unless the property is sold. The measure also states that no new property taxes may be imposed by local governments or even by referendum and that all new state taxes must be approved by a two-thirds vote of the legislature and new local taxes by two-thirds of voters.

Proposition 13 once again reaffirmed California's position as the nation's social laboratory. The same state that experienced the first race riots and student activism of the sixties now presented the nation with the tax revolt. New Jersey, Colorado, and Tennessee had already passed spending limits, but the California vote made the tax revolt respectable even in notoriously liberal Massachusetts, which later passed its Proposition 2½. Taxpayers in low-tax states such as Oklahoma put on the pressure for cutbacks. In 1979, fearing that high inflation could still fuel increases in government spending, California voters passed Proposition 4, forbidding state, county, and local governments from increasing spending beyond increases in the state's consumer price index, with an adjustment for population growth.

Nearly a decade later, it must be said that Proposition 13 broke the national pattern of increased government spending established in the 1960s. Although expenditures and taxes both had risen dramatically during his governorship, Reagan's anti-government rhetoric helped create the anti-tax climate; the revolt, in turn, added political weight to his anti-government presidential campaign. Perhaps even more dramatic in the long run, Proposition 4's automatic triggers created the climate in which Senators Gramm, Rudman, and Hollings could win approval of their 1985 law under which federal cuts to balance the budget are automatic if Congress does not establish priorities. The California propositions were citizen initiatives and the Gramm-Rudman-Hollings law a legislative solution, but each reflected such a loss of faith in the traditional political process that the decisions over taxing and spending were given over to automatic triggers and computer analyses.

Proposition 13 has resulted in rutted highways, reduced public school programs, shorter hours in parks, libraries that find it impossible to keep up their collections—and voters who still approve the tax cut. California has lost its position as a leader in governmental spending and social programming. Between 1978 and 1983 the Golden State fell from 14th to 29th in state spending per $1,000 of personal income and from 6th to 11th in per capita public spending.

Highways, the symbol of the mobile, car culture of California, and the public schools, once among the finest in the country, both have suffered terribly under Proposition 13. Despite its reliance on state highways for commerce and simple travel, California fell to last place among all states in expenditures for these major roads. In per capita spending on elementary and secondary education, California fell from 19th in the nation in the school year 1978–79 to 31st in 1983–84. Compared to other states whose high schools offer advanced classes in math, science, social studies, and foreign languages, many schools in California have been forced to pare back to the basics. Stanford professor Michael Kirst, who completed a study of 26 California high schools in 1983, described the state's schools as "lacking real depth in their course offerings." But as Morton Tenner, a principal in Highland Park in Los Angeles, observed, "People complain that we're not pushing the kids hard enough, but how can we if we don't even have enough money to offer the courses?"

Police and fire departments have fared better than public works, parks, or libraries, according to the California Tax Foundation. The continual public demand for greater crime control in California has made this a priority, but the large retirement benefits for police and firefighters also make those budgets high. In many counties, the only buildings put up since Proposition 13 have been jails, in order to comply with tougher sentencing requirements and court-ordered standards for housing of inmates. County-administered health, welfare, and social-service programs have been fairly well maintained, according to the California Tax Foundation, although social workers point out that their case loads have increased and charge that they no longer spend enough time on each case to provide high-quality service.

City and county officials did manage to avoid some of Proposition 13's consequences by violating the spirit of the law and finding money elsewhere. About a quarter of California cities raised alternative revenue through bonds, developer fees, and sales-tax increases, but counties had to content themselves with the state's making up 10 percent of their revenue losses from property taxes. Proposition 13 ironically achieved the opposite of the conservative goal of keeping government as close as possible to the people. Cities and school districts ended up more dependent on the state as they looked to Sacramento to make up for the loss in school funding. To add to the conservatives' woes, California so reduced the number of welfare-fraud investigators that the state was subject to federal penalties.

Despite the apparent cutback in government services, pollster Mervin Field found in 1983, five years after Proposition 13's passage, that 48 percent of Californians surveyed had not seen any change in services. A 1986 Field Institute report found that 42 percent, a higher figure than at any time since 1977, described the level of state and local taxes as being "about right," while only 20 percent felt they were too high, the smallest proportion since 1977. A majority (52 percent) still preferred cutting spending over increasing taxes if the state faced a budget deficit, even if that meant reducing services. When asked about increased spending for popular programs, however—to aid the elderly and the disabled or for local schools—large numbers supported increases.

Liberals, city officials, and public labor leaders still believe Californians committed heresy when they voted in Proposition 13. But are well-off Californians less caring today than in the past? The answer is very complex. Proposition 13 has helped homeowners, self-employed people, retirees, and upper-income people and may have hurt nonwhite newcomers. The only positive comment that urban-ologists will make about the tax revolt is that it may have discouraged sprawl because developers have to spend more on new roads and sewers. Some developers even charged that the costs were pushed onto unwanted newcomers. "While Proposition 13 support is part anti-government and part property tax revolt, it is also part drawbridge-mentality," said Democratic state senator John Gara-mendi, a supporter of higher state spending. "We're seeing an anti-newcomer attitude which could have a devastating impact on our state."

It must also be remembered that Proposition 13 was passed at a time when the Democratic governor, Edmund G. Brown, Jr., had won on an environmentalist "era of limits" platform. Brown did not sup-port Proposition 13, but he did implement it. "There were many errors made during the Jerry Brown era," Garamendi said, "particularly in not building for increased population. But the Brown era also taught us a sensitivity to the environment and human interaction with the environment. It doesn't mean that you don't build anything but it does mean you take the environment into account. The six to seven million people who will come to California in the next 15 years will come no matter what we're doing."

If California is to continue to be a first-class state, it must rediscover the historical attitude that allowed it to spend billions on water pro-jects and highways and to create the largest, and arguably the finest, public university system in the world. A consensus for a new wave of government spending could emerge if the spending cuts reach into the programs the broad middle-class needs. "Proposition 13 is like the Vietnam war," said Representative Tony Coelho. "The war ended when people saw white boys dying."

But the outside observer has to ask just what programs the Califor-nia middle class cares about and whether California's demographics have not changed enough to make the old pro-government political alliances unworkable. Politicians have been afraid to raise gasoline taxes to improve road maintenance. With predictions that California would become a "majority of minorities" by the year 2,000, more and more young Californians will be black, Hispanic, or Asian. Older California homeowners will indeed have to be convinced that they must spend money to educate these people.

The potential for a reversal of the tax cut lay in the fact that California liberalism still thrived on non-financial matters. In 1985, textbook control, long the ideological domain of ultraconservatives, was seized upon by moderates who led the state Board of Education to reject 20 science textbooks with watered-down descriptions of evolution. State superintendent of public instruction Bill Honig, an independent elected official who led the textbook fight, later announced he would take on the task of overturning the Proposition-13 and Proposition-4 spending limits in order to increase education spending.

The Military-Industrial Complex Supreme

Defense Secretary Caspar W. Weinberger and both of California's senators, Alan Cranston and Pete Wilson, dropped by. At least half a dozen members of Congress stayed for dinner, and one even stormed out momentarily when she found a seat had not been reserved for her. President Reagan and former House Speaker Thomas P. O'Neill, Jr., sent letters of greeting. After a cocktail concert by the U.S. Army Band, the party of 200, including some of the Pentagon's top brass, sat down to a menu of "salade crabes en gelée, veau cordon bleu et fraises au champagne."

Despite the lavish trappings and A-list guests, the May 6, 1986 event in the Caucus Room of the Cannon House Office Building in Washington was not a gala political dinner or a fete for a visiting foreign dignitary. It was simply the Sacramento Chamber of Commerce's annual "Night on the Hill."

The evening of entertainment capped the Sacramento chamber's nineteenth annual "fly-in" of business and civic leaders for two days of meetings with Weinberger and other Pentagon officials to keep federal defense dollars flowing to Sacramento's Air Force, Army, and Navy bases. Since the total economic impact of defense to the Sacramento area is estimated at $5.2 billion annually, such an effort is hardly surprising.

The Pacific states, but especially California, have gotten the greatest windfall from the doubling of defense spending during the Reagan years. California, home of the greatest number of military bases and defense plants, received $73.6 billion in defense and defense-related expenditures in 1985 alone, according to the Pentagon's own projections of outlays state by state—more than twice as much as its nearest competitor, Texas, which gained $32.1 billion. California ranks number one in every category of defense spending: Pentagon payrolls and purchases of goods and services, defense contracts, and the impact of consumer spending by Pentagon employees.

Four of the Pacific states—California, Washington, Hawaii, and Alaska—are among the nation's six most defense dependent economies. Only peaceminded, base- and munitions-poor Oregon loses out in the defense picture, ranking 35th in total defense spending and 46th in economic dependence on defense.

Even before the Reagan defense buildup, California's defense firms and even its cities had developed a cozy relationship with the Defense Department.

Despite the intense liberal criticism in California about weapons systems, the arms race, and military versus social spending, these stratospheric societal debates disappear into pure and simple economic development and job creation. Said Representative Mel Levine, who chairs the House Military Reform Caucus and represents defense-heavy Santa Monica, "Once you get beyond weapons systems about which there are deep philosophical questions—and noncontroversial weapons systems are the majority—then I'll do whatever I can to assist companies to get their fair share of the contracts. The way I square this is that a number of weapons are going to be built, and if a contract is going to be let, my contractors deserve the most aggressive advocacy possible."

Defense critics have charged that such schizophrenic actions by liberal congressmen end up increasing the size of the defense budget. Levine acknowledged that jobs "play a role" in the size of defense budgets, but said he believes "most members are willing to establish overall parameters."

By the late 1980s, however, defense critics are beginning to win more mainstream support from people who fear that their communities have become too dependent on defense. Even though economists say defense industries are no more unstable than other sectors, Californians remember the effects of the downturns in defense spending after the Vietnam War. From 1981 to 1985, according to an estimate by the University of California at Los Angeles, as many as 30 percent of all new California jobs were the result of defense and defense-related spending.

In the same Sacramento that sends its business leaders to lobby in Washington, California State University sponsored a debate with military contractors, Pentagon personnel, and peace activists on the pros and cons of heavy reliance on military money—and what they could do to soften the blows of defense cutbacks. "California is almost addicted to defense dollars," said state assemblyman Sam Farr, who sponsored legislation setting up a system to track the flow of military contracts into cities around the state. Farr calls the project "an early warning system" that will allow state government to anticipate which communities will be hit when certain projects are cut, and how many workers will end up jobless. "The White House takes credit for California's economic boom," said Farr. "Now, we want to be prepared when the winds are blowing in the other direction."

The Post-Manufacturing Economy

The California economy, the envy of America through much of the post–World War II era, glided through much of the Reagan era, surviving the early-eighties recession with little damage and leading the nation in growth through the subsequent recovery. California's diverse economic base—its business, financial, and high-tech centers in the north; the world's most productive agricultural region running through its core in the Central and Imperial valleys; and aerospace and defense-related manufacturing and research facilities in the south—continued to be a population magnet for both Americans and foreigners. But there have been signals of danger.

In 1986, a report by the congressional Joint Economic Committee declared that the policies of the Reagan administration had created a "bicoastal economy" in which the East and West coasts were prospering while the interior suffered. The theory held that Reagan's defense buildup and his advocacy of free trade and pared-down social spending had benefited the already rich coasts at the expense of the heartland. But Californians were already beginning to worry that all those Reagan defense billions may have masked the dwindling competitive advantages and growing problems in many other sectors.

Two 1986 California studies charged that the Golden State's manifest economic destiny was threatened by problems in every major sector, from traditional manufacturing to the military-industrial complex to high-tech to agriculture. California's economy is like "a fine luxury car cruising down the freeway with red warning lights on the dashboard. There are signs of massive problems ahead," concluded a report, "California and the 21st Century," commissioned by the state legislature's Joint Committee on Science and Technology, and compiled by the Public Policy Center of SRI International, a widely respected nonprofit research organization. The state "is losing its competitive advantage in key industries," the report found. Since Democrats controlled the legislature, the SRI study could be accused of partisan origins, but the main points were upheld by the San Francisco–based Wells Fargo Bank, whose "California 2000" study portrayed the state's current economy as robust but warned of "a tougher competitive climate" in the future and of "more difficult challenges."

Among the threats to California cited in both reports are the erosion of foreign markets, long-term declines in productivity, research and development funding skewed toward the military, declines in educational quality and state education spending in the aftermath of Proposition 13, and similarly pared infrastructure spending. Even more threatening, the SRI report found, was California's loss of "product life cycles"—from basic and applied research, product development, and manufacturing to marketing—to overseas competitors. The state continued to hold its own in the early research and development phases, but many new products are being manufactured overseas, where manufacturing facilities are newer and wage rates are lower. The SRI economists pointed out that the videocassette recorder, for instance, was developed in California, but is manufactured almost exclusively in Japan, Taiwan, South Korea, and other Asian countries.

"It is a fundamental misperception to assume that a post-industrial economy is a post-manufacturing economy," said the SRI report. "The production of goods remains critical to California's economy."

"If California becomes a service economy we just service somebody else's wealth and lose the ability to finance a standard of living that I think we'd like to have," said state senator John Garamendi, the Democrat who chairs the joint committee that commissioned the SRI report. "We'll have a two-tiered society—high and low services," he added. "And if you lose manufacturing, you also lose the ability to do research and you miss out on the next level of innovation."

Urban vs. Rural: Water and the Environment

> The water I will draw tomorrow from my tap in Malibu is today crossing the Mojave Desert from the Colorado River, and I like to think about exactly where that water is. The water I will drink tonight in a restaurant in Hollywood is by now well down the Los Angeles Aqueduct from the Owens River, and I also think about exactly where that water is: I particularly like to imagine it as it cascades down the 45-degree stone steps that aerate Owens water after its airless passage through mountain pipes and siphons.
>
> —Joan Didion, in *Aqueduct* (the magazine of the Metropolitan Water District of Southern California)

It's hard to imagine another culture in which a writer of the stature of Joan Didion would go into ecstasy about public works projects. But then few cultures have been as dependent on the transportation of water as California and few have had the dramatic and never-ending conflicts between powerful rural and urban interests.

Didion is, sadly, a rarity among Californians today in her knowledge of and fascination with water. Most Californians—and certainly visitors—drink water from the tap and travel the coast, missing the productive, though not very scenic, "agribusiness" valleys that extend from Sacramento nearly to the Arizona border.

But of all the buildings along Sunset Boulevard, none holds more power than the beautifully landscaped hillside palace of the Metropolitan Water District of Southern California. Without the "Met" the second largest city and metropolitan area in the country could not survive. And in the Central Valley and other agricultural valleys of California, water districts have far exceeded counties and cities such as Modesto and Fresno in economic importance and power. The state may grow an impressive 250 different crops and livestock commodities in its intensely farmed Central and Imperial valleys but many of the plants could not thrive in California's semidesert climate without water from the enormous system of 140 reservoirs and 2,000 miles of canals that transport water from the rainy north to fields farther south. The federal and state governments heavily subsidized these projects from the 1930s onward on the grounds that they were crucial to the general development of California.

As viewers of the movie *Chinatown* will recall, southern California land developers and farmers have always competed, sometimes violently, for the precious resource. The competition lay dormant for years, as all sorts of agricultural and municipal canals went forward, but the 1980s revealed that urban and rural water interests are once again on a collision course. Since the sixties, environmentalists have opposed the use of federal and state funds to build projects that benefit only a handful of landowners and defy nature. In 1982, the proposed Peripheral Canal to connect the Sacramento and California rivers fell victim to voter skepticism about the huge $3.1 billion cost. The project's water would have served agriculture just like 85 percent of California's current consumption.

In the mid 1980s, environmentalists began proposing that instead of building new projects, cities should buy agricultural water or pay agricultural water districts to reline their canals to save water which could then be sold to them. Since agriculture was in all sorts of trouble—water costs were rising due to public anger over federal subsidies and farm prices were low anyway—the idea sounded fantastic; that is, until the farmers remembered that the chief engineer of the L.A. Water Department, William Mulholland, secretly traveled up to the Owens Valley some 240 miles northeast of the city early in this century and bought up land with water rights attached. No matter how desperate they were in the eighties, California's farmers decided to turn down the city slickers' proposals. Urban-rural cooperation may well be the way out of California's water dilemma, but even U.S. Representative George Miller of San Francisco, one of the biggest opponents of the water interests, said "I'm for water marketing, but I'm not for Noah Cross [the evil protagonist in *Chinatown*] being the water master to decide who's going to get it and who isn't."

California's most dramatic water problem was the discovery in 1985 of dangerous concentrations of the toxic substance selenium in the Kesterson National Wildlife Refuge, used for drainage of one million acres of farmland in the San Joaquin Valley. Even the industry-oriented Reagan Interior Department forced the halt of drainage from some farms in the region, and unless a remedy is found land eventually will have to be taken out of production. "I don't see any significant expansion in agriculture in the future," said Jerald R. Butchert, manager of the Fresno-based Westlands Water District, which supplies water to part of the San Joaquin Valley. "The days of inexpensive water projects are over. I think we have a practical limit here based on costs."

While this water battle raged, California's urban masses were upset by even more visible threats to the ocean and desert. The developers and environmental groups spent most of the Reagan years fighting over whether to resume oil drilling off the Santa Barbara shore where a terrible spill occurred in 1969, killing birds and fish. There is really no question about which side the public is on since millions enjoy the Santa Barbara coast while only the oil companies stand to gain from the oil leasing, but the quarrel is a reminder that beautiful California has been one of the nation's premier oil-producing states. On the Mojave desert, however, there is real conflict between dirtbikers who have been used to tearing up the desert and environmentalists who want to prohibit such riding. The disagreement has gotten so nasty that Senator Cranston has had to step into the middle, defending the protection of the desert but distancing himself from the environmentalists' disdain for the working-class people who ride the bikes. As with so many things Californian, dirtbiking did little damage when the population was small, but with growth, the old ways can no longer be accommodated.

THE REST OF THE WEST

No grouping of American states appears at first glance to have less in common than the Pacific states of California, Oregon, Washington, Alaska, and Hawaii. They hardly form a geographically compact unit. From the desert that is California's southeastern extreme, it is exactly 3,765 miles to the Alaska island of Attu at the tip of the Aleutians—a seventh of the circumference of the globe. The distance from the northern extremity of Alaska at Point Barrow to Ka Lae, or South Cape, on the "big island" of Hawaii, is only a little less—3,622 miles.

Then there is the problem of disparate land area, population, and economy. Alaska is the biggest American state—an astounding 586,412 square miles, 77 percent greater than all the other Pacific states combined. The Great Land's population was only 534,000 in 1986, but it had grown so fast since 1980 (32.8 percent) that it lost to Wyoming its status as the least populated state. With its huge population, California—which has three times as many people as the other Pacific states combined—creates its own power and impulses and acts more like a colonial emperor than a neighbor to its fellow western states. It is like a great nation-state on its own.

Yet viewed from afar, the Pacific states do have many commonalities. All the western states played a role in "filling out" the idea that it was the "Manifest Destiny" of the United States to occupy the North American continent and beyond. California was the first prize, of course, granted statehood in 1850, more than 50 years before some of the land in between it and the rest of the country was admitted to the union. As the Oregon Territory, Washington and Oregon were fought over by the United States and the European powers until Congress finally decided it was worth adding these remote lands to the union. Alaska and Hawaii remained territories until 1959.

The smaller western states cannot compete with California in attracting publicity, but they are all leaders of social change. In Hawaii, every ethnic group is a minority, and the state has come closest to achieving the oft-stated American goal of a harmonious, multiracial, multi-ethnic society. There is no other state as free of class distinctions as Alaska, no other where a young person can rise as rapidly to the top in business, the professions, or politics. Washington has been the seedbed of radicalism in America since the turn of the century, when poorly fed and poorly housed loggers formed the Industrial Workers of the World, better known as the Wobblies. Washington owes its first settlement to the Oregon provisional government's 1845 decision to turn away a train of 80 overland wagons because they carried one black. Yet from the 1890s onward, Oregon has given birth to great

political reforms—in latter years environmental and land-use laws—
and has become a mecca for those people who yearn for simple life
styles in a physically beautiful place.

The Pacific states are all population magnets. Less than half the
inhabitants of California, Washington, Oregon, and Alaska were born
in-state as of 1980. In the 1980s, the Pacific states have continued to
grow, with California adding 3.3 million people between 1980 and
1986, the largest number of new residents of any state. Only Oregon
with its sluggish economy and a growth rate of 2.5 percent has grown
at less than the national average of 6.4 percent.

Many Americans and Europeans are attracted to the Pacific region
for its weather and life style, but a new wave of economically driven
immigration from Latin America and Asia has been introduced into
all the Pacific states except Alaska. Some suggest California has become America's Ellis Island of the 1980s: more than half of its net
migration, it is estimated, comes from outside the United States, with
the largest numbers of legal migrants arriving from Mexico, the Philippines, and South Korea. By 1980, almost one in five Californians was
Hispanic—more than when California was ceded to the United States
by Mexico in 1848—and one in twenty was Asian. Texas, New York,
and Illinois supply the largest numbers of U.S. migrants to California.
At the same time, the Golden State has become a major exporter of
residents to Oregon, Washington, Idaho, Arizona, Texas, Colorado,
New Mexico, and Oklahoma.

Residents of the Pacific states share the nation's highest levels of
educational achievement. Fully 19.5 percent of the region's inhabitants are college graduates, compared with the national average of
16.3 percent. And only 13.6 percent of the region's residents have an
eighth-grade education or less, compared with a national average of
18.4 percent.

All the Pacific states share the freewheeling and personality-
oriented politics that are so evident in California. In part, this stems
from Progressive-era reforms in California, Oregon, and Washington,
but the same pattern holds in Alaska and Hawaii as well. By national
standards, the state governments of the Pacific area are extraordinarily
progressive, both in their clear gubernatorial authority and highly
staffed legislatures and in the kinds of social programs they have
enacted. Alaska has given its governor more clear-cut authority than

any state except New Jersey, and Hawaii has become a hot-house of experimentation in new and responsive government forms, including the installation of America's first state ombudsman.

In partisan terms, only Hawaii, whose many ethnic groups and strong labor factions have been Democratic since statehood, now seems firmly in the hands of one of the two major political parties. The region's House delegation of 37 Democrats and 25 Republicans reflects the gain of four seats following the 1980 census—one each in Oregon and Washington and two in California. In the Senate, Republicans hold the upper hand by 6 to 4, with only Hawaii being represented by two Democrats, Spark M. Matsunaga and Daniel K. Inouye. Just as he emerged as a national figure during the Watergate hearings in 1973, Inouye emerged as an impassioned questioner and critic of Reagan administration management during the 1987 Iran-Contra hearings. The only Pacific Senate seats to change party hands during the eighties were in Washington. Republican Slade Gorton defeated Warren Magnuson in 1980 (only to be defeated himself after one term by former U.S. Transportation Secretary Brock Adams). In 1983, Republican Dan Evans was appointed and later elected to fill Henry Jackson's seat.

Democrats held the governorships in the four smaller Pacific states after the 1986 elections. Democrat John D. Waihee won a close and bitter race in Hawaii, proving that the state's postwar "machine" is still intact, while the former mayor of Portland and U.S. transportation secretary Neil Goldschmidt defeated a Republican in Oregon. Democrats also retained Alaska, electing Steve Cowper after a bitter primary fight in which the incumbent governor was defeated. The Democratic governor of Washington, Booth Gardner, remained in the position he won in 1984. Democrats kept control of both houses of the legislature in California, Washington, and Hawaii.

Economically, the only other western state approaching California's prosperity is Washington where the Boeing Company of Seattle makes money from both military contracts and building commercial planes, a field in which the United States still dominates the world. The eighties have been good for Boeing, but the company so dominates the economy that people in Seattle are upset by the growing popularity of the European Airbus and always live in fear of the occasional "Boeing bust." When California's 13 percent increase in jobs from 1979 to 1985 is eliminated from the picture, jobs in the rest of the Pacific states grew only 6 percent—below the 8.2 percent national increase. In the Pacific states as a whole, service jobs accounted for nearly half of all new jobs. Between 1982 and 1985, California's per capita income increase of 21.4 percent exceeded the national gain of 20.9 percent, but all other western states lagged. Alaska's increase of 5.1 percent was the nation's smallest gain in per capita income over the four-year period.

The Pacific Northwest states of Oregon and Washington have learned in the eighties just how difficult it is for remote American states to diversify their economies. Heavily forested, environmentally conscious Oregon grew so rapidly in the 1960s and 1970s that its late governor, Tom McCall, once told a group of conventioneers to "travel, visit, drink in the great beauty of our state. But for God's sake, don't move here."

Oregon did achieve some diversification through a 1970s boom in metals, machinery, finance, women's sportswear, and especially electronics, which Oregonians courted as the kind of "clean industry" they wanted for their state's future. But the early 1980s' decline in housing construction changed the tone of Oregon's public debate and proved just how dependent the state remained on its softwood timber industry. Only when housing starts increased did Oregon's economy begin a slow recovery, but this time it had to come to terms with growing competition from the southeastern states and from foreign countries more experienced in competing internationally.

Washington, a larger state in population, has a somewhat more diversified economy, but it has also demonstrated a dependence on traditional economic bases. The state's vitally important timber industry has experienced the same depression as Oregon's. Cheap electricity has been key to the Pacific Northwest economy since the construction of the federally sponsored great dams on the Columbia River in the 1930s. But utility bills have doubled and tripled in the wake of the troubles of the Washington Public Power Supply System (WPPSS), a consortium of public and private utilities set up to build five nuclear reactors.

So primitive is the Alaska economy that mineral and energy development remain dominant. Until the 1970s, Alaska, its great storehouse of resources and energy unexploited, labored under a weak economy and a cost of living made high by the necessity of importing all manufactured goods and much food. Federal government employment, including the military, was extraordinarily important to the state's economy. So important, in fact, that Alaska politicians have gone to great lengths to snag new military facilities. When New York won a coveted base for a new Army division in 1984 the decision piqued Republican Alaska senator Ted Stevens, then the powerful chairman of the Appropriations Subcommittee on Defense, who had lobbied vigorously for the selection of a site in Alaska. Perhaps to mollify Stevens, the Army decided to station a second light infantry division in Alaska, even though the division would be training to fight in Latin America, the Middle East, and Western Europe. To explain the apparent inconsistency of training the soldiers in an Arctic climate, the Army hastily added that defending Alaska from Soviet attack would be part of the division's mission.

The development of Alaska oil, following the sale of North Slope oil rights in 1969, did change the picture dramatically. Based on $900 million raised from the oil rights sale, the state began intensive capital investments; the state budget grew from $124 million in 1969 to $1.8 billion in 1981, and 90 percent of the money came from oil royalties and severance taxes. A special fund was established to invest oil revenues in major industrial projects, with each Alaskan getting an annual dividend check that ranged from a famed $1,000 covering 1981 to 1982 to between $700 and $800 toward the end of the decade. Alaska also abolished its state income tax. As oil prices dropped through the floor, conscientious legislators proposed abolishing the dividend payments and re-establishing the state income tax, but they soon learned just how attached Alaskans had become to living off what came out of the ground.

Hawaii, meanwhile, continued to try diversifying its economy beyond tourism and agriculture. Its biggest accomplishment was increasing the number of Japanese tourists, but it has also begun to market itself as a logical Pacific Rim business location halfway between the western U.S. and Asian time zones.

On the cultural side, the eighties were the state of Washington's decade to shine in the liberal light. Seattle always ranks lowest of major cities in the United States in church attendance, but those who do go tend to take religion very seriously and are likely to be liberal.

Catholic Archbishop Raymond G. Hunthausen so offended the Vatican with his liberal ministering to homosexual parishoners and others who disagreed with church policy that he was forbidden to perform some of his duties, and an auxiliary bishop was appointed to "help" him. Liberal Catholics in Seattle and elsewhere rose to his defense, however, and after a full church investigation, Hunthausen resumed full control.

On the governmental side, the women's movement got a big boost forward in 1983 when a Federal district judge in Tacoma ruled that Washington state had discriminated against its workers in those jobs held mostly by women because pay levels in those jobs were lower than in those dominated by men. The ruling, which included an immediate 31 percent pay increase, was eventually thrown out by the U.S. Court of Appeals in San Francisco, but as part of a settlement, Washington state agreed to put up $106 million in raises for those workers identified in job surveys as victims of sex discrimination. Even while Washington state workers waited for their pay increases, negotiators for the American Federation of State, County and Municipal Employees used the ruling to negotiate with other states and cities for "pay equity" between men and women. The advent of comparing such work as typing and nursing with running bulldozers is not without controversy, and it will undoubtedly be expensive for state governments, but even in the conservative Reagan era it appeared to be a social advance whose time had come.

PACIFIC PERSONALITIES: JACKSON, FOLEY, PACKWOOD, AND HATFIELD

The most powerful politician from the Pacific Northwest during the Reagan era was Henry "Scoop" Jackson, the Democratic senator from Washington. Jackson died in 1983, but his legacy lived on in one of the more curious turns in American foreign policy making. Jackson's last vote before he died was for an armaments measure, and that was fitting. Whether it was to protect the economic interests of his state—he was often called "the senator from Boeing"—or based on honest opinion, Jackson had been obsessed with national security

since the 1940s. But Jackson was equally devoted to using government to give people an equal break in life. His former aide Thomas
S. Foley once explained that Jackson's tremendous popularity was
due to a combination of advocacy for social programs (which attracted liberals and moderates), his own hard-work principle (which
mitigated his domestic spending votes in the eyes of conservatives),
and a foreign policy that looked after American interests first. "Jackson," Foley said, "ends up giving *them*—the conservatives—the lec-
ture about not trusting the Russians. So the conservatives feel for the
first time, 'Here's a Democrat we can trust.' "

Jackson remained popular in the state of Washington until his
death, but as the Vietnam War moved the Democratic party to
question defense spending and anti-communist foreign entangle-
ments, his followers were reduced to the "Jackson wing" of the party.
After Jackson ran unsuccessfully for the Democratic nomination for
president in 1976, many of them formed the core of the so-called
"neoconservative movement," principally writer Norman Podhoretz
and his wife Midge Decter. Until late in his second term, when the
President decided to pursue an arms control agreement with Soviet
General Secretary Mikhail Gorbachev, a string of Jackson's aides and
associates who had broken with the Democrats became some of the
most powerful executors of Reagan's conservative foreign policy. It
was in the Jackson camp that Ronald Reagan found Jeane Kirkpatrick, his ambassador to the United Nations; Elliott Abrams, assistant
secretary of state for human rights (and later for inter-American affairs); Kenneth Adelman, director of the Arms Control and Disarma-
ment Agency; Max Kampelman, head of the negotiating delegation
on nuclear and space arms; Richard Perle, assistant secretary of defense for international security policy; and briefly after Perle left, his
deputy and fellow Jackson protégé Frank J. Gaffney, Jr.

One former Jackson aide who was far from joining the Reagan
administration, however, became the new powerhouse from the
Pacific: Tom Foley, who had been elected to the House of Representatives from Spokane in 1964 and was chosen in 1987 as House majority
leader. Foley is sympathetic to arms control agreements with the
Soviet Union, but emerged as a leading House opponent of U.S. aid
to the Contras.

If there is any lesson from the Jackson–Foley connection, however, it is that the state of Washington is capable of producing national leaders who are men of their times. The son of a judge, and a lawyer himself, Foley seems to love weighing facts and figures and coming up with pragmatic solutions. During his early House years, Foley was close to many junior liberals. He chaired the Democratic Study Group in 1974, when it was a leading force in the fight for procedural reforms aimed at weakening the power of seniority. One result of those reforms was the overthrow in 1975 of the veteran conservative chairman of the Agriculture Committee, W. R. Poage (D.-Texas). Although Foley opposed the ouster, the move put him in the chairman's seat and made him a House insider.

Foley made a reputation for himself on the Agriculture Committee as a sophisticated market advocate who believed that production controls and income programs are short-term solutions. Named Democratic whip in 1981, Foley was forced to relinquish his chairmanship on the Agriculture Committee, but he was subsequently elected vice-chairman and continued to play an activist role. Some other members have charged that Foley got elected majority leader because he does not have a prickly personality. But that may be an important part of the job. "He is the ultimate moderate," said Representative Norman D. Dicks (D.-Washington), a longtime friend. "He is the epitome of the centrist who understands the art of the possible and defuses people who are violently opposed. He's cautious because he is so smart and sees all of the land mines."

While the Republicans controlled the Senate from 1981 to 1987, Oregon's two veteran Republican senators emerged from the usual minority ranks to become major committee chairmen: Mark Hatfield on Appropriations and Bob Packwood, first on Commerce, Science, and Transportation, and later on Finance. But as two of the most liberal Republicans left in the Senate, they also became thorns in the flesh of the Reagan administration.

Packwood, the junior senator, ended up building the most powerful reputation as he shepherded the 1986 Tax Reform Act through the Finance Committee. Initially cool to the idea of reform, he and former committee chairman, Senator Robert Dole of Kansas, worked hard and skillfully to come up with the compromises from their congressional colleagues and the administration. In doing so, Packwood retained his pet tax breaks for the timber industry and tax-free fringe benefits such as health insurance.

Packwood's tax bill success enhanced his prestige on the Hill and back home, but he shocked his Common Cause–type supporters by amassing a very un-Oregonian campaign war chest of nearly $7 million. Packwood himself deflected criticisms that special interests were trying to buy his influence by claiming "there is special interest after special interest that is hit in this bill [and many of them] contributed to my campaign!" Packwood might also have mentioned that he has developed national fundraising markets not open to most Republicans—mailing lists of Jews (with whom he is popular for his pro-Israeli stands) and pro-choice on abortion activists (who are thrilled to find a Republican supporter).

Packwood also angered the administration when, as chairman of the Republican Senatorial Campaign Committee in 1982, he accused President Reagan of harming the party by clinging to "an idealized concept of America" which excluded minorities, Jews, women, working-class people, and other groups. But he still claimed to support the president's legislation more than most Republican senators, pointing out that as chairman of the Commerce Committee he worked hard to deregulate the trucking, broadcasting, and interstate bus industries. On the sensitive environmental issue, Packwood has walked a fine line, (stopping dams on the Idaho-Oregon border and favoring efforts to protect whales and limits on aerosol cans and throw-away containers), but also helping the state's basic timber industry with its tax problems. In 1986, Oregon voters gave him his biggest margin to date, 63 percent.

Packwood was once a student of Oregon's senior senator, Mark Hatfield. Both men are roughly the same age and are considered liberals within their party, but their differences reflect the individualism for which Oregon politics has always been famous. Among the first troops to land at Hiroshima, Hatfield was originally elected to the Senate as an opponent of the Vietnam War. He opposes much military spending, and he cosponsored a nuclear-freeze resolution. While other Republicans criticized SALT II as favoring the Soviet Union and restricting the United States, Hatfield thought it was too limited in scope and power. He speaks of reducing military aid to Israel and of aiding Palestinian refugees. On domestic and economic issues, by contrast, Hatfield is more in line with his party. He tries to avoid alienating environmentalists, but has helped the timber industry by giving it more access to Oregon's vast forests. Hatfield is known as a deeply religious man who is opposed to abortion, but he is not a fundamentalist and has not cultivated nor received much support from the New Right.

In 1984, Hatfield's usually sterling reputation became the subject of unusual controversy because a Greek businessman who hoped to construct a trans-Africa pipeline paid the senator's wife Antoinette, a real estate agent, $55,000 in questionable commissions. The case dragged on into 1987 when an ethics panel ruled that Hatfield had done nothing wrong, but found that the businessman had tried to gain the senator's help and influence.

WESTWARD TO THE ORIENT?

The Pacific states owe a tremendous debt to Japan. If that country had not attacked Hawaii to start World War II, the Pacific states would be a shadow of their current selves. The Japanese threat forced the United States to build bases and big defense plants in California and Washington—giving birth to their industrial economies—and to recognize the strategic value of Oregon, Alaska, and Hawaii. Once the war was over, the newly industrial Pacific states and (then) territories established peaceable and prosperous trade relations with their foreign neighbors.

By the 1970s this close association had given rise to the theory that the future of the world lay with the "Pacific Rim" countries of Asia, Australia, and Latin America, and with free trade. The business leaders of the Pacific states had good reason to argue that free trade was beneficial; they had made billions of dollars selling their own manufactured goods and exporting those from other U.S. states while importing from Asia. Any form of protectionism, they argued, had to come from a weaker, backward, less competitive part of the United States. They saw—and still see—an unlimited frontier in the newly prosperous countries of Asia. Oil companies operating in Alaska still wish to export oil from the North Slope, a practice currently forbidden under

U.S. law. Forest product firms in Washington and Oregon note that the People's Republic of China now consumes 9 pounds of forest products per capita compared with 600 pounds in America and a worldwide average of 20 pounds.

California's Pacific trade helped the Los Angeles customs district surpass New Orleans in 1982 as the second largest in the United States, after New York. Seventy percent of California's international trade is with Asia, 7 percent with Latin America, and 5 percent with Australia and the Pacific islands; Europe still accounts for 16 percent of California trade, but its share is declining. The Asia trade even makes for intraregional competition. Seattle has tried valiantly to become a center for the reopened China trade, but has had a hard time competing with San Francisco, which has had economic ties with China on and off since the nineteenth century.

The eighties ended the West Coast's adolescent fantasies about the joys of free trade in an increasingly competitive world economy. Between 1981 and 1985, California's trade deficit grew from $1.8 billion to $20 billion, and there was a dawning recognition that while exports have been responsible for much of California's non-defense-related job growth in the eighties, the benefits have been offset by the deficit.

Between 1984 and 1987, Silicon Valley firms had laid off more than 18,000 workers, and since there were no signs that foreign competition or the global oversupply of semiconductors would abate, most economists expected the layoffs to continue. "California could become the electronic rustbelt of the 1990s unless its electronic, computer and communications industries are able to remain at the forefront of new product and process innovation and development," said the SRI report on the state's economic future.

Convincing Californians to embrace anything that would smack of trade restrictions and might offend foreign buyers is still a hard job, as I learned watching Representative Coelho try to promote the "fair trade" bill to the Turlock, California, Sunrise Rotary Club. "I'm a free trader, but I'm not a damn fool," Coelho told them. "We're permitting foreign nations, particularly Pacific nations, to come in and steal our industry. They're coming in and taking what we've developed and producing it much cheaper. High techers a few years ago were the biggest freetraders, and now they're the biggest protectionists."

Whether it was the 7 A.M. time of the gathering, or the Republican-minded Rotarians' reaction to the Democrat Coelho, the group registered little response to their congressman's comments. Coelho's Central Valley audience had good reason to consider protectionism. The high value of the dollar, compounded by a global oversupply of many farm commodities, had taken a great toll on California agriculture: from a high of $4.2 billion in 1981, farm exports dropped to $2.7 billion in 1985. Domestically, Mexican wheat and foreign specialty crops have begun to compete directly with American farm products, and California farm imports exceeded exports by $600 million in 1985. In the Central Valley surrounding Fresno, in such smaller towns as Modesto, Merced, and Atwater, farmland was taken out of production, and land prices have plummeted from as much as $15,000 an acre in the late seventies to $2,500 an acre in the late eighties. Except for cotton, which has been hurt most severely by competition from China, California's agricultural economy has not fared as badly as the rest of agricultural America because the industry is diversified and concentrates on high-value products such as fruits and vegetables. But even so, "markets have dropped off tremendously," said Leland H. Ruth, president of the Sacramento-based Agriculture Council of California. "Third World countries are now marketing crops in direct competition with our people." Ruth predicted that measures introduced in the California legislature to restrict foreign imports—usually on the basis of quality and use of pesticides that are illegal in the United States—will find greater sympathy in the future.

Protectionist measures still cannot pass in the western United States without a real fight. There is something almost romantic about the westerners' confidence in free trade. Listen to the views of Mike Mansfield, former Montana senator and U.S. ambassador to Japan under both Carter and Reagan: "Over a hundred years ago, Walt Whitman said, 'Westward to Oregon.' Today were he alive, he would probably say, 'Westward to the Orient.' The next century will be the century of the Pacific and the development of that huge basin comprising four South American nations, all of Central America, all of North America, Australia and New Zealand and all of East Asia including Japan and the islands between, an area which holds most of the world's people, friendly governments and peoples. . . . It is here in the Pacific and East

Asia, where it all is, what it's all about, and where, in my opinion our future lies."

But by 1987, such romantic notions had obviously run their limit. It fell to Ronald Reagan—the president from the Pacific and an avid free trader throughout his political career—to issue, however reluctantly, the first U.S. trade sanctions against Japan since the Second World War.

THE
MOUNTAIN STATES:
The Boom Goes Bust

Here in the Mountain West, space and nature shape us. Despite our differences, we are made a hopeful people, as the mountain men and the overland travelers and just yesterday's homesteaders were hopeful. As the gold-seeker and the mining magnates and the cattle kings were hopeful. Not always honest, mind you, not always capable or wise or successful, but almost always hopeful and hence astride of life.

—A. B. Guthrie, Jr.

Parachute, Colorado. Evanston, Wyoming. Coalstrip, Montana. For close to a decade after the 1973 Arab oil embargo, these hamlets on the prairie horizon symbolized the new Mountain West. While the United States prepared to make itself "energy self-sufficient," the towns nearest the oil, gas, and minerals boomed like the nineteenth-century Gold Rush. Only the strong, the desperate—and journalists—needed apply.

The journalistic pack eager to report on the "rape of the West" and the lively goings-on got so big that the Colorado School of Mines set up boom-town bus tours. I remember getting off such a bus in Evanston on a blistering day in the summer of 1981. There was a mixture of horror, greed, and hope in the air.

Evanston's population had swelled from 6,400 to 11,500 in a year and a half, and the city council filled us with tales of traffic jams as bad as Boston or New York; of job-seeking families who squatted on

open land in mobile homes, campers, cars, and school buses; of construction managers busing their lonely workers to the fleshpots of
Nevada; and of more prosaic plans to build an industrial park to keep
the economy going once the boom was over. "Coffee-cup" government had given way to planning and zoning, and wildlife was endangered by $9-to-$15-an-hour workers whose only recreation was to
cruise across the state every weekend "with wife, baby, and a gun rack
in a four-wheel-drive vehicle." Complain they might, but most Evan-
stonians seemed quite happily wrapped up in reliving the quick profits
and romantic lawlessness of the Gold Rush days. High prices, drifters,
drunken brawls, even prostitution were all part of the package.

Then world oil prices fell, and just as suddenly and predictably as
the old-timers said it would, the boom went bust. Today the streets
of Evanston are quiet, and the ephemeral nature of the modern Mountain dream is clear. As they look toward the 1990s, the energy boom
towns and most of the eight Mountain states—Montana, Wyoming,
Colorado, Utah, Idaho, Arizona, Nevada, and New Mexico—are
resting, regrouping, trying to come to terms with *not* fearing the
"phenomenal, cancerous growth rates" predicted by Richard D.
Lamm of Colorado, the region's most environmentally outspoken
governor.

This deep economic crisis has provided the greatest challenge since
the Great Depression to the Mountain West's commitment to unfettered free enterprise and its reputation as the most reliably Republican
region of the United States. The era of Reagan and the Republican-
controlled Senate has left most of the Mountain states worse off
economically and environmentally than when it began. The Reagan
military buildup has pumped money into Colorado, Arizona, New
Mexico, and Utah, but it has not made up for the region-wide effects
of low oil prices and a farming and ranching economy so deteriorated
that landowners have sold their precious water rights to cities and, in
a few cases, taken down fences to graze wild animals for hunting. By
1986, the economic outlook had become so bleak that a *Wall Street
Journal* article suggested the Mountain states were developing into a
northern and a southern tier, with the northern states, their fortunes
closely tied to energy, mining, and agriculture, unlikely to prosper in
the rest of this century.

The depression in the energy industries hurt the worst. Thousands of workers left their homes in small mountain and prairie towns to look for work in Denver, Phoenix, Salt Lake City, and Albuquerque or farther afield in California. Instead of mining and construction jobs that paid $9 to $15 per hour, they found minimum-wage jobs as security guards and maids. The young and fit tried to solve the problem by going into the military. In the mining sector alone, nearly $2 billion in wages were lost.

The prettiest of the boom towns, such as Parachute, remarketed themselves as retirement havens—a far cry psychologically and financially from oil centers. The ever-optimistic Mountain state promoters liked to say the high-tech-oriented cities of Denver, Albuquerque, and Salt Lake City fared better, but the expense accounts and free spending of the oilmen were sorely missed. In the Denver of 1986, an oil executive friend could no longer take me to the Petroleum Club for lunch because his firm had canceled his membership; the carpenter who restored the same friend's historic house reported that half his clients had canceled their plans.

The Reagan record is equally dismal on the environment, the biggest social issue in the West. Western conservatives lauded the appointments of the strident, confrontational Interior Secretary James G. Watt and the equally conservative Environmental Protection Agency administrator Anne Gorsuch Burford. And they argue that, after a generation of dominance by overly protectionist federal environmental policies, the Reagan years have restored the balance in federal policy making to reflect the very real needs of mining companies, ranchers, and concessionaires in national parks. But there have been no short-term economic rewards for the administration's hardline pro-industry stands, especially Watt's leasing and selling of federal coal and minerals to multinational energy companies at the lowest prices imaginable. Meanwhile, the administration stalled proposals to protect the ecosystem of Yellowstone National Park and reduce airplane flights that disturb the quiet of the Grand Canyon, and discouraged designation of new wilderness areas.

In politics, the Mountain states maintained a much more independent stance in the eighties than is generally recognized. It's true that all the Mountain states have voted Republican for president since 1968, and President Reagan received some of his highest percentages in the Mountain West. But on their home turf, westerners vote for the man—or woman—not the party, and were splitting their tickets long before the rest of the country caught onto the idea. From Montana to Arizona and New Mexico, the voters are highly educated, vote regularly in high turnouts, make hard choices between individual candidates, and view party affiliation, much less machine politics, as an anachronistic, undesirable remnant of the eastern states. This independent streak goes back as much as half a century when Montanans defied political tradition to elect the first congresswoman and Wyomingites the first woman governor.

During the Great Depression, which hit this region hard (half of Montanans were on relief), the Mountain states voted for Franklin Delano Roosevelt in almost all elections (though even Roosevelt lost Colorado twice and Wyoming once). And again, in 1964, Democrats nearly swept the region. Arizonan Barry Goldwater's strategists assumed his right-wing stands would have great appeal in the Mountain states. Only his home state gave him a majority, the rest voted for Lyndon B. Johnson.

Democratic presidential candidates still face two obstacles in this part of the country. It is now almost 50 years since Mountain state voters felt desperate enough to vote for Roosevelt. Nearly a quarter-century after Goldwater's defeat and after two Reagan administrations, one has to wonder whether any Republican candidate would be too conservative for Mountain state voters. While this thinly populated region fielded not one, but two 1988 Democratic presidential candidates, Senator Gary Hart of Colorado (who nearly won the 1984 nomination away from former Vice-President Walter Mondale), and Governor Bruce Babbitt of Arizona, it's also important to remember that neighboring westerner George McGovern's 1972 presidential bid was rejected even in his home state of South Dakota. Even regional loyalties may not be enough to penetrate this Republican bastion.

The Democrats' problems are both cultural and ideological. Westerners simply do not think in terms of class consciousness and redistribution of wealth as vehicles for social change. The hopeful attitude Guthrie described is not just Rocky Mountain hype. As *Atlantic Monthly* writer Nicholas Lemann discovered when he visited Grand Junction, Colorado, in 1985, a large percentage of the people in the

Mountain states have adapted to frequent moves "in a constant hope for the big score—or if not the big score, some kind of score."

This mobile work force ranges from college-educated engineers and teachers to the "boom-town trash" on whose hard, physical labor much of the country depends: truckers, oil-rig roughnecks, construction workers, and the women—married and unmarried—who follow them. These and traditional western migrants—ranch hands, rodeo performers, carnival barkers—are often romanticized by outsiders, but the reality of their lives is stark indeed, as was brought home to the nation by a 1985 traveling exhibit of the work of photographer Richard Avedon. Stripped of their ten-gallon hats and rodeo settings but retaining the soot of mines or the grime of a drilling site, Avedon's subjects demystified the West, revealing the vulnerable but gritty people behind the image of the idealized cowboy and agrarian utopia. Avedon's subjects may be beaten, but they are not broken. And they are reluctant to consider themselves an exploited working class that can be organized in traditional Democratic party terms.

The Democrats' second problem is whether they will ever again offer the region an economic reason to elect a president of their party. Roosevelt's New Deal rewarded the Mountain West with the hydroelectric plants and irrigation projects which made the region's fantastic postwar growth feasible. Today the national Democratic party, in ideology if not in practice, has forsaken most of these projects as environmentally damaging. In the process, the Democrats have won the environmentalist vote, but that vote is not large enough to tilt a presidential election. The Democrats' interests in urban problems and minorities are seen here as commitments to other places. Unless the national Democratic party stops writing off these states as too Republican and too small to count and comes up with a program to diversify their economies, the Mountain West will remain the staunchest Republican territory anywhere in presidential politics.

In Congress the Republican dominance is less extreme, and in the governors' mansions, an entirely different story. After the 1982 congressional elections, the region's 24-member House delegation (enlarged in 1980 by a new seat in each of Arizona, Colorado, New Mexico, Nevada, and Utah) was 16 to 8 Republican, and the Senate delegation 11 to 5 Republican. In Idaho, Utah, Nevada, and Wyoming, Republicans made up the entire congressional delegations. By the time the 100th Congress took their seats in 1987, however, Democrats held 9 of the 24 Mountain House seats and 6 of the 16 Senate seats. Only Wyoming's delegation remained entirely Republican. In 1986, Coloradans elected another Democrat, Representative Timothy E. Wirth, to the Senate seat vacated by Gary Hart. In Nevada, Representative Harry Reid used his state's anti-Washington sentiments to convince the voters in 1986 that a candidate hand picked by retiring Nevada Senator Paul Laxalt, Reagan's "best friend," had too much of a Washington taint to deserve their favors.

When the GOP controlled the Senate from 1981 to 1986, Mountain state senators became the most powerful regional bloc in the body, holding five chairmanships: Banking, Housing and Urban Affairs (Jake Garn of Utah), Budget (Pete V. Domenici of New Mexico), Energy and Natural Resources (James A. McClure of Idaho), Labor and Human Resources (Orrin G. Hatch of Utah) and Veterans' Affairs (Alan K. Simpson of Wyoming). With the Democratic takeover of the Senate, all Mountain state committee chairmanships were gone, and the region was once again clinging like a lifeline to its one House chairman, Interior head Morris Udall of Arizona.

During these same vaunted Reagan years, environmentally minded Democrats occupied the governor's office in *all eight* Mountain states. The Democrats owe their good fortune to both their own good candidates who rarely emphasize the national party's ties with labor unions and minorities, and to the state Republican parties' tendency to pick unsophisticated state legislators to run for high office.

Reagan's long years in the presidency had little or no effect on the Mountain state governorships. After the 1986 elections, Montana, Wyoming, Idaho, Nevada, and Colorado still had Democratic governors; Idaho even put Cecil Andrus, the governor who had resigned to become President Carter's Interior secretary, back in office. Utah and New Mexico did switch to Republicans while Reagan was in office. So did Arizona, electing one Evan Mecham, a perennial candidate who managed to slip into office in a three-way race. Described by a local columnist as "a guy from the wrong side of the tracks who's scratched his way to the top," Mecham abolished the state's observance of Martin Luther King's birthday and appointed a bizarre assortment of right-wing ideologues to head state departments, thus ruining Arizona's growing reputation for thoughtful, progressive governance.

Yuppie Heaven

It was no accident that Gary Hart found his political base among the "yuppies"—young urban professionals—in his victory over Walter Mondale in the 1984 New Hampshire Democratic primary. As the vast baby-boom generation was settling down from the 1960s through the early 1980s, Denver was one of their destinations of choice, and Hart had learned to appeal to them as early as his 1974 Senate campaign.

The electorates of Colorado and the other Mountain states are ahead of their times in the best and worst ways. The people of the Mountain states are younger than the people of any other region of the country and more highly educated than all but residents of the Pacific states. They are also highly mobile. As of 1980, a full 56 percent of the region's residents were born out of state (compared with 37 percent nationwide).

Compared with the East Coast, the Great Lakes, and the Plains states, where many of the new Mountain residents were born, raised, and educated, this region has garnered an unfair share of highly educated, youthful human energy to work on the problems of their region. But one cannot yet be certain how or whether all this talent can be harnessed to solve western problems. The boomers' libertarian inclinations cut across party lines, of course, and in this already independent region, the baby boomers can turn the electorate from the thoughtful to the undependable.

The baby-boom migration to the Mountain West must also be divided into two waves. There are the protectors, who came in the 1960s and early 1970s, lured by the region's natural beauty, and the exploiters, who came later to cash in on the energy boom. The results could be seen in the differences in the 1974 Colorado elections when Hart, Lamm, and other liberals were swept into office, and 1980 when Hart won by only two percent.

The protectors and the exploiters may further be divided into the yuppies, the relatively small percentage of baby boomers who are lawyers, doctors, accountants, and successful business people and what pollster William Hamilton has called "yuppies' cousins"—a much larger group of less affluent baby boomers who have gradually adopted the educated elite's liberal social mores but do not share its education, high-paying jobs, and economic security.

The mettle of this generation of Mountain residents will be tested over the coming years as they face the fact that they migrated to this region in a period of extraordinary economic growth, but have settled in a place that is difficult, and sometimes downright hostile, to human habitation. In this time of economic trouble, all the people of the Mountain states must confront the five timeless and basic facts of their political and economic lives: a mountain-desert climate, vast spaces, small populations, absentee ownership, and dependence on volatile international markets to price their resources, agricultural commodities, and yes, even computers. And they must also cope with urban air pollution and threats to the very environment that attracted people to these states. The seriousness with which the Mountain boomers respond to this challenge will say much about the generation's national potential.

As they take their leadership roles, the baby boomers and other new Mountain residents may find the presence of so many outlanders more important than they think. We often forget that mobility and growth carry a price. Politicians recognize this even if it has helped them get elected. Leaders as prominent as Udall, Hart, and Goldwater have found it a constant battle to win name recognition among the constant stream of newly arrived voters, much less educate them about the serious issues the region faces. Activists charge that too many newcomers, young and old alike, use the Mountain states as an escape from problems they had faced back home. Many newcomers of all ages dismiss the region's history, with its tales of prospecting, mining, and irrigated agriculture, as irrelevant to modern times. In that history lies a spirit of problem solving, compromise, and practical politics that is timeless. If the Mountain migrants don't study that history and take up their proper roles, they risk living out the terrible prediction of the late crusading Denver editor Eugene Cervi, who saw Colorado, together with its mountain neighbors, becoming a "withdrawal" state—a refuge for the wealthy, fleeing from confrontation with every real problem of the modern world.

THE INTERIOR FRONTIER

What do we want with this worthless area—this region of
savages and wild beasts, of shifting sands and whirlwinds of
dust, of cactus and prairie dogs? To what use could we ever
hope to put these great deserts and these endless mountain
ranges?

—Senator Daniel Webster, 1852

For close to a century, Webster's prognostication had a ring of truth
to it. There were the gold and silver rushes of the nineteenth century,
of course. And the mountains, forests, and desert were early recognized
as a local joy and a tourist destination, especially for people in need
of clean, dry air. But for generations, only a small number of people
could find enough work to survive in the Mountain states. Most of
the land was too dry for grain farming, and vast acreages were required
for cattle and sheep ranches.

To the nation, the Mountain states were a huge burden. Great
dams, aqueducts, and reservoirs, so costly that only the federal government could afford to pay for them, had to be built to provide water
for even minimal agriculture and moderate-sized cities. The federal
government kept title to nearly half the land because no settler could
figure out how to make a living on it.

Traveling through the Mountain West in the mid-1940s to write
Inside U.S.A., John Gunther noted that Colorado was so inbred, its
level of state aid to education so low, its provision of health services
to its large rural population so minimal that the state was guilty of
"Olympian inertness."

In those years, the Mountain states exported people with brains,
youth, and talent to the West Coast and the high-paying jobs that
started with World War II. This problem was somewhat relieved in
Colorado and Arizona as they began to attract substantial military
payrolls and space-age industries, but as late as 1970 Governor Forrest
Anderson of Montana succinctly named five "human resource" problems which bedeviled his and the other Mountain states: (1) outmi-
gration of working people; (2) a resulting small return on heavy
educational investment; (3) a burdensome per capita tax load resulting from sparse population and vast spaces, much of it owned by the

federal government; (4) a colonial status imposed by out-of-state control of an almost purely extractive economy; and (5) the commercial disadvantage of distance from the market place.

Even Montana throbbed with new life and new people during the energy boom of the 1970s, but the sparseness of population and power can still be felt. Former Governor and Senator Milward Simpson of Wyoming has called his state "the land of high altitude and low multitudes." The population density per square mile in Wyoming is the lowest in the nation, Alaska excepted, but Simpson could have been speaking of the entire Mountain region. From the Canadian to the Mexican border, the Mountain West stretches 1,260 miles, three times the distance from Boston to Washington. From Colorado's eastern border to westernmost Nevada is 950 miles. Altogether, there are 863,524 square miles in this vast expanse of sagebrush and mountain, 13 times as large as New England, five times as large as California, and equal to the combined area of 13 European nations. Yet even today, after the great population surge of the last generation, the region is home to only 12 million people.

Powerlessness is palpable in the Mountain states. A case can still be made that, despite the diversification of the postwar period, these states remain what they have always been: wards of the federal government and pawns of absentee private business.

The land in federal hands—ranging from 30 percent of Montana to 86 percent of Nevada—includes mountains, forests, and desert, all of which play vital roles in the region's grazing, mining, and tourism industries. When one adds the billions the federal government spends in the West each year—on land and forestry management, water resources, aid to agriculture, military installations, and the whole array of present-day federal programs, it turns out that the West is getting a lot more in services than it pays back in taxes. Denver is, naturally, one of the federal government's regional office capitals. That these eight remote states have been able to garner so much federal largesse is a remarkable political accomplishment, but there is a constant awareness in the region that political power in sheer numbers is still elusive. This huge area, making up 30 percent of the national land mass, is represented by only 24 House members, a little more than 5 percent of the body.

Home-grown economic power is rare. Multinational energy companies based in New York, Los Angeles, and Houston make the biggest economic decisions in the region; the people of the Mountain states face formidable odds in confronting them, and even when they do, the companies are increasingly subject to the vagaries of the international market place. *Fortune* found only seven companies large enough for its list of the 500 industrials in 1987 and five of those were in Colorado. Big banks are equally rare. Financing of huge energy deals is still arranged in New York City; Denver's financial claim to fame is a penny stock market. As a result, even the debate over an oil import fee is conducted mostly by companies headquartered elsewhere.

The Mountain states do much better in the *Inc.* magazine rankings of small, growing businesses, but those companies do not provide the established corporate base enjoyed by older parts of the country. Denver, for example, had 1,200 energy companies in the early eighties, but many consisted of an executive, a geologist, a secretary—and an unproven future. Most of the high-tech plants are branches of California firms, and some of the locally headquartered high-tech companies have gone through spectacular bankruptcies. Strangely enough, the city with the strongest sense of self-determination may be little Boise, Idaho, home of the great corporations Boise Cascade and Morrison-Knudsen, and of J. R. Simplot's potato and mining empire.

The Politics of Schizophrenia

Distrust of government comes naturally to the Mountain West. Baronial cattle ranches and the mining interests had no use for governmental regulation. The pioneer life offered opportunity to the men and women strong enough to make it on their own far from civilization. But it also demanded self-reliance—and self-protection from the animals and the misfits the frontier attracted. Thus was born the western attachment to firearms and the opposition to the national gun control movement that emerged after President Kennedy's assassination. Ethnic discrimination was not unknown, but there were few ethnics to discriminate against in this homogeneous, masculine, Anglo society. The only exceptions were the Hispanic communities in the Southwest and a few mining towns (the biggest was Butte, Montana) where Irish and southern European immigrants viewed themselves as a laboring class subject to discrimination.

But early westerners violated their conservative inclination, sometimes out of convenience, sometimes out of desperation. From territorial days, western leaders contended it was the obligation of the federal government to pay a large chunk of the cost of the dams and aqueducts that were vital for both agriculture and cities to grow. At its best, their reasoning went back to the theory of Manifest Destiny—that the people of the United States should populate the North American continent from coast to coast and keep out European powers—and at its worst, they simply wanted use of tax money from other regions to make their backers and themselves rich. Like the South, the Mountain West distrusted Wall Street. Westerners railed against discriminatory freight rates, low farm prices, and other evidence of the power of "eastern interests."

Arizona's former senator Barry Goldwater has come to symbolize the conservatism of modern western politics, but he too supported federal sponsorship of water projects, and his rise broke a tradition of development-minded Democrats who held sway when the Democrats had Congress under almost uninterrupted control. The man who really brought home the bacon for Arizona was the durable Carl Hayden, chairman of the Senate Appropriations Committee until his retirement in 1969 at age 93 after more than a half-century on Capitol Hill. Two other Democrats, from neighboring New Mexico—Dennis Chavez and Clinton P. Anderson—used their Senate power to transform their state from a sleepy winter tourist sun spot to a center of nuclear and space-age research and development. Many of the Mountain states, normally Republican in their voting habits, made it a point to keep one or even two Democrats in the U.S. Senate through the 1970s to protect their federal flank. Thus Wyoming's Gale McGee, Idaho's Frank Church, Nevada's Pat McCarran, Utah's Frank Moss, New Mexico's Joseph M. Montoya, and Montana's Mike Mansfield and Lee Metcalf established long and notable careers. Some of these men made a national mark far broader than parochial western interests. But for the most part, parochial interests prompted voters to send them to Washington in the first place.

The House Interior Committee was headed for 14 years by Wayne Aspinall of Colorado's Western Slope; he obtained money for so many federal dam and reservoir projects in Colorado that even his home-state boosters admitted some of them were uneconomic and should never have been built. The first clear signal that this political and economic partnership had run its course came in the 1972 primary when Colorado Democrats threw out the aging Aspinall in favor of a young environmentalist. In a pattern that would repeat itself in other western elections, Colorado's general electorate did not agree with the Democrats' break with tradition and chose a Republican in November. Aspinall's defeat came as a shock, however, to the timber, grazing, and mining interests, who detested the growing questions in Washington over the construction of dams, the unlimited exploitation of minerals, and the low fees that ranchers were paying to graze their animals on federal lands. The "feds," traditional westerners charged, were suddenly being manipulated by outsiders, usually easterners, eager to tie up the West for the pleasure of rich backpackers.

As the Aspinall election showed, the debate over proper federal policies in the West was—and is—as much between the region's own growing urban populations and the rural people who make their living from the land as between easterners and westerners. The first federal official to develop modern policies for the region was Stewart L. Udall, an Arizona House member until President Kennedy appointed him Interior secretary in 1961. Over the years, the Interior Department, the great federal patron of the West, began to champion environmental protection, promotion of tourism, rehabilitation of rangelands, wilderness designation, and the setting aside of federal land for the recreation of the Mountain West's growing urban populations.

It was a western senator—Idaho's Frank Church—who led the floor fight for the landmark 1964 Wilderness Act. Representative Morris K. Udall (D.-Arizona), elected to Congress when his brother became Interior secretary, rose to the chairmanship of the House Interior and Insular Affairs Committee and shifted the committee toward environmental protection with the cooperation of at least some of the Mountain states' representatives who sat on the committee. The 11 members from the Mountain states, together with 10 members from the Pacific states, form a western majority on the committee.

By the late 1970s, Mountain state voters felt so secure in their fantastic new energy wealth they had no trouble in throwing out the kind of senators who had based their careers on bringing home federal bacon. The influx of new voters, the constant stream of criticism from the increasingly influential environmental organizations, and heavy Republican criticism of these same Democratic senators for their role in higher federal taxes and federal regulation contributed to the demise of this conservative Democratic era. In 1976, Utah's Moss, New Mexico's Montoya, and Wyoming's McGee were all defeated by anti-government Republicans; Arizona's Paul J. Fannin, who retired, was replaced by another relatively conservative Democrat, Dennis DeConcini, after a bitter Republican primary. The defeats of Church in the 1980 Reagan landslide and Nevada's Howard Cannon in 1982 completed the rout of the old conservative Democrats. But Republican media consultants still reserve their greatest reverence for the key television ad aired in Malcolm Wallop's 1976 campaign against McGee: a porta-potty was strapped to a horse as an announcer sarcastically informed voters that federal labor laws promoted by McGee's party would require them on roundups.

SEVERANCE TAXES: LEGACY OF THE BOOM

If the baby boomers do have a claim to early political accomplishment in the Mountain states, it is in the legacy of the ʝ'severance taxes" on minerals passed over the mineral industry's heated objections during the boom of the 1970s and kept even in bust times. In one of the greatest assertions of state political power in the postwar era, all the Mountain states finally stood up to protect themselves from the environmental rape, abandoned ghost towns, and out-of-state exploitation that had marked their history.

This willingness to tax minerals, most of which are exported to serve larger urban centers, is also a sign to the political independence of the modern Mountain states. Earlier generations of legislatures had been overwhelmed by the mining companies and their usually Republican vassals in the state legislatures. As an Anaconda copper lobbyist once said of the Montana lawmakers, "Give me a case of Scotch, a case of gin, one blonde and one brunette, and I can take any liberal."

Both the gargantuan size of the mining companies' proposals and changing times contributed to the new political atmosphere. The development of western coal was logical since the American people had drifted westward, and the Mountain states and California both needed more power. In 1970, for the first time in American history, a western mine—the Navaho strip mine of the Utah Construction and Mining Company near Farmington, New Mexico—became the country's largest single producer of coal. By 1971, nearly one million acres of public and Indian coal lands across the West had already been leased for strip mining by coal and petroleum companies. And the railroads, which had been given sections of land as encouragement to build track a century ago, found themselves owners of immense coal supplies.

Coal gasification was seen as a way to replace the country's fast-depleting reserves of natural gas in wells, and the West was the place with the coal. By federal government estimates, some 77 percent of the country's total of economically strippable coal lay west of the Mississippi. Wyoming's reserve of low-sulphur (and hence less-polluting) coal is eight times as large as West Virginia's and Kentucky's put together. The regional shift in U.S. coal production in the last 15 years is startling to behold. In 1970, only 44.9 of the 612.7 million tons of coal mined in this country came from west of the Mississippi, but by 1985, 316.9 of the 886.1 million tons were mined in the West.

As the boom intensified, the political climate for tough environmental laws and severance taxes improved. As Montana state senator Tom Towe put, it, "The copper kings, who became fabulously wealthy, did not leave their money to Montana. The only thing I can find they left in Montana was $20,000 toward the construction of a theater inside the state prison.* We are determined to leave future generations something more than unknown environmental problems and a depressed economy."

The records vary state-by-state—Wyoming, Montana, and New Mexico have proven far tougher on mining than Colorado and Utah—but the mechanisms for environmental protection and collection of severance taxes are in place everywhere. These laws are a testament to the pioneering efforts of the environmental movement and to the energetic politicking of the baby boomers, many of whom

---

*Even the prison theater reached a bad end. In the 1960s, prisoners tore it apart in a riot. Montanans are now trying to raise money for its historic preservation.

had traveled and gone to school elsewhere. They realized the land and life at home were things to cherish, and became determined to stop the brutal, colonial exploitation. As Michael Jacobs, now editor of the Grand Forks *Herald* in coal-rich North Dakota, wrote in 1974, "The coal men who come to this frontier are like the buffalo hunters who came to the frontier in another time. They killed the bison and left the stench of rotting carcasses and mounds of bleached bones. They made the survival of civilization impossible. Unlike the buffalo, though, coal can't be replaced. Coal beds can't be rebuilt. Coal is a one time harvest."

Perhaps even more impressively, the lawmakers have defended the severance taxes against actions by both the energy consuming states and their own hard-pressed citizens. When Montana passed a whopping 30 percent coal severance tax and Wyoming a 17 percent tax, the incensed utilities and energy-consuming states jointly mounted a campaign to paint the energy states as "a kind of United American Emirates" that were profiteering at the expense of energy-poor parts of the country. But the western states stood united, and the coal severance taxes survived a Supreme Court challenge to their constitutionality and congressional maneuvers to limit the taxes on coal from federal and Indian lands to 12.5 percent.

In 1981, when Republicans gained control of the Montana legislature for the first time in 10 years, there were immediate proposals to gut the environmental laws and energy taxes, but they went down to defeat. Similar fates met such attempts in other states. In 1985, after coal demand had plummeted in the face of lower oil prices, Montana did grant a 10 percent credit for a two-year "window of opportunity" so companies could prove they could sell coal if the price were lower. But the framework remained, so that if the demand was strong, Montana would extract its proper price for the loss of its nonrenewable resource.

During the boom, the severance taxes paid for environmental cleanup, roads, schools, and other modern improvements in the energy towns. When the boom went bust, the Mountain states at least had a nest egg to maintain services and make some attempt, however feeble, at economic diversification. By the late 1980s, Montana's trusts alone contained over $350 million.

The severance taxes are not a simple panacea. They can be considered liberal only to the extent that the states have shown a willingness to tax business and the only major source of wealth in the state; they are not the same as the states' citizens deciding to tax themselves to help the unfortunate. When energy and mineral prices go down, the tax revenues go down too. But both the economies and the ecologies of the energy-producing states seem fragile and uncertain. Who knows whether the reclamation of the coal lands will last over time? Or whether the wildlife so dear to westerners will survive the onslaught of population growth and mineral exploitation? At the very least, severance-tax self-protection is surely warranted.

REAGANITES IN RETROSPECT:
JAMES WATT AND ANNE GORSUCH BURFORD,
THE LAND AND THE AIR

It already seems a long time since Reagan's first Interior secretary, James G. Watt, and Environmental Protection Agency administrator Anne Gorsuch Burford threw the environmental movement and the national press into almost daily fits over their pro-business ideology and management snafus. Like a cowboy and a cowgirl riding matching conservative horses, these two Wyoming-born Colorado residents arrived in Washington vowing to take the eastern, liberal establishment and its environmental movement head on.

Watt started out by directing that the bison adorning the Interior secretary's official seal be flipped so that after facing left for the Interior Department's first 132 years, it now faced right. Burford, meanwhile, declared that her top priority as the nation's environmental protector would be to relieve American industry of the "overburden" of environmental regulation. Within three years, both were declared unfit for public life and driven from their offices. But their sagas— now complete with autobiographies—are colorful reminders of the early, heady days of the Reagan presidency when conservatives' self-confidence knew no bounds.

Watt and Burford, more than any other appointees, symbolized the Reaganites' plan to take over the federal government, not only from the Democrats, but from the remains of the Republican party's liberal wing. To the frustration of western ranchers and many businessmen, the national environmental movement had roots as strong in the Republican party as the Democratic. It was the Republican president Teddy Roosevelt who promoted the national park system, and the Nixon administration that created the Environmental Protection Agency. Liberal, patrician Republicans have often defended both wilderness and the urban environment not only against big business, but against pro-growth labor unions as well. Whenever a Republican sat in the White House, the liberal wing of the party claimed Interior and EPA as "their" agencies.

Western pleasure at Watt's appointment must be viewed in terms of the times. The entire West had broken with the national trend in 1976 and voted for the losing Gerald Ford. Before Inauguration Day, 1977, word got out that President Carter had demanded that aides develop a long "hit list" of western water projects to be "zerofunded" on the grounds that they were environmentally degrading and financially extravagant. Whether Carter ordered the list out of pique or conviction, the idea of summarily stopping already authorized projects struck westerners as the height of arrogance, and a withdrawal of federal commitments. The entire western power structure—from the anti-government Goldwater to the environmentalist Lamm—rose up in what may have been the last great western stand. As with so many Carter actions, it was the style, not the substance, that proved objectionable. Neither Congress nor Reagan approved of some of the projects to which the Carterites objected, and Carter's policy of asking the states to share in the up-front costs of water projects was adopted by the Reagan administration. The difference was that western members of Congress and Reagan never drew up a "hit list" or said they were bad ideas.

But the insult changed the West's relationship with Washington. National public opinion polls showed the West replacing the South as the region of the country which felt most out of tune with the federal government. In 1979, western resentment hit its high mark in a "Sagebrush Rebellion," which made the cover of *Newsweek*. The Nevada legislature declared state sovereignty over 49 million acres of territory owned by the Interior Department's Bureau of Land Management, and legislators in 13 other western states introduced similar bills.

The rebellion faltered after Governor Bruce E. Babbitt of Arizona pointed out that the states would never be able to manage so much land and would sell it off to ranchers who would overgraze it and restrict access for hunters, fishermen, and sportsmen. But westerners of all ideological persuasions would probably agree that as long as the federal government remains the biggest landowner in the West, the conflict will always be there. Nevada legislator and sagebrush leader Dean A. Rhoads was speaking for the conservative side but voiced a regional—if not universal—belief when he summed up the situation: "It's impossible for a landlord who's 3,000 miles away to manage."

Reagan, the pro-development western traditionalist whose environmental attitude was summed up in his comment that "trees pollute," never courted the Republican environmentalists, and in September 1980 heads of most of the leading environmental organizations assembled in the White House Rose Garden and endorsed President Carter for re-election. The Carter commitment marked the first time environmentalists had forsaken their bipartisan lobbying position in favor of one presidential candidate. To Watt, this formal politicization of the environmental movement was confirmation of his view that "What I call 'commercial' environmentalists are hard-core, left-wing, radicals, manipulating the press. They have a conspiracy of shared values. Their real objective is partisan politics to change the form of government."

If Reagan agreed with Watt's political and environmental views—and there is no evidence to the contrary—no man was better suited to the task ahead. Watt already had political reasons for wanting to take on the environmental establishment. As an Interior Department bureaucrat, Watt had been assigned by the Nixon White House the job of getting the governor of Alaska, Walter Hickel, confirmed as Interior secretary. On the job, Hickel turned out to be much more of an environmentalist and anti–Vietnam War activist than anyone ever dreamed, and Nixon finally fired him. From Watt's viewpoint, merciless environmentalist pressure was responsible for the change in Hickel, just as it was for Wyoming Republican governor Stan Hathaway's 1975 nervous breakdown and resignation shortly after grueling confirmation hearings for the Interior job. During the Carter years, Watt—whose father hated the New Deal and whose grandfather came west when the region was still unclaimed territory—served as president of the Mountain States Legal Foundation, an organization financed by Joseph Coors, the ultraconservative Colorado brewer who also started the Washington-based Heritage Foundation. Mountain States started out fighting environmental groups, but also challenged government agencies, affirmative action, and the proposed Equal Rights Amendment.

As it turned out, Watt's conservatism ran deeper than politics. He had undergone a conversion to "born-again" Christianity and leaned toward a literal interpretation of Genesis 1:28—"And God said unto them . . . replenish the earth, and subdue it; and have dominion over . . . every living thing." When asked about preserving wilderness for the benefit of "future generations," Watt replied, "I do not know how many future generations we can count on before the Lord returns." His responsibility, Watt said, was to strike a proper balance between the country's vast "natural resources base" to ensure that "people are provided for until He does come."

In Watt's case these beliefs meant cutting the federal budget for purchasing parklands in half, offering 1.3 million acres off the shores of northern and central California for oil and gas exploration, "phasing out" the U.S. Office of Surface Mining, which is responsible for overseeing strip-mine regulations, and ignoring Congress's order to study whether millions of acres of federal land should be designated as wilderness.

To the environmentalists, Watt was a fox put in charge of the chicken coop, and they greeted this onslaught with all the political and legal muscle they could muster in Congress and the courts. The Reagan years solidified the environmental movement into a real political force, but the legacy of the Reagan years, said Chuck Clusen, president of the Wilderness Society, "is a very bad one because the discretionary powers that the Interior and Agriculture departments have over public lands is immense. Watt leased coal at fire sale prices, and in the year 2010 it will be very easy to show the impact of the policies of these eight years."

Watt's policies were not all crazy. He raised national park entrance fees, which are still minor compared with the costs of traveling to the parks, and a subsequent government investigation showed that the money was used to improve facilities. Many middle-of-the-road people were willing to listen to his argument for limiting the prohibition on mining and drilling in wilderness areas to 15 years while those areas are surveyed for possible mineral content. "If we determine that there's a cobalt deposit that could reduce our dependence on Russia for our military needs, then we could open up a 100-acre tract or a 500-acre tract out of the 200 million acres of wilderness," he said. "The gravest threat to the ecology is to put a lid on energy and mineral development until demand reaches the crisis stage."

But Watt's nasty, confrontational side made even those who thought the government might have become overzealous in protecting the West wonder whether he was a proper custodian of the nation's natural areas. "I don't like to paddle, and I don't like to walk," he told a convention of park concessionaires. On the issue of whether there should be flights or quiet in the Grand Canyon, Watt said that on the fourth day of his raft trip down the Colorado River, he was "praying for helicopters. There is no way you could get me on an oar-powered raft on that river—I'll guarantee you that."

Watt's running commentary drove Wilderness Society chairman and former Wisconsin senator Gaylord Nelson to declare that "the Secretary has gone bonkers," but Watt retained the support of the president until he started baiting liberals and the press on issues bigger than the environment. A careful rereading of the stories surrounding the Beach Boys affair shows that Watt was right when he charged that the environmentalists and the press were willing to jump on any personality issue to drive him from office. In response to demands from Parents for a Drug-Free Youth, a group supported by Nancy Reagan, Watt planned to curb drug use at Fourth of July events on the Mall in Washington by cancelling rock groups in favor of military bands and—for reasons never explained—Las Vegas nightclub singer Wayne Newton. When the *Washington Post* noted that the Beach Boys had often headlined the event, Watt suddenly became the man who wanted to ban the Beach Boys. The White House had defended his anti-environmentalist comments, but Watt learned the limits of being a Mountain conservative in a White House dominated by California image-makers well aware of the popularity of the Beach Boys. Nancy Reagan declared her personal support for the Beach Boys, and Watt emerged from the White House, publicly humiliated, holding a plaster trophy of a foot with a bullet hole in it.

Humor gave way to disgust several months later when Watt characterized a coal commission he had appointed as "every kind of mix you can have. I have a black. I have a woman, two Jews and a cripple. And we have talent." Watt had already been required to apologize for warning the Israeli ambassador that if liberals of the Jewish community opposed the administration's energy development policies, "there is a great risk . . . America will be prevented from being the strong protector and friend of Israel that we are and want to be." Even mining companies feared a public backlash. The Senate planned a bipartisan resolution condemning him, and after Senator Robert J. Dole (R.-Kansas) said, "We just can't stand every two or three months Mr. Watt making some comment to offend another 20 or 30 or 40 million people," Watt declared that his "usefulness" to Reagan "has come to an end."

His congressional nemesis, Representative John F. Seiberling (D.-Ohio), asserted that Watt's tenure would "rank with the Teapot Dome in terms of mismanagement of the Interior Department—the only difference is that Watt is giving assets away because of ideology, not venality." Environmentalists had mixed feelings about Watt's retirement. They lost a perfect enemy, whose very name was a gold mine in their membership and direct-mail fundraising appeals. Watt's successors, William P. Clark and Donald P. Hodel, maintained the same pro-development agenda, but proved too smooth to attack.

Watt, meanwhile, became the first Reagan official to write his memoirs. In *The Courage of a Conservative* (Simon & Schuster, 1985) Watt revealed surprisingly little of the behind-the-scenes operations of the administration, but his book is a highly readable guide to conservative positions on every subject from abortion to farm aid. "Modern conservatives," Watt wrote, "acknowledge that a kind of second revolution took place when, under Franklin Roosevelt, the federal government stepped in and took charge during the emergency of the Great Depression . . . seek, not to dismantle the welfare state, but reform it," and "oppose the growing bureaucracies of big government *and* big business."

Watt's main issue—the changes in our cultural values since the country was founded by English Puritans who limited the role of government—is a very appropriate subject for discussion in a society that has absorbed immigrants of every nationality and uses government to cope with modern problems. Watt maintains that our pluralism is endangered by European communist and Marxist influence, but I finished the book shocked by Watt's narrow definition of the *true* conservative constituency. Watt rejects big business, southerners with mixed feelings about racial integration, and Catholic bishops who oppose abortion—the last because they are too "inundated with European concepts of economics and history" to "have any appreciation of conservative fiscal theories and how they work for the laboring class." With western ranchers apparently the only truly trustworthy brethren, it is not surprising that Watt finds his brand of frontier conservatism threatened. It is amazing that such a narrow man should have been considered fit for a national leadership position in a country as diverse as the late-twentieth-century United States.

At Watt's suggestion, Reagan named Anne McGill Gorsuch, a 38-year-old Denver lawyer and former state legislator, as head of the Environmental Protection Agency. Gorsuch's credentials in the conservative club were unquestionable. In the Colorado legislature, she was best known as a leading member of a faction so committed to deregulation and conservative social policies they were called "the House crazies." In Washington, she signaled her disdain for her new agency by initially working out of an office in Watt's Interior Department. She arrived in Washington, not only as Watt's protégée, but the companion of Robert Burford, a Colorado cattle rancher and state legislator, who became head of Interior's Bureau of Land Management, one of the most powerful agencies in the West. At the height of her official troubles in 1983, she and Burford took time out to be married.

By any standard, Gorsuch's background in environmental protection was limited. She had been a member of a Colorado legislative committee examining a measure to control toxic wastes, and had been instrumental in killing the proposal. She had sponsored automobile inspection and maintenance legislation aimed at controlling Denver's air pollution, but only after EPA had threatened to cut Colorado's funding, and she opposed inspection for auto emissions controls because "I don't believe there are any adequate data to show that it works."

Reagan demoted the EPA job to below the Cabinet rank it had under Carter, but Gorsuch was still the second-highest-ranking woman in the early years of the Reagan administration, below only

United Nations ambassador Jeane Kirkpatrick. Gorsuch accepted the EPA job as the second-toughest job in town and because her first choice, director of the Office of Management and Budget, had gone to David Stockman. She cooperated with Reagan's cuts in the EPA budget, recommended "streamlining" the Clean Air Act, and immediately ordered the EPA staff—which she regarded as a collection of overzealous bureaucrats—to freeze all contract-letting, cancel all public appearances, and stop talking to any members of Congress. For her own staff, she hired eight lawyers, seven of whom had worked for industries regulated by EPA. Business leaders were thrilled, but less than a year after her appointment, they were complaining that Gorsuch was slow to reach decisions while her contentious manner was giving environmental groups a base of appeal to the general public.

What triggered Gorsuch's demise, however, was not policy, but politics—internal politics and private agendas within the Reagan administration. It all began with Rita Lavelle, a Reagan staffer from his California days, whom, Burford later claimed, she was forced to hire. Lavelle was put in charge of the $1.6 billion Superfund, created in 1980 to finance cleanups of the nation's most hazardous waste dumps and prosecute companies for dumping waste illegally. Reporters discovered Lavelle was lunching in Washington's most expensive restaurants with lobbyists for the very companies she was regulating. This led to a congressional investigation and charges that she and Burford held up funding for cleanup of a hazardous waste site in California because the agency feared then-governor and Democratic Senate candidate Edmund G. (Jerry) Brown would claim credit for bringing the money into the state. Members of a congressional subcommittee, claiming that they had evidence that EPA had not assessed high enough fines against illegal dumpers, demanded to review sensitive law-enforcement records.

EPA permitted the congressional investigators to see some of the documents, but then pulled back on the "executive privilege" grounds which had become so famous in the Nixon administration. At this point, according to her interpretation of the events, Burford, the good soldier for President Reagan, became a victim of the administration she loved. According to Burford's account, she withheld the documents only because White House and Justice Department attorneys relished a historic confrontation over executive privilege. Burford claims she questioned the wisdom of the policy at the time, but White House Chief of Staff James A. Baker reprimanded her, saying "Anne, are you going to be a prima donna about this?"

The rest of her tenure turned into a series of legal maneuvers. The House cited Burford for contempt of Congress, which carries penalties of a $1,000 fine and up to a year in jail; the Justice Department filed suit in U.S. District Court to block enforcement of the contempt citation on executive privilege grounds. But the Justice Department's case was, Burford said, "without a doubt the sloppiest piece of legal work I had seen in 20 years of being a lawyer," and eventually the White House told her the Justice Department could no longer provide her with legal representation because it was required to investigate EPA. Finally overwhelmed, Burford resigned in mid-1983.* She was succeeded by William Ruckelshaus, EPA's first administrator, a liberal Republican who was trotted out to restore the agency's respectability, and later by Lee Thomas.

Never one to shy away from expressing her opinion, Burford summed up her tenure at EPA in a 1985 speech. "I approached it as a manager . . . and that simply won't fly with the eastern press corps," she said. "It won't cut it. They want a tree-hugger." Asked what advice she would give anyone considering accepting a high-level government appointment, she said, that No. 1 is "don't be female," and No. 2 is "if you want to make a change in government, then be prepared to go down in flames." Burford's "relationship" with the administration continued into 1986 when the Justice Department agreed to pay $198,000 of her lawyers' bills, but only after she gave up the right to sue the White House and Justice officials who had advised her to take the hardline position on executive privilege.

In her autobiography, *Are You Tough Enough?* (McGraw-Hill, 1986), Burford reveals herself as a hard-nosed but still naive westerner so unfamiliar with Washington that she ended up in a seedy motel when she first came to town. In relating the details of her life, Burford reveals the contradictions of a traditional Denver woman turned power figure. She is thrilled at her husband-to-be's insistence on buy-

---

*Lavelle was eventually convicted of two counts of perjury, one count of filing a false statement with the EPA, and one count of obstructing the investigation of a congressional committee. She was sentenced to a minimum-security prison in California.

ing her a $2,000 outfit to make the senators know she is a "class act" at her confirmation hearing, and is awed by the foreign travel her EPA job includes.

Unlike Watt, Burford gives no philosophical origins of her conservatism, but she does not hide her disappointment in Reagan. In the midst of the executive privilege battle, when she told him the agreement was not working out, "his response was a stunned silence. I don't mean to make too much of the prepared-script analogy, but it does seem he has great difficulty dealing with an 'unscripted' response." Of Reagan's commitment to the environment, Burford points out that he never made a major environmental address. "I took the job because I wanted to bring a politically conservative approach to solving the management problems of environmental protection," she concludes. "And I took the job because I thought Ronald Reagan shared that philosophy. Having to face the fact that he does not is probably the hardest thing I have had to do, and I am still uncomfortable with it. Ronald Reagan has always been a personal and political hero of mine, and concluding that he doesn't care about the environment hurts."

MOUNTAIN MEN—AND A WOMAN—IN POLITICS: SENATORS HART AND LAXALT . . .

For the first time in its history, the Mountain West has begun producing politicians who are known more for their national roles than for their success at garnering an unfair share of the federal pork barrel. While the Republicans controlled the Senate, New Mexico's Domenici, chairman of the Senate Budget Committee, won national respect for his management of the budget process, and Wyoming's Simpson managed against all odds to win passage of a new immigration bill, a matter of only the slightest interest to his constituents. And these men are only supporting players to the Mountain politicians who play the biggest games on the national scene.

The most prominent political personality to emerge from the Mountain states in the Reagan era, Colorado Democrat Gary Hart, is already history. Senator from 1975 through 1986, winner of the 1984 presidential primaries in 24 states, Hart was the front-runner for the 1988 Democratic presidential nomination until reporters from the *Miami Herald* followed a tip and watched him spend most of a spring 1987 weekend with model Donna Rice. Hart dropped out—temporarily.

I worked for Hart on his campaign in 1974 and on his Senate staff in 1975 and must write a few words to put this situation in perspective. The signs of trouble could be seen very early in Hart's political career, but he was so successful as the photogenic candidate that everyone cast them aside. The rumors of Hart's involvements with women other than his wife, so common in political campaigns, were secondary to his relations with everyone from his staff to other senators. Hart was always friendly (unlike many senators, he encouraged his staff to call him by his first name), but I have never met another politician who made so few references to his childhood; in fact, I can recall none. The saddest part of Hart's unwillingness to talk about his background is that his life—birth in a small Kansas town, education at Bethany Nazarene College in Oklahoma and Yale divinity and law schools, work as George McGovern's presidential campaign manager in 1972, and election to the Senate in the post-Watergate election of 1974—contains all the pathos and upward mobility that the American people love.

The issue of the propriety of the press staking out someone's house aside, Hart's downfall was not entirely his own making. Questions about Hart's personal life were triggered by several changing facts in American politics: the public knowledge that President Kennedy had carried on an affair with a woman who was also involved with a mobster; the calculating spectacle of Ted and Joan Kennedy's campaigning together for the White House, only to divorce shortly after they failed; Hart's own public separations from his wife; and the women's movement, which has opposed the use of women as objects of pleasure. But the whole episode, including the *National Enquirer* pictures of Hart, maracas in hand in a Bimini nightclub, showed beyond question that there was another side to the intellectual face that was presented to the world. Men with no public ambitions would guard against such pictures even if the moment were truly innocent.

In the midst of this tacky display, it is easy to forget that Hart did make intellectual contributions to our political life. As a liberal, he won unexpected praise as a student of military reform and in 1986 earned widespread intellectual respect in the diplomatic and defense communities for a proposed U.S. foreign policy of "enlightened engagement" in the post-Vietnam era. In wishing him farewell from the Senate, a *Washington Post* editorial praised him for opposing the three-year tax cut with which President Reagan began his term, the Gramm-Rudman-Hollings budget process, and protectionist trade legislation. "As a senator, Gary Hart did a good job," the *Post* concluded.

There are precedents for the rehabilitation of talented men in American politics, though usually not in elected office. One is Kentucky's Edward F. Prichard, Jr., the most brilliant mind in the state and destined to be governor until he was convicted of stuffing ballot boxes in 1948. For the rest of his life, Prichard made his contribution as the author of legislation that bore the names of lesser men. But Hart showed no interest in a slow road to redemption. With his ever-supportive wife, Lee, at his side, Hart re-entered the race in December, 1987, as the first liberal Democrat to run against the press.

The title of Mr. Western Republican during the Reagan era has undoubtedly gone to Senator Paul Laxalt of Nevada. Co-campaigners for Goldwater in 1964, and neighboring governors, Reagan and Laxalt were a perfect regional and ideological match for political friendship. As Reagan's "best friend" in the Senate and "general chairman" of the Republican party during Reagan's presidency, Laxalt achieved stratospheric social and political status in Washington. Whether Laxalt ever made use of his power to achieve any serious goal is another question. As *Congressional Quarterly* put it, "if Laxalt is more than an amiable conduit between the two centers of Republican power, the evidence is concealed from view." Laxalt will be remembered for telling Reagan that Interior secretary—and fellow westerner—James Watt would have to go and for convincing Reagan to abandon the multiple-launch basing system for the MX missile, which would have placed it in the Utah and Nevada desert. But in the halls of Congress, Laxalt's greatest accomplishment was as floor leader of the conservatives' failed attempt to nullify the Panama Canal treaties. When it came to legislative output, Laxalt seemed to follow his ideological compatriot, Barry Goldwater of Arizona, whose aim was "not to pass laws, but to repeal them."*

Laxalt retired from the Senate in 1986 and began testing the presidential waters as a reincarnation of Reagan. On the surface, he appeared to be the perfect combination of the free enterprise ethic and social conservatism that embody Republican ideology today. A Catholic and the father of seven children, Laxalt was opposed to abortion (unlike Democratic Catholics Mario Cuomo of New York and Bruce Babbitt of Arizona) and had been a strong backer of the Family Protection Act, a failed piece of legislation which sought to restore "traditional morality" in America by re-establishing prayer in the public schools, forbidding use of federal funds to promote homosexual or feminist values, or even "the intermingling of the sexes in [school] sports activities."

But under closer scrutiny, Laxalt also had several serious, probably insurmountable, problems for a presidential candidate. The *Sacramento Bee* wrote that money had been skimmed, probably by organized crime, from casinos Laxalt operated between his terms as governor and senator. Laxalt sued, and the *Bee*, in an out-of-court settlement, agreed to say that it could not find conclusive evidence. Even if no taint remained, Laxalt would still have had to confront his promise to defend Nevada's legalized gambling *and* prostitution of which he once said, "You're never going to eliminate the girls. It's a very old profession and a very lucrative one in Vegas." To the old-fashioned, Catholic, paternalistic, Laxalt (he is the son of a Basque immigrant sheepherder), these views did not seem contradictory; and they meshed perfectly with the free-wheeling, hypocritical political culture of Nevada in which even many Mormons dismissed the fact that they indirectly owed their livelihood to the tourist lure of the gambling casinos. But Laxalt was also divorced and remarried,

---

*Any account of Mountain state political personalities must, of course, include Barry Goldwater whose pioneering, unfearing commitment to conservatism from the early 1950s and disastrous 1964 presidential campaign laid the groundwork for Ronald Reagan's political respectability. Goldwater's age, ill health, and support for Gerald Ford for the 1976 Republican nomination kept him from the inner circle when a real conservative finally made it to the White House, but who can forget his conservative call-to-arms in 1952 when he asked "What kind of Republican are you, anyway? Well, I am not a me-too Republican. . . . I am a Republican opposed to the superstate and to gigantic, bureaucratic, centralized authority."

a problem for Catholic endorsements. And perhaps even worse, gambling is anathema to "born-again" evangelical Christians, now a key constituency for any Republican to win the presidency. The "born agains" may have voted for an actor-turned-governor of the most populous state in the union, but the day they and millions of more liberal Americans entrust the country to an ex-casino operator would be strange indeed—as Laxalt soon learned. After one of the shortest campaigns in American history, Laxalt dropped out of the race.

. . . Governors Lamm and Babbitt . . .

When he left office in 1987, Colorado's Richard D. Lamm was the nation's senior governor. There have been many senior governors, but only one Dick Lamm. For 12 years, as columnist Neal R. Peirce has written, Lamm was "the nation's prophet governor."

The chief sponsor of Colorado's liberal 1967 abortion law and successful opponent of hosting the 1976 Winter Olympic Games in the state, Lamm came to the governorship like a 39-year-old silver-haired savior of a state that had always been in the hands of development-minded politicians. Taking office after the same post-Watergate 1974 election that put Gary Hart in the Senate, Timothy Wirth in the House, and antiwar activist Sam Brown into the state treasurer's office, Lamm was the immediate darling of the national press, which declared that the "eco-freaks" had taken over Colorado. That analysis proved short-sighted as the energy boom brought new and more conservative voters to the state, but Lamm soon became that rarest of governors from a small state: a national figure. At first, Lamm seemed mainly interested in promoting the environmentalist values that he had championed as a state legislator, though he broke with the environmentalists to defend the region—and gain more national attention—when President Carter established his "hit list" of western water projects. But around 1980, Lamm said he underwent "a kind of Copernican change in my perception. . . . There was the mounting trade deficit, the United States becoming a debtor nation. When I became governor, we were competing with Arizona, California and Illinois. And suddenly it was Seoul, Taiwan and West Germany. I decided the biggest threat to Colorado's prosperity was not what went on in the state capitol. It was in negative national and international trends."

Lamm's own rhetoric became so negative he earned the moniker "Governor Gloom." He railed against global overpopulation, the deterioration of the nation's roads and bridges, declining national productivity, low teacher pay, the trade deficit, and the federal budget deficit. But nothing got him in so much hot water as his 1984 remark that the hopelessly ill elderly have a "duty to die" rather than use society's resources on high-tech medical equipment. Lamm later claimed his point had been sensationalized while doctors said such actions are already taken. Lamm's overarching theme, he said, was that "history will show this generation has not kept faith. It has not, like all before it, left the nation better off for those who follow."

Lamm was undoubtedly courageous in taking on the pet views of every political constituency from lawyers (there are too many) to Hispanics (U.S. immigration laws should be tightened). But after all the intellectualizing—speeches, articles, and so many books that one season he had two books with two coauthors put out by two unsuspecting New York publishers—it must be said that Lamm was more pundit than politician. Goals such as statewide land-use planning, higher mineral severance taxes, and substantial improvement in Denver's air quality all eluded the Lamm administration. Lamm blamed the lack of accomplishment on his conservative, Republican legislature. "It is a never-ending irony to me that I can be elected governor of this state, then reelected by a substantial margin, but can't get through the legislature the policies which almost everyone agrees are necessary to protect the state," he said. But in 12 years of extraordinary popularity, Lamm had shown little or no inclination for building the coalitions necessary for any governor to achieve objectives. The Michigan-born, California-educated Lamm always seemed, like many environmentalists, arrogantly distant from the common people of Colorado who made their living from the land and the mines. A fellow western governor told me that after all his years in Colorado, Lamm still viewed the environment "like an easterner. He never learned to fear it." Lamm did deliver the governorship into the hands of a like-minded Democrat, Roy Romer. But on the issues there is no Lamm legacy.

Arizona's Bruce Babbitt, governor from 1978 to 1986 and a Democratic presidential candidate in 1988, left the opposite impression of Lamm. For a presidential candidate, Babbitt is one of the more obscure of politicians, but as a governor, he had an outstanding record in identifying major problems and pressing solutions through a legislature firmly in the hands of the opposing party. Babbitt did just that, not once, but twice, on the testiest issue of all in Arizona: water.

Babbitt's roots are pure Arizonan—he was born into a pioneer family that settled near Flagstaff in the 1880s to operate Indian trading posts—but he exposed himself to the broader world. Babbitt spent the 1960s excelling as an undergraduate at Notre Dame and earning a master's degree in geophysics in England and a law degree at Harvard. As a member of a Gulf Oil geological expedition to Bolivia, Babbitt was affected by the human deprivation he witnessed and decided to chuck geophysics in favor of Harvard Law School and a career of social concern. He joined the 1965 civil rights march on Selma, Alabama, and went to work for the federal Office of Economic Opportunity (OEO), the flagship agency of Lyndon Johnson's War on Poverty, first in Austin, Texas, and then as assistant to the director of VISTA (Volunteers in Service to America) in Washington. In his War on Poverty days, Babbitt traveled all over the Southwest, organizing blacks, Mexican-Americans, and the poor and telling the traditional Anglo power structure that the price of federal aid was serving poor and minority neighborhoods and including those groups in decision making.

Even while working in federal anti-poverty programs, Babbitt became disillusioned with social change delivered from Washington. "The war on poverty bore some good fruit, but what I learned was you can't force thoroughgoing social change from the top down," Babbitt told the *National Journal*'s Ron Brownstein. "The whole war on poverty had a certain arrogance . . . It could not be a lasting process of change when it depended upon GS-7s hired in Washington dispensing federal money with terms and conditions that they prescribed in local communities."

Returning to Phoenix in 1967, Babbitt practiced law until he decided "the attorney general has the largest law firm in the state devoted to the defense of racial discrimination, and what it really ought to be is a public-interest law firm." Babbitt was elected to the office in 1974, attacked land fraud (a perennial issue in Arizona where most big money is still made from development), prosecuted the Mafia murder of *Arizona Republic* reporter Don Bolles and was catapulted to the governorship in 1978 after the unpopular Raul Castro resigned to become ambassador to Argentina and the secretary of state, Wesley Bolin, died in office. That fall, he was elected to the first of two full terms.

When Babbitt took office, Arizona had for generations been pumping more water out of its underground aquifers than was replenished by nature. As early as 1927, the subsiding water table had caused cracks as deep as 400 feet, some running for miles; by the 1980s, there were more than 100 such fissures. This "overdrafting", as it's known in the West, was causing not only obvious environmental damage, but raising the cost of pumping water out of the ground. Any change in water pumping or regulation, however, threatened people's livelihood and property rights—and raised their political hackles. But in 1980, after months of negotiating with farmers, miners, utilities, and cities and of not-so secretly urging the Carter administration to threaten to hold up the Central Arizona Project if the situation were not corrected, Babbitt won passage of a regionally unprecedented ground-water management act. To gradually reduce ground-water pumping, the law established a statewide management and conservation program, provided civil and criminal penalties for violations, and required statewide registration of wells and strict conservation measures in Phoenix, Tucson, Prescott, and Pinal County. Six years later, Babbitt managed, cajoled, and pushed some more until he got a clean water act passed.

In 1986, Babbitt decided against running for Goldwater's Senate seat in favor of aiming right for the U.S. presidency. His campaign would test whether the party and the country were ready for a western governor committed to social justice, but who questioned the federal government's role as much as many conservatives. Democrats, Babbitt said, "must reconcile" their "progressive tradition" with "fiscal reality." An early supporter of taxing social security benefits, Babbitt proposed a "means" test on all federal programs. He argued the test would be the way to maintain commitments to social justice and keep spending down; critics charged that limiting federal programs would

destroy the middle-class constituency which made the programs politically feasible.

Long shot and dark horse were the only appropriate words to
describe Babbitt's candidacy. He had little national base on which to
build a following and had also earned the distrust, if not the enmity,
of organized labor in 1983 when he mobilized the state police and
National Guard in a copper mine dispute. Babbitt did have a link to
traditional Democratic ethnics in his Catholic faith, but his position
on abortion is one word: "pro-choice," and as he told me, he doesn't
think that the religious affiliation of the candidate has meant anything since Kennedy won the presidency. Media gurus and party
leaders complained that Babbitt lacked charisma to stir an audience.
That might be different if he were running for president of Mexico,
however. As a border state governor, Babbitt took a special interest
in U.S.-Mexican relations and the causes of Hispanic Americans.
Reporters who followed him on the trail noted that Babbitt is a man
of feeling and eloquence—when he campaigns in Spanish.

. . . And Representatives Udall and Schroeder

Without question Morris Udall has the most accomplished legislative
reputation of any Mountain state politician in Washington today.
The descendant of one of the most distinguished families in Arizona's
pioneer "dirt aristocracy," Udall was a professional basketball player
turned lawyer when his brother Stewart left his Tucson congressional
seat in 1961 to become President Kennedy's secretary of Interior.
Morris ran for his brother's seat, and his decency and wit quickly won
him the affection of his colleagues. If he had not been a critic of the
seniority system, Udall would probably be the Speaker of the House.
Denied that office, he concentrated on legislation and became the
most prolific author of environmental legislation in Congress. Chairman of the House Interior Committee since 1977, Udall fathered the
federal strip-mine law, the division of Alaska lands between development and wilderness, and the first major addition to the wilderness
system since its inception in 1964—8 million acres in 20 states. Environmentalists have long faulted him for continuing to support the

Central Arizona Project, but even his championing of that—probably the price for his other out-of-Arizona environmental actions—was a political accomplishment in an age in which winning congressional approval of water projects is tougher and tougher. Udall is also the father of the law that regulates campaign finance, limits expenditures, and requires disclosure.

Udall ran for the presidency in 1976, but was outgunned by Jimmy Carter. In recent years, Udall has forged ahead with his congressional career in the face of Parkinson's disease, which often leaves him in obvious discomfort. He easily won a 14th full term in the House in 1986, but was widely expected to announce it would be his last.

The only woman in Congress from the Mountain states is Democrat Patricia Schroeder of Denver, Colorado. Considered by Republicans and conservative Democrats to be a peacenik-envirofreak-feminist when she was elected in 1972, Schroeder immediately asked for and received a seat on the Armed Services Committee from which she protested the Vietnam War. To the amazement of both liberals and conservatives, Schroeder is still on the committee, waging her lonely battles against pro-military sentiment and high defense spending, but now winning such victories as getting the Pentagon to report regularly on weapons cost overruns. Schroeder is also chairman of the Civil Service Subcommittee, her piece of the federal pork barrel since Denver is a regional headquarters for many federal agencies.

Schroeder's real forte is women's issues. She has worked for better pension rights for foreign service spouses and the divorced spouses of military personnel and promotes stronger laws to enforce payment of child support. Schroeder's feminist successes prove that Americans are still willing to use government, even in a conservative era, if they believe strongly enough in the cause. After fellow Coloradan Gary Hart's withdrawal from the presidential race Schroeder began exploring a 1988 bid of her own, hoping her Iowa roots would give her a boost in that state's important caucuses. The campaign took off among feminists, but was not strong enough for her to declare a formal candidacy. Historians will remember that it was Schroeder, frustrated at Ronald Reagan's popularity in the face of slip-ups, who termed him "the teflon president."

South by Southwest

After the South and New England, the Mountain West has the strongest regional consciousness of any group of states. The mighty Rocky Mountain ranges and the jagged line of the Continental Divide stretch through them from one international border to the other; only Nevada is not actually in the Rockies, and it is still mountainous. Get a Denverite, Phoenician, Utah Mormon, or Montanan into conversation, and you are almost certain to hear the same tales of how the West is different from the rest of the country. The spaces are wide, you will be reminded, and people from the big cities of the east and California "just don't understand."

Westerners wear their westernness so lightly, however, that the sense of regional solidarity rarely carries political weight or results in the sort of cooperation that could solve some of these states' common problems. "The West is not a region in the chauvinistic sense," Arizona's Babbitt once explained to me. "The South is a region welded together by history, a civil war, a sense of having to stick together to survive. There's little of that in the West. Most westerners are national in outlook, notwithstanding the efforts of many of us over the years to portray the West as an oppressed region. Bernard De Voto and Walter Prescott Webb and the great writers of the West attempted to prove that we were the victims of historic oppression and exploitation and bring us together with a sense of indignation over our colonial oppression. But it didn't wash."

In pioneer days, the Mountain states were fiercely competitive for both federal dollars and tourists. In the postwar era, the governors and other state officials have developed an exhausting list of cooperative organizations, culminating in the union of 16 Pacific, Mountain, and Plains governors in 1976 when President Carter threatened their water projects. But lacking a visible and immediate federal enemy, they have found no equally compelling issue in the last decade.

There are, of course, logical reasons why the Mountain states find it difficult to come together. The eastern reaches of Montana, Wyoming, Colorado, and New Mexico are all part of the Great Plains and about as unmountainous as any territory in the United States. Each

of these states does have not-so-subtle economic and political differences. Colorado remains the leader of the Mountain states in the
economic and political sense, and Denver still serves, as George Sessions Perry wrote decades ago in the *Saturday Evening Post,* the "doctor, lawyer, merchant, and (political) chief, as well as banker, butcher,
teacher, and supplier of transportation, markets, entertainment, culture, and shelter for the transient" to not only the state of Colorado,
but the entire Rocky Mountain region.

But in the bust end of the energy cycle, Arizona, which grew 22
percent between 1980 and 1985, overtook Colorado as the most populous state of the region. Arizona's ever-expanding retiree communities
and high-tech industries and nearness to California business and markets have made it the most stable of the Mountain state economies.
By 1987, however, Arizona could feel the bust, and even construction
lost jobs.

New Mexico, the only Mountain state with a large non-Anglo
population, testily combines the remnants of a ranching culture with
a high-tech world that started with the atom bomb's development at
Los Alamos during World War II. The atomic economy was only the
beginning of an Anglo influx that has reduced the native Hispanic
population from 45 percent in 1945 to 37 percent in 1980.

Nevada is primarily a sin-and-fun appendage of California in which
gambling (or the gaming business, as it's called locally) directly em-
ploys 32 percent of Nevadans while another 25 percent work in related
businesses. "If you can't do it at home, go to Nevada," Las Vegas
still advertises in national magazines; that may be fine for tourists, but
a lot of people have decided Nevada might offer permanent answers,
and their neuroses have contributed to the highest alcoholism rate in
the country and a suicide rate twice the national average. Nevada lost
its status as America's only state of legalized gambling when New
Jersey voters in 1978 authorized casinos in Atlantic City, but the
chambers of commerce promoted Nevada's pro-industry tax position,
luring warehousing, product distribution, and high-tech facilities.

Neighboring Utah's dominant Mormon religion gives it quite a
different social profile. Utah has the highest birth rate in the United
States, 29.5 births per 1,000 people, more than twice the national
average—and its own set of odd social phenomena such as the lowest
rate of illegitimacy and the highest rate of pregnant brides. But the

ups and downs of mining and energy development (industries run outside the Mormon establishment) can also be seen in Utah's growth rates: the state's population rose 18.9 percent in the 1960s compared to a fantastic 37.9 percent in the booming 1970s and back down to 14 percent in the first six years of the eighties.

Mormonism increasingly dominates Idaho's culture, but this oddly shaped state is also tugged by Washington and Oregon since it lies within the Columbia River basin and relates economically to the Pacific Northwest. Idaho must also live with the dubious distinction of being the base of the Aryan Nation, and other neo-Nazi groups that find the isolated location and homogeneous population to their liking.

If the Mountain states are to come out of their economic depression it will take a new type of leadership, said Harry Fritz, a University of Montana history professor and state legislator. "We're in the worst economic situation since the '30s. It's going to take a lot of education in the school of hard knocks to make people wake up. We've got good leadership in terms of brains, but they just can't get that majority coalition together in an era of real fiscal withdrawal."

One place to begin might be with greater regional cooperation among these far-flung states in which distance and small populations makes it so expensive to provide government services. There is, for example, not one great university in the entire eight-state region to play the cultural- or economic-development role of the great private universities on the coasts, the "public ivys" of California and the Midwest, or the University of Texas at Austin. If precious higher education monies were not scattered among so many smaller state universities and colleges, perhaps a great university with the potential payoffs of Stanford or the University of Minnesota could be built.

The Mountain West could also gain much from mutual coopera- tion to solve the region's urban problems. The Mountain people live more like the rest of the country than is generally recognized. While the great open spaces lure the people, the new residents have settled in a few cities where there are jobs. Two urban counties—the sun industry, agriculture centers of Maricopa (Phoenix) and Pima (Tuc- son)—hold 75 percent of the population of Arizona, Maricopa alone providing 64 percent of the state's jobs. In Colorado, 78 percent of the population now lives in the Denver-Boulder, Colorado Springs, Fort Collins, and Greeley metropolitan areas, all along the front range of the Rockies. In Nevada, Clark County (Las Vegas) and Washoe County (Reno) have 82 percent of the population. In Utah, 64 percent of the people live in Salt Lake City and the cities scattered around it in the fertile, narrow Wasatch Mountain valley. The Mountain metropolises suffer the worst air pollution problems in the country outside Los Angeles. That their residents have proven so unwilling to combat this problem is a singular and collective travesty. Annoyed by the obsession of national mayors' groups with winning federal grants, the mayors of the West have begun to meet on their own. But the day they act on solutions to western urban problems is yet to come.

FROM THE FARM TO THE CITY:
ADVENTURES IN THE WATER CULTURE

What is at the *heart* of the West? Where is the center from which the shaping force and power radiate? The answer is simple if we would only see and accept it. The heart of the West is a desert, unqualified and absolute.

—Walter Prescott Webb

"The dream has come true," said Governor Bruce Babbitt. "It's not pork barrel," said Senator Dennis DeConcini, "It's an investment in America." Thus Arizonans on November 15, 1985, dedicated the federally sponsored Central Arizona Project, a 200-mile-long cement ditch to bring Colorado River water from Lake Havasu on the California border to Phoenix and, one day, Tucson.

Such celebrations have always been among the most special and official of occasions in the West, but there was a defensive, nervous quality to the opening of this latest exercise in desert defiance. Arizonans could now rest assured that Phoenix and Tucson would continue their endless expansion across the desert. The state's traditions of making money off the land could continue unabated for the foreseeable future. But the opening ceremony only reminded the farmers, land developers, and other landed interests in the region that the C.A.P., as it is called in these parts, just might be the last of the big federally financed water projects. No other federal water project that reached the construction stage encountered as many environmental, political, and financial obstacles as the C.A.P. Only a single-minded Arizona congressional delegation—and the House Interior Committee chairmanship of Morris Udall—kept the project from sinking in a sea of criticism; even those forces might not be able to save some of the final, ambitious links that would raise its full cost to $3.5 billion. No other state can count on such a combination of political might in the water arena today.

Sophisticated westerners know that the stark reality of the West's dryness will be the region's perennial dilemma as long as it remains committed to growth. And they know that the allocation of water is no less sensitive today than when John Gunther wrote, "Water is blood in Colorado. Touch water, and you touch everything; about water the state is as sensitive as a carbuncle."

Average annual precipitation in the eight mountain states is only 12 inches, barely escaping the true desert mark of 10 inches. Often there are droughts that last over many years. The Colorado River, coursing through much of America's most arid and water starved territory, has ranged from record flood-year levels of 22 million acre-feet down to as little as 4 million acre-feet in a drought year. (For the uninitiated, an acre-foot of water is the amount it takes to cover an acre to the depth of one foot.) The distinguished western analyst, Wallace Stegner, has argued, "I would prefer to call [the West] a series of deserts and semi-deserts separated by the snow fountains of high ranges, and with a rain fountain along its Pacific shores, but with Webb's insistence on aridity as a basic unity, I do not quarrel." Even in Montana, the coolest and northernmost state of the region, grass would not grow on the state capitol lawn in Helena without continuous and intensive irrigation. John Wesley Powell, the great conservationist, spoke well when he told the Montana Constitutional Convention in 1889 that "all the great values of this territory have ultimately to be measured to you in acre-feet."

Millions of westerners, exploiters and environmentalists alike, could not drink water, much less earn a living, without the storage of spring runoff from the high mountains for use during the long, hot, dry summers and beyond. The Bureau of Reclamation has been doing just that ever since it completed its large masonry dam on the Salt River in Arizona in 1911, a first step in making possible the farms and city of modern Phoenix. Former President Theodore Roosevelt recognized its importance and came to dedicate it even though Arizona would not achieve statehood for another year. Over the succeeding decades, the West became dotted with dams which are crucial to its agricultural and municipal water supplies.

Two decades after Salt River came the mighty Hoover Dam in the precipitous gorge of the Colorado River's Black Canyon in Nevada. Hoover was the first of the great multi-purpose dams, not only storing water for the people of southern California and the great vegetable and fruit basket of the Imperial Valley, but also providing flood control, massive electric power generation, and the spacious recreation area on the desert called Lake Mead. In the postwar years, four great storage projects rose in the Upper Colorado River basin—Glen Canyon (Lake Powell) in Utah and Arizona, Flaming Gorge in Utah and Wyoming, the Navajo in New Mexico and Colorado, and the Curecanti on the Gunnison River in Colorado. The construction of large-scale diversion projects went forward, piercing the walls of the Rockies to supply Denver and the Colorado Eastern Slope, and the Uintas to bring water to Salt Lake City and the Wasatch Front. Colorado won approval of the federally financed Fryingpan-Arkansas project to water its thirsty southeastern reaches; New Mexico got its San Juan–Chama Project to divert Colorado River water for irrigation in the Rio Grande River basin and for municipal supplies for Albuquerque. Along the Middle Snake River within the Columbia River basin on Idaho's western border rose three dams in Hells Canyon. Montana got its Hungry Horse Dam on the Flathead River and the Yellowtail Dam on the Bighorn, largest and highest dams in the headwater tributaries of the Missouri River. The Central Arizona Project was the last great prize in this game of vote trading. "Getting the C.A.P. was sort of like Arizona getting its manhood," one local leader observed at the dedication.

Support for water projects was as uniform as religious dogma until the 1960s when environmentalists and politicians from other parts of the country began to question the logic of the national government financing multi-million-dollar reclamation projects to provide water for crops such as cotton which are already in great enough supply to require government subsidy. In even more cosmic terms, they began to protest the disturbance to the fragile mountain ecology. Over time, the environmentalists have prevailed in many cases. The Central

Arizona Project's original justification was to save Arizona agriculture from its dropping water table, but the law now says that none of the water may be used to expand agriculture; 50 percent of the water will go to farms, but as Arizona cities continue to grow even those acre-feet will end up in municipal hands.

Dam-bashing reached a high point, of course, with President Carter's hit list, which emerged as *the* symbol of Democratic insensitivity to the West. Big western growers and land developers were thrilled to make big donations to Reagan, who pledged to overturn Carter's environmentalist opposition toward water projects and Carter's proposal that states pay 10 percent of the cost of water projects. The westerners didn't count on competition in the form of Budget Director David Stockman, whose purist conservative vision sought the total elimination of federal public works projects. Nor did they expect the Reaganites to promote cost sharing, upping the proposed local ante to as high as 35 percent. "The era of building large dams like Glen Canyon and Hoover is over," said Wayne Merchant, Reagan's deputy assistant Interior secretary for water and science. "Our role now needs to change to one of facilitating the wise use of water as a resource."

Reagan's budget staff also agreed with a Carter-style plan to limit water subsidies for farms over 960 acres, and with Congress, prevailed. As one western editor described the difference between the two presidents, "Carter told us we were bad people. Reagan told us, 'I love you, the nation just can't afford it.' "

Reagan's Interior Department did issue rules allowing 10,000-acre farms to get more cheap water, but in the budget battles the White House position on these subsidies was never clear, and Congress overturned them. Both the subsidies and cost sharing say much about water issues and political sensitivities in the West. Environmentalists contended that requiring states and local governments to pay a larger share of the full costs of water projects would put an end to them. But Bureau of Reclamation officials in Phoenix told me they were not horrified by the proposal. Industrial, municipal, and hydroelectric power users have long been required to pay back the government for the full costs of the projects, reclamation officials said, and farmers paid the percentage the Bureau of Reclamation deemed they could afford. The costs of public recreation were split evenly between the federal and local governments while only flood control and delivery to Indians were totally federal expenses.* The difference is that they must now pay the costs up front.

Thus one is left wondering whether cost sharing would really curb water projects, as the environmentalists contend. If not, is it just a way for environmentalists to make their supporters think they are doing good? And since Reagan didn't suffer for his shift on cost sharing, does water really have political power in the West today?

The latest proposal to solve the West's perennial thirst is water marketing—allowing farmers and rural landowners, who own 85 percent of western water rights, to sell their precious commodity to cities whose residents and businesses can afford to pay more for it. Economically troubled farmers, water-hungry cities, and dam-hating environmentalists have all praised the idea, but it has also engendered understandable opposition.

If water is sold to the people or places that can afford to pay the most for it, Phoenix, Denver, Albuquerque, and Salt Lake City will get more water while vast rural expanses will give up not only their current agricultural base, but long-term prospects for economic diversification as well. Individual water rights would also take precedence over a rural community's desire to maintain a local water supply large enough for either agricultural or industrial development. In remote La Paz County, Arizona, financially pressed farmers have found economic salvation by turning their lands into "water ranches" for sale to cities and speculators. But the local chamber of commerce fears that such sales will not only ruin the area's cotton, grain, and alfalfa economy, but end any chances for attracting industry. "To say 85 percent of water rights is in agriculture is like saying 85 percent of gauze is in hospitals," said La Paz County's lobbyist in Phoenix. "It sounds like waste. But is it wrong?" The issue gets even testier when

---

*Indian water rights have emerged as the new wild card both of American Indian affairs and western water policy. The same 1964 court decision that clarified Arizona's rights to the Colorado River also established the rights of Indians to part of that water. The case inspired other suits which have set water rights for other tribes. How Indians will use their water is not yet clear; the reservations could turn into an environmentalist inspiration or an employment center for engineers. One indicator was the Navajos' vote in early 1987 to throw out Peterson Zah, the small-is-beautiful-minded chairman elected in 1982, in favor of Peter MacDonald, the development-minded former chairman Zah had defeated.

marketing proposals involve interstate transfers. Farmers in northern Colorado, for example, hoped to sell their water to San Diego, but the state of Colorado has sued to keep the water at home. The upper basin states have become so afraid of the thirst of more populous lower basin states they have begun formalizing their claims to water.

After an August visit to Phoenix, I came away wondering just what kind of an environmental accomplishment water marketing would be. In their quest to save some bird-nesting areas and mountaintops, the environmentalists may have made a pact with the devil. Water marketing totally avoids the question of urban growth and could easily confirm the old western adage that "water follows money." Hot, dusty, polluted cities are being created in this part of the country, and given the pro-business atmosphere, many Americans will have no choice but to move to them.

Cutting back on irrigated crops sounds so logical, but agriculture may well be made a scapegoat. On a helicopter flight over Phoenix, the cotton fields provided relief from the dome of auto-induced air pollution which covers the city. Larry Jarnigan, a cotton farmer whose lands on the edge of Phoenix are rapidly becoming housing tracts, said, "Environmental groups think we're poisoning society. But is agriculture so damn bad? They say how wasteful, how inefficient and how polluting farming is, but they never tell you how much water an acre of developed land uses." Officials of the Salt River Project, whose landowners are converting their lands to housing and offices, confirmed that the comparative efficiency of water use depends on how intensely the land will be developed—and that as the land gets more scarce and expensive, the number of houses per acre will go up. Jarnigan has made lots of money developing his land ("Your last crop is always houses," he joked). He said he would still prefer to farm but noted that state officials have become "so damn afraid of this water thing" that they are making it very tough to build new golf courses that are the centerpieces of the winter tourism and retirement home businesses. "If they're not going to permit more golf courses, they're not going to worry about agriculture," he concluded.

I had stayed at the famed Biltmore Hotel, which lies within the jurisdiction of the Salt River Project where the fifties-style and earlier homes still have old-fashioned lawns. Each day, I went from one

complex of office buildings, parking lots, and paved roads to another
and toured the newer residential areas with their governmentally
mandated "desert landscaping" of gravel, rocks, and cacti. My eyes
were relieved to see the now-belittled greenery of the Biltmore area.
Perhaps desert landscaping is fine for the elderly who are thrilled they
don't have to mow or shovel the rocks, but I felt sorry for the pre-
schoolers whose play areas are so limited.

At the time of my visit, the entire Valley of the Sun was fighting
over whether to turn the jagged, ugly, dried-out Salt River bed into
a water-and greenery-filled park to be called Rio Salado. Desert lovers
denounced the project as yet another artificial, water-intensive, tax-
financed bonanza for real estate developers. There's always that danger in the fast-growing Southwest, but if Phoenix is to be a major city
it must have recreation land somewhere.

If this lack of interest in urban affairs continues, the environmentalists could lose out to the pro-water-use forces they hate. The engineers
and dam builders still have enough grand plans that Oregon and
Washington members of Congress won an extension of a 1968 moratorium that forbids federal studies of diversion of water from the Columbia River; there is still talk of bringing water from Canada or
Alaska to the Mountain states. But even more shocking, the engineers
refute the environmentalist claim that all the logical sites for dams
have been used. Modern technology means "there is no such thing as
a bad dam site," said an irrepressible Bureau of Reclamation official.
"There are only expensive sites. The Central Arizona Project is the
last of the great western water projects in our generation, but 50 years
from now motivations will be different, and there will be more water
projects in the West—and in the East."

Back to Butte

Of all the old mining towns scattered around the West, none could
ever compare with Butte, Montana. The world's greatest copper producer from the 1880s until well into the twentieth century, Butte in
1915 had a population of 70,000 and was the biggest city between
Minneapolis and Seattle. The years brought a decline, and finally the
closing of the Anaconda Copper operations in 1983, but it is a pleasure

to report that in this region which thrives on the new above all else, Butte is a model of resiliency and resurgence.

Butte is everything the Mountain West is not: old (founded in 1864) big (still over 23,000 people), dense (all were packed onto a few hills above the copper pits), ethnic (Irish, Italian, Serb, Croatian, Finnish, Jewish, and German to name but a few), and working class (the Butte Miners Union was founded in 1878, and the city soon became known as the "Gibraltar of Unionism"). Befitting its status as the largest of the old mining camps, its history is the most dramatic and infamous of all: the feuds between the copper kings who pioneered the place and controlled early Montana politics, the bloody ups and downs of the labor unions which managed to pit the mine owners against each other and gain a foothold, and the tragedies of the mines themselves—from the decades of fires and accidents underground to the environmental degradation of the massive aboveground Berkeley Pit, opened in 1955 and inching closer and closer to the city center when operations ceased.

If ever there was a city that gave the appearance it had little to work with when a mine closed, it was Butte. Butte is no jewel-like Aspen or Central City waiting to be boutiqued for the tourists; the scale of abandonment is closer to New York's South Bronx or Chicago's South Side. First there is the gaping hole of the pit itself, 7,000 feet long, 5,600 feet wide, and 1,800 feet deep setting the scene for the city. Butte's abandoned buildings on "the richest hill on earth" include multistory department stores, movie theaters seating hundreds of people, and office buildings and retail stores. In Chicago or St. Paul, these buildings could be turned into condominiums or artists' housing, but here there is no population base for that sort of thing. That they exist at all is a miracle; a decade ago the city fathers considered abandoning the entire hill in favor of "the flats," where the inevitable shopping mall and new housing are located.

Butte was also the ultimate company town, controlled from Anaconda's offices in New York and Denver. Its wealth was sucked away by the copper kings for high living and socially prestigious causes such as the Los Angeles Symphony Orchestra, the Stanford University Library, the Corcoran Gallery of Art in Washington, D.C., and the University of Virginia Law School. There is no copper-based charitable foundation in Montana, and even the mansion of copper king

William A. Clark is open only because a local woman operates it as a restaurant to pay for its upkeep. No wonder Montana was so willing to pass a tax on coal in the seventies.

When the mine was closed, Butte was devastated; there had been a thousand and one battles against the mine, but it was still the lifeblood of the town. But Butte was not some upstart boom town like nearby Billings, which has still to recover from the bust in coal prices. The next few years revealed both Butte's advantages and the true grit that comes from dealing with violent strikes, distant capitalists, and true class conflict.

ARCO, which had bought the Anaconda Copper Company in 1976, continued to pay its $4 million per year property taxes on the mine, giving the city a base from which to operate. Second, Butte suddenly realized it was not only the home of the copper mine, but also Montana Power, the utility which had once been in league with Anaconda to rule the state. Employing 1,000 people, Montana Power pledged to stay in Butte even though it was considering moving to one of the younger, cleaner Montana cities. Montana Power itself was diversifying into automation, telecommunications equipment, and especially international mining ventures through its Western Energy unit. Martin White, the president of Western Energy, is a local boy who graduated from the Harvard Business School and came home. White claims he would not move Western Energy's headquarters because of the presence of Montana Tech, the local university that specializes in training mining engineers, and he has become *the* local civic booster, pledging to build a high-altitude skating facility that he says could be used for Olympic training and could mean as many as 200 jobs.

The city, meanwhile, concentrated on reopening the mine and put together the Butte Economic Futures program. To help small businesses such as Roundup Powder, which makes blasting powder for mines, the city established a business incubator to save money on bookkeeping, secretarial, and computer services as well as providing management advice. Noting that Butte is both a railroad and highway crossroads, the city also built a grain terminal to give Montana farmers a broader market and is trying to add storage and marketing facilities for other Montana products.

In 1985, the city received another dose of self-esteem when it

managed to place a 90-foot statue of the Virgin Mary on a peak atop
the Continental Divide. First conceived in 1979, and put up totally
with donated time, money, land, and equipment, "Our Lady of the
Rockies" was finally lifted by an Air National Guard team into place
3,500 feet above the city.

Reopening the mine was the greatest challenge. The federal Environmental Protection Agency coveted the pit as a toxic dump site; the
state of Montana claiming that Anaconda owed back severance taxes,
was reluctant to transfer the mining permit; and all the while high
utility rates, taxes, and labor contracts kept the cost of production at
$1 per pound when the world price of copper was 65 cents. Governor
Ted Schwinden indicated he wanted the laws followed, but the mine
reopened, and gradually the state, the city, and the school district
(which had to forego taxes) reached agreements. The mine was sold
to a Montana construction company, and three thousand people
applied for 300 jobs paying an average of $10 per hour and $3 in fringe
benefits plus profit sharing. The wages were high by today's standards
in depressed Montana, but the situation was a shocker since Anaconda always had 850 or more employees averaging $20 per hour
before they ceased operations. The mine also opened union-free, but
no one expects that to last in a town with a union tradition so strong
that the school district, city, hotels, bars, and even a Wendy's are
unionized.

Butte and neighboring Anaconda, where the company's smelter
stack still stands, have developed ambitious plans for an historical
park in which the two cities would be linked by the old railroad that
once carried copper ore between them. As in the Deep South, Butte
and Anaconda have had the questionable advantage of so little development that the historical legacy has been left largely undisturbed; the
park would be a rare opportunity for future generations to experience
nineteenth-century industrial America.

The man who gets credit for this remarkable turnaround is Don
Peoples, Butte's city manager through good times and bad. Peoples
has angered other cities with his ability to get grants, and leaders from
other Montana cities still speak a bit resentfully about Butte's well-
organized handling of the state legislature. When the mine closed,
Peoples took the bus several hundred miles to Pueblo, Colorado, an
old steel mill town, to see how they had handled the loss of several

thousand jobs a couple years earlier. "We learned a lot of lessons from Pueblo," he says. "They really worked on thinking differently about themselves. Butte had for years been the laughing stock of Montana. Today Butte is the place in Montana."

While the old-timers in Butte proudly offer the visitor a pasty, the miner's traditional lunch, Peoples is equally proud that Butte has enough yuppies to patronize the Uptown Cafe, a nouvelle cuisine restaurant featuring escargots, sole with pecan butter, and tenderloin with green peppercorns. "We have to make this thing cook on our own," he says. Cook it will. Peoples is the best of the west—unpretentious, hard-working, and hopeful.

THE
PLAINS STATES:
The Commodity Culture

"**P**asserby, look about you and question," commands a statue of the pioneers in downtown Oklahoma City. "Where else within a single life span has man built so mightily?"

Across the street stands Leadership Square, a poignant reminder of the fragile condition of America's premier agricultural and energy-producing region. Planned in the seventies when both oil and wheat prices had skyrocketed, Leadership Square's twin towers of 21 and 16 stories opened in 1984 totally tenantless. With a huge American flag flying between its two reflecting glass wings, Leadership Square looks as if it would be irresistible to the patriotic yet glitzy oil community, but three years after opening day, only 52 percent of its 713,000 square feet were rented. The situation, said one national real estate broker, is "typical of the Oil Patch go-go mentality. Everybody wanted to have the biggest building. Everybody wanted their names up in lights."

Leadership Square's vacancy rate is typical of the agonies of the nine-state Plains region that lies west of the Mississippi and east of the

Rockies and extends from North Dakota and Minnesota to Texas. Commodities rule the economy just as surely as they do in any Third World country. And in the eighties times have been tough, or as they say in this part of the country, real tough. Small oil producers have gone under and small farmers have lost both their land and their way of life in the severest societal dislocation the Plains has seen since the Great Depression.

Oklahoma, at the geographic center of the region, has seen the problems from both ends. Oklahoma's northern half is like its northern neighbors—settled by New Englanders and midwesterners who traditionally vote Republican and make their living on wheat, cattle, and oil and gas. Oklahoma's southern half is like the southern Plains anchor of Texas—settled by southerners who usually vote Democratic and grow soybeans and cotton but are also affected by oil and gas.

We don't often think of this particular group of states as a region. Texas, after all, was a part of the confederacy, and Oklahoma is its economic colony. The Lone Star state does include the moist, low plain along the Gulf of Mexico and the mountains near El Paso, but geographically most of Texas lies within the Prairie and High Plains typical of the region. It was, in fact, an illustrious Texas historian, Walter Prescott Webb, who wrote the classic definition of the region in 1930: "In the new region—level, timberless, and semi-arid—the people were thrown by Mother Necessity into the clutch of new circumstances. Their plight has been stated this way: east of the Mississippi, civilization stood on three legs—land, water, and timber; west of the Mississippi, not one but two of these legs were withdrawn—water and timber—and civilization was left only one leg—land."

Together, the northern and southern Plains states make up an American agri-energy fortress—if the nation cares enough about them to maintain it. The northern outposts are Minnesota and North Dakota, running some 700 miles along the Canadian border. Proceeding southward on the Mississippi River tier, one comes to farm-rich Iowa and variegated Missouri. On the western tier are the lonelier lands of South Dakota, Nebraska, and Kansas, then Oklahoma and the megastate of Texas.

Agriculture dominates the northern Plains economy as oil does the south. But both types of commodities are found throughout the region. Texas is the nation's number-one cattle producer, and Oklahoma one of the top five wheat producers. During the seventies, energy deposits brought temporary wealth to North Dakota, Kansas, and the other northern states. The Plains states also share the loss of people on farms and small towns, a phenomenon lessened only a degree during the heady agri-energy boom of the seventies.

In the last decades of the twentieth century, the northern and southern Plains have been united by ups and downs of the worldwide commodity trade, as the prices of oil, minerals, and raw foodstuffs rose astronomically and then plummeted, hitting them like a sledgehammer. The Plains states produce so little else. Their manufacturing is tied to farm equipment and food processing, their banks and law firms to oil and gas, their state budgets to agriculture and energy-based taxes. There are a few urban pockets of prosperity such as Minneapolis–St. Paul and Dallas and Austin, Texas, but even their very modern high-tech companies have been threatened by growing international competition.

In its free-enterprise, free-trade, anti-inflationary mindset, the Reagan administration has tried to avoid any action which would raise the prices of the products of this region. Congressional pressure on agriculture became so intense that Reagan had no choice but to agree to send billions of dollars in federal subsidies to the area. But on oil, the bargain-basement prices have prevailed, probably providing the key to the low inflation of the Reagan years. With the oil industry split between the smaller independent producers, who have been going bankrupt, and the big processors, who believe they will gain an even stronger position, Congress has been unwilling to act.

Of all the regions of the country, the Plains states found it the most difficult to help themselves cope with the eighties. Most of these states started programs to help farmers in danger of losing their lands. Nebraska joined other farm states in making corporate farming illegal. But these programs could not solve the basic problems of overabundant farm production and low international prices for both grains and oil. The Plains states' task was, in some ways, more difficult than their neighbors. Industrial states could help industries modernize, but no one was complaining that American agriculture was inefficient. More government-funded research was likely to push food production even higher. States could promote agricultural sales overseas, and they did.

But in the mysterious world of international grain trading, how could anyone really tell whether the Japanese or Chinese ended up buying Kansas or North Dakota wheat?

In politics, this agony produced a resurgence of the economic populism that has always been the region's only real counterweight to conservatism—both Democratic and Republican. But the decade also led three very establishment Plains politicians to run for president in 1988: Vice-President George Bush, who started his career in Texas, Kansas senator and former majority leader Bob Dole, who posed the greatest threat to Bush, and Missouri Democratic representative Richard Gephardt, who sought labor support through the severest questioning of free trade in decades. With Iowa the home of the first presidential caucuses and Texas the largest state in the Super Tuesday primary, the entire Plains region had reason to be excited about the process. But the mercurial agricultural and energy policies of the last four presidents—Nixon, Ford, Carter, and Reagan—were enough to engender cynicism and self-protection in anyone living on the Plains.

BACK ON THE FARM

Film historians may record the eighties as the decade that American movies rediscovered rural America. The real-life difficulties of small farmers and newspaper headlines of farm bankers committing suicide provided the grist for a series of tearjerkers—*Country* and *The River*, among others. Actresses Jessica Lange, Sally Field, and Jane Fonda testified before Congress seeking socialist-style intervention for farming. But another—and equally thought-provoking, if comedic—view of farm life came in 1987's *The Secret of My Success* starring Michael J. Fox. As a handsome, light-haired, newly minted college graduate, Fox leaves his parents' seemingly prosperous midwestern farm for the bright lights of New York. He encounters the usual closed doors, but by the end of the movie has gone from a job in the mailroom of a distant relative's company to fending off an eighties-style hostile corporate takeover, being seduced by his boss's wife, and winning an MBA girlfriend who is overwhelmed by his "natural" business prowess. The movie is a fantasy, of course, but it carries an inadvertent social comment. The other guys in the mail room are native New Yorkers, but "ethnics" with heavy accents. Only after the farm boy succeeds, does one of the local city boys begin the climb upward. He may grow up a great distance from our powerful urban centers, but it's clear that the aggressive, all-American farm boy has an easier time connecting to the corporate culture than does an "ethnic" son of a factory worker.

These contradictory images begin to illustrate the varied lot of midwestern American farmers today. Urban and suburban Americans, who now make up 97 percent of our population, tend to categorize farmers in one of two extreme terms they understand: rich, upper-class landowners, or exploited working class. The truth is farmers and ranchers are both, neither, and somewhere in between. They are their own distinct class—landowners, to be sure, but often so cash-poor (and these days sometimes in hock up to their necks) that they have less security than salaried urbanites. It's also important to remember that the Plains states are the great bastion of the medium-sized farm from which most farm owners and their families have (at least until now) made their living from working only on the land. This makes them different from the southern sharecroppers or small farm owners who often take jobs in textile factories or the like, or the California corporate farmers who may employ migrant workers by the hundreds to harvest their crops.

In the postwar era, the Plains farmers also strived to become modern people, and they succeeded. They have bought the newest farm equipment, both to relieve their own physical labors and to be as productive as possible. They really do drive those $40,000-plus tractors, combines, and plows, but they become incensed when urban reporters compare the cost of these pieces of industrial equipment with Cadillacs. They would invite anyone to spend a day in the dirt and dust and then decide whether their tractors with air-conditioned cabs are more luxurious than air conditioning in an auto factory or restaurant kitchen. As more and more of their crops are exported, they have abandoned the isolationist and stridently anti-communist politics that marked their region. And for the most part, they have also taxed themselves to create adequate to fine public universities to educate their children. Yet the sad fact is that if Michael J. Fox's farm-boy character had wanted to make his fortune taking over his father's farm in the eighties, the story could have easily turned into a tragedy.

Populism to Internationalism

To understand today's farm situation, one must go back, but not too far back. It was little more than a century ago that the first homesteaders ventured into this land. What they found was grass—a seemingly boundless sea of grass, tall in the more humid eastern section called the Prairie Plains, shorter in the arid High Plains further to the west. The land was at times as level as any land on earth, then rolling, but never mountainous. Only an occasional stand of trees along a stream bottom, often cottonwood or burr oak, broke the rhythm of the grass with its broad variety of wildflowers.

The homesteaders also came upon a natural environment of startling extremes. This was a land of fiercely cold winters and furnace-like summers, of relentless winds, blizzards, tornadoes, thunderstorms, and prairie fires, of vast skies and celestial pyrotechnics, a region of infinite spaces that almost dared man to tame it. The Plains Indians had lived nomadic lives in delicate balance with the countless millions of buffalo and prairie dogs who had held the land as their own.

The settlers, however, saw the prairie as a challenge for their plows, and thought little of the difficulties that awaited them. And in the somewhat more humid and benign prairie Plains nearer the Mississippi, they were able to establish an agriculture of corn and livestock that prospered magnificently in the affluent meat-consuming economy of the years after World War II and endures to this day. The abundant outpouring from the farms here is interrupted occasionally by the dry spells, though the droughts have not been quite so severe as those farther to the west.

The most severe aridity occurs on the High Plains west of the 98th Meridian, which one can trace from a point some 50 miles west of the North Dakota–Minnesota border straight south to Texas. The High Plains extend westward to the foothills of the Rockies. Within this massive climatic belt, the settlers found that in turning up the prairie, they had destroyed the deep grass roots that had formerly given the land stability. They also found their land could be transformed into a storm of dust that darkened the midday sun. Many indeed fled in terror during the worst droughts.

Prices proved to be an even bigger barrier to rural prosperity than the elements, and in the 1870s the American populist movement emerged to oppose low farm prices, high railroad shipping fees, high interest rates and tight management of the money supply. It was not the first farm protest in the United States, but populism, based in both the Middle West and the South, posed a stronger challenge to the eastern, urban-based capitalist system than any rural movement before or since. Envisioning an economic system which benefited "the people" over elites, farm and labor organizations formally organized the Populist party in 1891, with the goal of replacing the Democrats as the nation's second political party through an alliance of farmers from the South and the Midwest and industrial workers in the East.

In 1892 at a convention in Omaha, the Populist party adopted a platform calling for the free coinage of silver and many liberal economic reforms such as banking regulation, the graduated income tax, and the eight-hour workday. The same year, James B. Weaver, the Populist candidate for president, won more than a million votes, and the party continued to gain momentum. In 1896, however, the Populists began to lose their identity when the Democrats adopted the free silver platform and nominated the same presidential candidate as the Populists, William Jennings Bryan. Bryan lost to Republican William McKinley, and the Populist party continued its decline as farm prices rose and the desired alliance between farmers and laborers went unrealized.

The Populists' ideological weak point had always been their willingness to blame any "them"—whether they were corporations, bankers, Jews, or any other racial or ethnic group—for common Americans' economic woes. In all the Plains states, however, populist sentiments became the bedrock of belief in the federal government's role in bringing stability and modern services to rural areas. Populism, not labor unions or ethnic politics, elected the Plains Democratic governors, House members, and senators who helped write the New Deal legislation that attempted to stabilize rural America.

The U.S. government has ended up playing a more central role in agriculture than in any other sector of the economy. The justification is that farming is a particularly risky business and a particularly vital one. After drought, dust storms, and depressed farm prices drove many farmers out of business, politicians began to believe that the "invisible hand" of the free market was not enough to guide agriculture. The origins of modern-day U.S. farm programs go back to 1933 when Roosevelt's New Deal introduced the Agricultural Adjustment Act. Under its terms, the producers of many crops—including wheat, corn, cotton, peanuts, tobacco, and rice—were required to reduce production in order to eliminate surpluses and increase prices. In return, the federal government agreed to keep farm prices up by buying certain crops when prices were low. The purposes were twofold: to keep farmers in business through temporary adversity and to ensure a steady supply of food to the consumers. Over the years, the details changed, and additional programs were added—agricultural research, dams and aqueducts to provide water in desert and mountain areas and electricity where it had not existed before, crop insurance and disaster relief. The fundamental purpose of the nation's farm policy has remained the same: to help farmers stabilize their lives despite the vagaries of weather and the market.

Farm programs are nearly incomprehensible to nonfarmers, but really can be summed up in a few sentences. The government sets two prices for most farm products, a "support price" and a "target price." These prices were originally set to assure farmers a standard of living in "parity" with farmers' incomes between 1910 and 1914. The standard has been changed over time, but the concept remains sacred, as every presidential candidate soon learns. Farmers who wish to participate in the government's programs sign up at their local Agricultural Stabilization and Conservation Service office. If the market price paid by grain elevators and other private buyers around the country is lower than the government "support price," then a farmer who has signed up for government programs takes a loan on his grain from the government on the theory that if enough farmers keep their grain off the market temporarily, prices will rise. If the farmer is later able to sell the crop for more than the loan, he pays back the loan and sells the crop, but if the price has not risen, the law permits him to leave the crop in the government's hands and keep the money. If market prices are low, the support price does force up the market price in the United States because grain dealers have to come close to competing with the government in order to get any grain at all. But if the U.S. market prices become too high, then American farm products cannot compete on world markets. For this reason, the government established the "target price," which is deemed to be the fair price farmers would receive in a more perfect world. When the market price is not as high as the target price, the government makes the farmer a "deficiency payment" for the difference. In the internationally competitive 1980s, this can amount to a considerable amount of money. In late 1987, for example, the target price for wheat was $4.30 per bushel while the support was $2.10. To try to bring supply and demand into some balance and to keep the government's costs down, the Agriculture Department also has the right to demand that program participants reduce the number of acres they have planted.

Under this system, agriculture was more or less stable from World War II until 1972. Soil conservation practices, irrigation from underground wells, and other technological advances transformed the Plains from dust bowl into the great breadbasket. A few important environmental trouble spots such as the depletion of the Ogallala aquifer in the High Plains of west Texas, Oklahoma, and Kansas developed out of this period, but in general the vagaries of both the weather and the market were overcome. Try as they might, however, the government's farm programs could not protect small farms from the advance of big technology. General tax laws, in fact, helped larger operators—as well as nonfarmers—invest in more and more land and equipment. During the Eisenhower administration of the 1950s, the number of farms in the country declined by 20 percent. In the 1960s, under Kennedy and Johnson, the figure declined 33 percent, and in the first three years of the Nixon administration, another 10 percent.

Then, in 1972, President Nixon and his Agriculture secretary Earl Butz attempted a revolution in agriculture: to "get the government out of agriculture" by turning food into an export product. Ideological conservatives and some farmers, usually highly successful ones, had always objected to the government's presence in agriculture. "Handouts" to farmers, they argued, were not fair to the taxpayer and reduced economic efficiency. The Republican party paid lip service to these ideas, although farm-state Republicans in Congress protected their careers by voting for every farm program from price supports to rural electrification. When the Soviet Union, under the pressure of failed harvests and wishing to offer its people more consumer goods, offered to buy practically all the U.S. agricultural products it could get, Butz and Nixon leapt at the idea. Butz promised a new future for farmers and told them to plant "fence row to fence row."

At first the international sales seemed like a dream come true for both the Republicans and the farmers. Oil prices were high, and oil-producing countries in Latin America and Africa began importing more food as did the newly industrialized countries of Asia. Grain prices skyrocketed, and with it land and equipment sales. Small farms became economically viable, and sons who were going off to college or to the city to work suddenly saw big profits and changed their life plans. The rural good times coincided with the college graduation of the first of the postwar baby boomers, and hundreds of thousands of talented young lawyers, doctors, architects, and government bureaucrats who had grown up in small Plains cities went home to establish themselves.

The first signal of the fragility of this new economic order came less than a year after the Soviet grain deal had been signed. In June 1973, soybean prices got so high that there were fears of a food shortage, and President Nixon embargoed shipments. The soybean situation was typical of things to come. A mysterious ocean current called "El Niño," which hits the west coast of South America every six or seven years, lasted longer than usual and caused a drastic shortage of anchovies, which are used worldwide as a protein-rich feed supplement for poultry and livestock. Animal feeders, unable to buy either anchovies or traditional feed grains—which had been committed to the Soviet Union—turned to soybeans, sending the price from $3 per bushel to $12.90. The dangers of these policies became clear when, after Nixon established the embargo, the soybean-consuming Japanese got scared and entered into a joint farming venture with the Brazilian government that has grown to a $300 million enterprise with a goal of producing 100 million tons annually by the year 2000.

The soybean embargo was only the first presidential curb on exports used to achieve other goals. "Moratoriums" on grain exports were imposed in 1974 and 1975, and President Carter imposed an embargo on grain exports in 1980 in response to the Soviet invasion of Afghanistan. Agricultural experts said each embargo had little effect on farm income, but the embargoes gave the United States a reputation as an unreliable supplier. By the 1980s, a bad reputation was something the United States could ill afford. Canada, Argentina, Australia, and the European Economic Community had gotten heavily into grain exporting and quickly took up any markets the United States abandoned for political reasons. Finally, the Third World was taking advantage of the "green revolution" in seeds and planting techniques. Self-sufficiency in agriculture became a matter of national pride, and farm subsidies swept the world. Sandy Saudi Arabia, which had once imported millions of bushels of wheat, became an exporter.

Congress and the Carter administration, meanwhile, raised target prices and loan rates, which pleased the farmers because they quite correctly believed their long-term welfare had been assured. Since market prices were so high at the time, and many farmers were either not participating in the program or paying off their loans to sell at market prices, the increases were a cost-free way to make political points with farmers. When Carter established the Soviet grain embargo, he offered farmers a big increase in price supports for wheat and corn to offset their losses. The sins of the seventies thus set the stage for the incredible chaos of the eighties.

THE REAGAN YEARS AND THE FUTURE

By the time Reagan took office, every trend responsible for the export-based agricultural prosperity of the early seventies reversed itself and other negative developments set in. The OPEC countries' pricing agreements collapsed and with it their ability to import food, and the Latin American countries found themselves deeply in debt and using their foreign exchange to pay interest rather than to buy food. The high prices of the seventies had also produced a glut of nearly every agricultural commodity. Europe, Canada, Argentina, Australia, and other countries found it very easy to compete for sales because the exchange rate for the dollar was so high, and when they did not, they used special programs to help poor foreign countries buy their goods. U.S. agricultural exports fell from a high of $43 billion in 1981 to $26 billion in 1986.

Despite these apparent problems, the Reaganites started out with a campaign to end all government agricultural subsidies. Office of

Management and Budget Director David Stockman showed no sympathy for the growing problems in rural America, saying "For the life of me, I can't figure out why taxpayers should be expected to refinance bad debt willingly incurred by consenting adults who went out and bought farmland when prices were going up and thought they could get rich." Stockman's strict conservative economics left no room for the idea that farming was somehow special or for the fact that farmers who lost their land also lost their homes and way of life. Reagan's first Agriculture secretary, John Block, offered a more realistic view when he said "We in agriculture built our own trap. We're all responsible: the farmers who bid up the land; the so-called experts who said 'Buy another piece of land—they ain't making any more of it'; the lending institutions that couldn't shovel the money out the door fast enough. We all fell into the trap and expanded too fast." Under pressure from Congress to do something about the deteriorating farm economy, Block and his team developed the famed "payment-in-kind" or PIK program of giving farmers—in exchange for cutting back on acres planted—certificates of ownership for government-owned grains. The farmers were able to use the certificates to pay off their loans—essentially getting paid twice for the same grain—or they could sell them or trade them, sometimes at a premium, to other farmers who wanted them to pay off their own government loans. The program did reduce grain stocks, but it didn't really increase world prices since both U.S. harvests and foreign production remained heavy.

Inflation was still high enough that, in the 1981 farm bill, Congress increased the support prices even higher. This move, combined with the strong dollar, would make U.S. agricultural goods more expensive than those of other countries in the international markets. In an attempt to counter this trend, the 1985 farm bill reduced the "support" price, which had an effect on the price of U.S. products on the international markets, but increased the size of deficiency payments to make up for the loss. The bill also created the first U.S. export subsidies.

By the latter half of the decade, however, one-third of America's 600,000 farmers were in financial trouble, and both private and government-connected agricultural lending institutions were in terrible shape. The two-thirds of farmers who remained solvent were experiencing a markedly reduced standard of living. To stay afloat, even the staunchest conservatives had signed up for the government programs, and federal farm subsidies had risen from $4 billion in 1981 to $20 billion in 1987—faster than defense spending. Since farm programs are "entitlements"—that is, as in social security, anyone who qualifies must get his money—big farmers who could make it on their own as well as little guys signed up. Farmers were limited to $50,000 in subsidies, so many began subdividing their properties among family members to qualify for more money. General Accounting Office studies found that 30 percent of all farm subsidies went to the largest one percent of all producers, and that farmers making less than $100,000 per year received only one-third of the government payments. By 1989 it was estimated that farmers would get 70 percent of their income from Uncle Sam compared with 25 percent in 1984.

Urban lawmakers became furious over this increase in farm spending when almost all other domestic welfare programs were barely surviving. Farm-state senators and members of Congress who had used all their power to save their constituents defended the massive increases as a short-term necessity in a glutted world market. Some defended big farmers' participation in the program, saying that big farmers' lands produce a lot of food and that in participating in the program big farmers also had to cut back on the number of acres they planted.

To the end, the Reaganites blamed Congress for the chaos in agriculture and pursued their goal of getting the government out of agriculture. In 1987, when the multilateral trade talks opened in Geneva, the administration offered to end all U.S. farm subsidies, including the agricultural extension service, if other countries would abandon their subsidies and establish a worldwide free market. Some Europeans responded that the U.S. proposal would destroy the continent's agriculture, which, in many countries, makes up a higher percentage of the gross national product than in the United States. Such a radical change would take years (after Reagan has left office) to institute, but an equally big obstacle might be resistance from U.S. farm groups.

The Reaganites' radical—though failed—approaches to farm policy produced an equally radical leftist approach from Senator Tom Harkin of Iowa, who had formed a populist caucus in 1983 when he was a House member. Harkin has argued that "driving down world food prices will reduce Third World food production and stifle those nations' new base for economic expansion." Newly industrialized, growing nations are America's most-promising cash customers, Harkin argued, also noting that "the European Economic Community has made a decision to have family farms. We cannot force them to abandon those policies." Harkin has trotted out the old populist idea of production controls based on a farmer referendum, but other members of Congress seem to think the idea is too old-fashioned in the now-internationalized economy.

Harkin's views are backed up, however, by the Reverend David Ostendorf, organizer of Prairiefire, the activist farm group based in Des Moines, and Maurice J. Dingman, the Catholic bishop of Des Moines. Ostendorf argues that Americans have looked upon land as "simply another commodity to be used, exploited, owned, obtained and accumulated for the primary benefit of the self, not for the benefit of the broader community." Ostendorf believes that land is "a base of the covenant relationship between God and the people of the community of faith." Land, he said, is a "gift," and "one does not treat a gift—especially one of the most basic gifts of God besides life itself—as mere property." Citing the Hebrew law of the Jubilee Year (Leviticus 25:10–24), which directed the Jews to return the Promised Land to the families who originally received it by lot, Dingman has called for farmers to become unified and large corporate farms to be discouraged through higher land taxes for bigger landowners.

Where, one is tempted to ask, will all this end? That is precisely the wrong question. Both farmers and consumers could save themselves a great deal of emotional energy if they would realize that any changes in the government's farm policies are likely to come within the framework of current programs. Politicians may say the current subsidies are short term while the United States recovers its export markets, but if that recovery doesn't happen, no one expects the senators and congressmen from the nine Plains states and others to sacrifice their careers on an ideological altar—right or left.

Cool-headed economists point out that U.S. farm programs have had two great consumer successes that no one wants to destroy. They have guaranteed a food supply at relatively cheap prices and avoided the gluts and scarcities that plague so many countries. Americans spend only 16 percent of their disposable income on food, and if the cost of federal farm programs is included, another 5 percent, making a total of 21 percent—still less than any other industrialized country. A good argument can also be made that the current system inadvertently helps poor people because food prices are kept low while the tax-paying middle class subsidizes the farmers. The decision to pursue export markets also bodes ill for reducing the U.S. government's role in agriculture since, as economist Martin Abel has written, "in most countries of the world, agriculture is viewed as a public utility to be regulated in the interest of society." The current levels of farm support—producer subsidies, import barriers, and export incentives combined—range from under 9 percent of farmers' income for beef in the United States to more than 75 percent for dairy, rice, and wheat farmers in Japan.

The gross worldwide imbalance between supply and demand and the controversy over the government's rising expenditures will keep the debate alive. But it's pointless to look for a savior in the farm situation. The last three administrations—Nixon-Ford, Carter, and Reagan—have all proven that presidents place agriculture's welfare second to foreign policy and political expediency. Nixon's export plan and the embargoes that followed disrupted farming more severely than any event since the Great Depression. Carter, the peanut farmer-turned-engineer, proved quite willing to ban exports to the Soviet Union in order to look tough, and his Agriculture Department loaned too much money to marginal farmers. Reagan has driven an unrealistic hard line on free-market theory, but put ideology aside to create incentives to export to the Soviet Union when he thought it might keep the Senate in Republican hands.

The farmers, ranchers, and processors have too many complementary and competing interests to reach any consensus. They now range from the Republican-minded Farm Bureau, the Democratic-leaning Farmers Union, and the less partisan National Grange to the increasingly powerful commodity groups such as the National Milk Producers Federation, the National Cotton Council, and the National Association of Wheat Growers. To these may be added the consumer and food safety groups that have grown up since the 1960s, and anticapitalist farm groups—such as Ostendorf's Prairiefire—that often get church and foundation money to protect farmers at the lowest end of the economic spectrum.

At this point, all of these groups are involved in a kind of holding pattern to keep agriculture in as good a position as possible. Some analysts see the worldwide trend toward self-sufficiency and the debts of Third World countries as permanent obstacles to the export of American agricultural products. In their minds, only a catastrophe can make American agricultural products more valuable. World hunger has been reduced extraordinarily over the past 15 years except for relatively small areas of Africa, according to the World Bank. But I have stood in the shantytowns of Rio de Janeiro and Lima, and in the neighborhoods of Beijing, and wondered about this supposed worldwide trend of food self-sufficiency. If goals were established to increase the quantity and variety of food people eat in the Third World, if the environmental impacts of some of their large-scale agricultural projects were seriously assessed, and if some arrangements were made to help pay off their debts, then American foodstuffs might become more valuable. In the meantime, the situation cries out for leadership to overcome the havoc that technology and world events have wreaked upon the food producers of our time.

JIM HIGHTOWER: MR. AGRICULTURE?

In today's highly educated, well-dressed political society, it's hard to find the kind of fiery populist that used to put the fear of God into the urban establishment. An exception is Texas Agriculture Commissioner Jim Hightower, who flies around the state resplendent in the standard western suit, cowboy hat, and boots and persists in a self-described "kick ass populism" that "taps a deep strain of populist resentment of the powers that be—the banker and the bosses, the politicians and the press, the big boys, and what generally is referred to as 'the bastards.' "

"Reagan's idea of a good farm program is 'Hee-Haw,' " Hightower says. "The President promised farmers a seven course meal and it turned out to be a six-pack and a possum." When the Reagan administration planned to freeze the federal farm programs, he said, "we're in danger of the PIK [payment-in-kind] program becoming an ice pick that is going to be driven through the heart of our family farm system."

This coarse, funny language, delivered in a north Texas twang, has provided relief, if not hope, to frustrated farmers and made Hightower far more famous in rural states than the rhetorically dull Democrats on the House and Senate agriculture committees. A sharp critic of Reagan's plans for reductions in federal loans on commodities, Hightower's own national program called for mandatory production controls (subject to producer referendum) that would limit total U.S. production and federal loan programs structured to encourage "small and medium-sized" farms and discourage big corporate operations.

Hightower has transformed his $20 million, 565-person agency from a sleepy bureaucracy into a thorn in the side of the state's powerful agriculture establishment. With a staff culled from state agriculture departments around the country, the agency has cajoled Texas supermarket chains into buying produce from local farmer cooperatives rather than from out-of-state suppliers, has started an export program that sold $78 million worth of Texas livestock last year, and has set up 40 farmers markets around the state. Hightower has tried to push farmers into growing more high-profit specialty crops such as blueberries and gourmet onions and won passage of a multi-million dollar bond program to help finance local food processing facilities.

His strident advocacy has attracted some enmity from big Texas farmers. When the agency tightened restrictions on pesticides, it sparked an unsuccessful effort in the legislature to strip the department of its regulatory powers and downgrade the commissioner's post to an appointed slot. His national politicking—he chaired the Democratic National Committee's Agriculture Council in 1984—is not entirely popular either, but Hightower strongly defends his activities. The agriculture establishment would prefer "an agriculture department checking the scales and inspecting the eggs and not making any noise," he said. "Legislators have complained that they don't like me going to Washington to fight the federal government, but to me, that's where the battle is." On that front, Bob Dole has termed Hightower "noisy but ineffective."

Hightower's Texas agricultural opponents appear powerless to unseat him since his political base is urban. "It's a folksy but intelligent image, communicated in a way that attracts urban voters who wouldn't normally fit the populist profile of the message," said John Hildreth, executive director of Common Cause in Texas.

His life is far from that of the old-time populist. Hightower was born into what his official biography describes as "an old family of scrappers from the rolling prairies of North Central Texas," and he worked as an aide to former Texas Democratic senator Ralph W. Yarborough, Jr., but he also studied international relations at Columbia University in New York and in 1970 founded the Washington-based Agribusiness Accountability Project. The then-long-haired Hightower wrote two anti-corporate books, *Eat Your Heart Out* and *Hard Tomatoes, Hard Times*, and staged rallies against Nixon administration Agriculture secretary Earl L. Butz before returning to Texas as editor of the crusading *Texas Observer*. His personal life is also unconventional for a populist. Hightower has lived for many years with a feminist who refuses to marry him—though, as one Austin-based correspondent put it, his day-to-day life is a lot more home-based than the average Texas state legislator's.

Don't look for Hightower to sit in the Agriculture secretary's chair in Washington, however. He has already said he is uninterested in the position and readily acknowledges he has set his sights on the the Senate seat of Republican Phil Gramm in 1990. But his preferred career path may also indicate that it's a lot easier these days to criticize the government's agricultural policy than it is to do something about it.

URBAN POCKETS OF PROSPERITY:
A PANOPLY OF PRODUCTS

Cities, rare and strange creatures on the Plains, are the region's only hope of maintaining its population. The homesteaders did not like cities, viewing the grain traders' mansions as symbols of their economic exploitation and gaudy saloons as temptations to iniquity. The World War I song "How You Gonna Keep 'Em Down on the Farm after They've Seen Paree?" was written about midwestern farm boys who had never before been treated to the delights of a sophisticated city. More people still live on farms in the northern Plains—30 percent in North Dakota and Nebraska—than in any other region except the South, and between 10 and 15 percent of the people still work in agriculture. But nearly every farm family has a child living in Minneapolis, Dallas, or the like. The Plains farmers may not like it, but the situation is better than in the 1930s, when the Great Depression caused thousands to flee to the West Coast, and in the 1940s, when hundreds of thousands more fled westward to work in defense plants, never to return.

A list of Plains cities must begin with St. Louis, the "last city of the east" from which Lewis and Clark and thousands of settlers set out, and where a museum of western expansion is appropriately located. But the pioneers could not get along without railheads and distribution centers for their cattle and grains, so Kansas City, "the first city of the west," the Twin Cities of St. Paul and Minneapolis on each side of the Mississippi, and Fort Worth, "Cowtown U.S.A.," grew up. They joined San Antonio, Texas (founded in 1718 by the Spanish), as the region's vital centers. A string of smaller cities developed slightly farther west: Des Moines, Iowa; Omaha, Nebraska; Wichita, Kansas; Oklahoma City and Tulsa, Oklahoma; and Austin, Texas. Sad to say, the cities stopped in the middle of the region; all the way from the Canadian border into Texas, the belt west of the 98th meridian is still devoid of a single large city or important university. These groupings leave out only Dallas and Houston, the region's modern southern powerhouses; these two cities are among the ten largest metropolitan areas in the United States, but they did not turn into real cities until oil and urbanization transformed the Texas economy in the 1930s.

The variety of jobs available in the Plains' cities of the eighties—in manufacturing, law, accounting, engineering, and government—is a marvel to anyone who knew these places as the urban backwaters of the country. The diversification did not come easily. The movement of people out of the region altogether in the thirties and forties and the "coastalization" of our society after World War II left the Plains behind in jobs, scientific skills, population, and wealth. The problem was most acute in the western tier of Plains states (the Dakotas, Nebraska, and Kansas), but it affected the easterly tier as well.

The stability in agriculture in the fifties and sixties gave the Plains

cities the wealth to diversify while the modernization of food processing made it a vital necessity. Just as technology changed farming, it
changed the way agricultural products are handled. Meat slaughtering and packing, for example, have moved from Fort Worth and
Kansas City (as well as the Great Lakes city of Chicago) to smaller
cities closer to feed lots.* Truck transport made rail yards less important. Much northern Plains industry remains tied to food processing,
brewing, milling, and farm-equipment manufacturing but Plains cities
have also developed specialties that have little or nothing to do with
agriculture—Minneapolis in computers and Wichita in light aircraft.

This seeming independence from the land has produced new varia-
tions on the old urban-rural split. In the eighties, these cities have
sometimes thrived even when agriculture has been in a depression.
Minnesota Democratic-Farmer-Labor governor Rudy Perpich spoke
frequently of the "two Minnesotas"—the thriving Twin Cities and
the depressed farming areas and mines near Duluth. The Plains are
lucky not to have to cope with the decline of the heavy manufacturing
that made their Great Lakes neighbors so much richer for so long. But
the newer industries are also subject to foreign competition. Minneapolis and St. Paul have found themselves caught up in the worldwide semiconductor glut, and Wichita's Cessna factories have to
compete with Brazilian aircraft makers. In these same years, the Plains
cities ironically have discovered that their agricultural past is a tourist
draw—a phenomenon gleefully reported by Kansas City native Calvin Trillin when he described his city's rediscovery of its American
Royal stock show.

*Slaughtering, cutting, and packing meat may be less in the public eye than when they were
located in union-conscious Chicago, but despite the advance of technologies seem to be just as
dangerous. With their plants now removed from the big city, pro-union atmosphere and their
profits threatened by the decline in meat consumption, packing companies throughout the
Middle West have become some of the nation's biggest union busters and objectors to federal
occupational health and safety laws. In 1987, the government proposed a $2.59 million fine
against IBP, Inc., the nation's largest meat-packer, accusing it of omitting accidents from
medical logs during a two-year period at its largest plant (in Dakota City, Nebraska) and, then
adding 832 injuries to the logs a week before federal inspectors gained access to the plant. "This
is the worst example of underreporting injuries and illnesses to workers ever encountered by
OSHA in its history," said Assistant Labor Secretary John A. Pendergrass. Representative Tom
Lantos of California, who had been conducting hearings on the question, said the conditions
evoked the horrors documented in Upton Sinclair's novel, *The Jungle*. "It's a nightmare,"
Lantos said, "an absolute nightmare."

The most vigorous, forward-moving urban economy in the postwar Plains has been Minnesota's Twin Cities. Finance, insurance, and services have boomed there as companies such as Honeywell, Inc., Minnesota Mining and Manufacturing Company, and Control Data Corporation defied the state's inland location and developed national and international markets. Giant agribusiness firms such as General Mills, Inc. and Pillsbury Company kept their home offices in Minneapolis and St. Paul as they diversified from milling into products and services.

Minnesota's history of small farms and small businesses, as opposed to a single dominant industrial interest, and the extremely large extent of home-state ownership, is believed to have played an important role in its economic vitality. Minnesotans are not so certain about the future, however. The giant retailer Dayton-Hudson's decision to ask the Minnesota legislature for protection from hostile takeovers demonstrated how tough it is for a civic-minded, successful firm to maintain its posture in today's unregulated business environment.

Minnesota's industrial competitor on the urban Plains is Missouri, and the defense dependence of its biggest metropolitan area of St. Louis reveals much about the region as a whole. Home of several *Fortune* 500 headquarters, including the aerospace giant McDonnell Douglas, St. Louis is largely responsible for Missouri's ranking sixth of all the states in defense payrolls and prime contract awards. In 1985, Missouri got $8.8 billion. Either because Missouri doesn't have the plants to carry out the work at home or because its defense suppliers are smart enough to spread the work to congressional districts in other states, Missouri drops to 14th place when subcontracting is taken into consideration. Defense is still responsible for 7.5 percent of Missouri's economy, however—the 12th highest percentage in the country.

Minnesota is the only other Plains state to get substantial defense money, and it gets only $6.3 billion, for a ranking of 22nd. Bases, starting with the Strategic Air Command at Omaha, dot the northern Plains, but defense spending in these states is a pale shadow of the money flowing to the coasts and Texas. South Dakota's $678 million places it dead last in defense spending, below Wyoming and North Dakota. Iowa gets a relatively large amount—$2.93 billion, but with only 3.9 percent of its economy related to defense, it ranks as the least defense-dependent state in the country. Most of the Plains states are among those that Pentagon opponents contend are being sucked dry by defense spending.

Texas and Oklahoma:
Troubles in "Big Awl" Country

The southern Plains states of Texas and Oklahoma share wheat and cattle, oil and gas. But here the similarities with the northern Plains end. Cotton and other hot-weather food such as watermelon and pecans grow on the southern Plains. And "awl"—mercurial in its price—dominates the economy above all else.

It still may not show, but the eighties have brought true humility to the bragging Texas and Oklahoma oilmen who were so hard for the rest of the country to live with during the seventies. To the people who once brandished bumper stickers reading "Let a Yankee Freeze in the Dark," the list of humiliations was unending. Oil prices below $15 per barrel brought Texas's jobless rate above 10 percent in June 1986, its highest figure in post-Depression history. The rig count in Texas and its Oil Patch neighbors of Louisiana and Oklahoma, a critical indicator of drilling activity, declined from 1,170 to 459 in just one year. "There are fewer rigs in the entire U.S. today than there were in Oklahoma alone four years ago," said Oklahoma's governor at the time, Democrat George Nigh.

The downward spiral in oil erased the Oil Patch's advantage of financing its state government through energy-production taxes paid indirectly by out-of-state consumers. In 1987, Governor William Clements of Texas ended up approving a $5.7 billion tax increase, raising the state sales tax from 5.25 to 6 percent, raising the corporate franchise tax and the motor-vehicle sales tax and imposing a $110 annual fee on professionals. The bill also made permanent a 15-cent-per-gallon gasoline tax enacted the year before as a temporary measure.

The situation revealed how recent and fragile was the affluence and modernity that had come to this part of the country. As late as 1930, most of Texas drifted along—rural, agrarian, and poor. Almost 60 percent of its 5.8 million people lived on farms or in small towns, making their living principally from cattle and cotton. In those years, Texas closely resembled the Southern states with which it had been grouped since joining the Confederacy in the Civil War—over the objections of General Sam Houston, who as a result was removed from the governorship by slave-owning pioneers.

The first great Texas oil strike was made in an inconspicuous mound of earth called Spindletop, near Beaumont on the Gulf Coast, in January 1901. But Texas's real road to affluence—and separation from its southern heritage—came in the early 1930s, when the east Texas oil field was discovered. It remained the largest in the United States until the Alaska North Slope strike in the 1960s. The oil field spawned Texas's petrochemical industry and provided the capital for the state's industrial diversification. During World War II, military bases sprouted, and in the postwar years Texas became the country's second-largest defense contractor, after California.

Texas's final push forward came in the 1960s when John B. Connally, who had been appointed Navy secretary under President Kennedy, returned home to run for governor and make Texas competitive with the East and California in education and business growth. Connally and his friends in the tightly knit Texas oil-insurance-finance-manufacturing-agribusiness establishment were determined to make Texas a Class-A state and not, in the words of one of their associates, "to go the route of Mississippi, Alabama, and Louisiana." By the time Lyndon B. Johnson served as president and Connally as governor, a new Texas had been born: aggressive, investing heavily in higher education, oriented to the space age. Connally was responsible for expanding the University of Texas into one of the nation's top teaching and research institutions. The federal government poured in millions of dollars in defense contracts and located the National Aeronautics and Space Administration's Manned Spacecraft Center in Houston.

The oil shortage and Organization of Petroleum Exporting Countries' accord in the 1970s increased the value of Texas oil 5 times and gas 10 times. The state boomed and mocked the rest of the country which suffered under the weight of the new prices. Congress responded by instituting a windfall profits tax to counter the oil import fee and oil depletion allowance which had once caused conservative economist Milton Friedman to write, "Few industries sing the praises of free enterprise more loudly than the oil industry. Yet few industries rely so heavily on special government favors."

In the early 1980s, after the OPEC agreement collapsed, global prices fell; the world seemed awash in oil, and new exploration in the United States became unprofitable. By the late 1980s, the windfall profits tax was not being collected anymore, and some factions of the industry had begun asking for the reinstitution of the oil import fee or a floor price on crude oil on the grounds that America's increasing dependency on cheap, imported oil (37 percent in 1986) was a danger to national security. Their efforts made little headway partly because Exxon, the largest integrated multinational oil company, opposed any form of federal price support. The Reagan administration would have none of the national security argument, and one of Vice-President Bush's worst moments came when he publicly expressed a Texan's concern about low oil prices, and as a loyal Reaganite had to take back his words.

In an interview, Oklahoma Republican chairman Tom Cole made a compelling case for some type of floor price. Investors had lost so much money and believe that oil investments are so risky, he said, that "if the Arabs jack up the price, you're not going to get anybody to invest." To the argument that import fees are nothing more than oil protectionism, he argued Oil Patch–fashion that such "pure market" arguments are fine for textiles, but not for a vital necessity like oil.

None of the arguments seem to matter. Texas's attitude in the seventies had left Americans in other regions nearly totally unsympathetic to the Texans' plight. New Englanders, who, by dint of location, are the most dependent on imported oil, oppose any import fee as staunchly as when a fee existed. To the horror of the industry, some economists and environmentalists responded to the national security argument by suggesting that the way to deal with the question was to increase the gasoline tax or impose an industry-wide oil excise tax which would cut domestic consumption and raise tax revenues. The 1986 elections brought advocates of the oil import fee to prominent positions in the Congress—House Speaker Jim Wright and Senate Finance Committee chairman Lloyd Bentsen, both of Texas; and Senate Energy and Natural Resources Committee chairman J. Bennett Johnston of Louisiana—but the atmosphere was so negative that they couldn't deliver for the industry as had Lyndon Johnson, Speaker of the House Sam Rayburn, Senator Robert S. Kerr of Oklahoma, and, in his earlier years, Senator Russell Long of Louisiana.

By the late 1980s, even the famed Hunt brothers and former Governor John Connally were trying desperately to hang onto some of their money. The oil bust destroyed Texas's blustering, larger-than-life, easy-money image and revealed a state whose status as largest in the union until Alaska's entry and history as an independent republic had permitted it an unrealistic self-confidence. "This has never been a really rich land," noted *New York Times* Houston bureau chief Robert Reinhold. "From the arid western reaches to the lush eastern pine forests, Texas has always for most been a state where hard work and grit were needed to making a living." For all the bigger-than-life, money-and-glamor imagery, Reinhold noted, Texas's per capita income was five percent below the national average in 1970, rose to only slightly above during the best of times, and fell to two percent below in 1985. Texas incomes are below those of most of the northern Plains states, where life may be more staid, but even in these troubled times is more stable.

In the future, Texas has no choice but to diversify. Its crude oil supplies are dwindling, and America's concern for energy conservation has also reduced demand. Even Texas's vaunted tradition of entrepreneurship turned out to be more oil related than anyone thought, requiring a new look at what really makes business grow. But Texas still has many business advantages—low taxes, minimal government regulation, and strong opposition to labor unions.

Texas's great urban centers have begun to respond to the challenge of a new age. Diversified Dallas has been the mecca for people from worse-off places in the Southwest, and it liberalized its image in 1987 by electing its first woman mayor, Annette Strauss. In its weakened state, the oil capital of Houston is finally taking a second look at its ugliness. San Antonio has the boon of having the most successful young Hispanic politician in the country, Henry Cisneros, as its mayor. But these cities' futures will not be easy. In Austin, where the University of Texas and the state government protect the economy, speculators have lost their shirts on "raw" land (without water or sewers) they expected to buzz with high-tech plants; the Austin economy has, in fact, gotten so bad that landlords have reduced rents and restaurants cut their prices.

Perhaps it is best now to remember that the majority of Texans were never much like the rich, aggressive characters on "Dallas." Texas is also home to poor blacks who have migrated from the poorer Southeast, to Hispanics who labor in the vast farms of south Texas, and to poor whites everywhere from the cities to the ranches of west Texas. Visitors lured by the wealth and glamor of Texas don't see many of those people. One day in the state capitol in Austin, I watched a class of junior-high-school students who obviously had journeyed a great distance to see their state government in action. Their thin bodies, mended clothing, and oiled, slicked-back hair, were a reminder that vast stretches of the Lone Star State have never been touched by the wealth that flows from the ground.

THE TEXAS SCHOOLS GROW UP

If the agonies of oil and agriculture can have a positive legacy, it will be the reform of the Texas educational system.

For the third most populous state of the union, with pretensions toward world-class status, the Texas school system has been shameful. Despite the state's enormous oil wealth, until recently its per student spending was near the basement of all U.S. states; the differences between rich districts and poor were enormous, and many of its teachers were poorly educated. To top off the situation, textbook selection had become dominated by a right-wing, elderly couple, Mel and Norma Gabler, who frequently objected to modern interpretations of evolution, the civil rights movement, the role of women, and foreign affairs.

The textbook issue came up first. In 1980, when Hollywood producer Norman Lear founded People for the American Way to oppose the New Right and its conservative social agenda, his staff noticed that Texas had become the focal point of the New Right's attempt to influence the content of textbooks. A quirk in Texas law permitted citizens to object to textbooks under consideration by the state's textbook review committee, but not to testify on behalf of textbooks. Since 1961, the Gablers had been reading texts and causing rejections or changes in 10 or 12 books per year. Since Texas buys 10 percent of the textbooks published annually in the United States, publishers could ill afford to write off the Texas market, so they altered their books according to the guidelines. In one of the most famous incidents, a textbook publisher removed a text reference to the famous Leakey family's work on prehistoric humans in Africa because some Texans thought the Leakeys were too closely associated with evolution. The deletion became embarrassing public knowledge when the reference was taken out of the chapter, but left in the index.

People for the American Way "discovered the Gablers" in 1982, according to its Austin-based lawyer and executive director, Mike Hudson. "Far from being this little interesting couple in Texas," said Hudson, "they were really a focal point for right wing activity in Texas. They would do these reviews and then market them to other states. They would lead seminars on education at national 'family' forums in Washington and were plugged in with Jerry Falwell and Phyllis Schlafly."

When People for the American Way set about publicizing the Gablers' connections its leaders discovered, somewhat to their surprise, allies among Baptists, United Methodists, Catholics and scientists; the Texas Anti-Censorship Coalition resulted. Happily for the Coalition, exposure of the Gablers coincided with national concern about the "dumbing down" of textbooks (that is, the practice of taking stimulating and controversial material out of textbooks).

Under scrutiny, the Gablers came off as reactionary, paranoid, and backward—damning traits in a Texas that was beginning to see science as the key to its future. The Texas school board, which selects the textbook review committee, agreed to a rule that allowed testimony in support of books as well as against them. People for the American Way's records show that the Gablers have not been successful in instituting any changes since 1984, and Texas emerged from its dark ages to throw out the best-selling health textbook in the nation because it did not contain enough information on the reproductive system.

While the Gabler case was garnering national publicity, Texas was beginning a long-term school reform movement that would far surpass the textbook issue in consequence. As the agri-energy economy worsened, there was the dawning recognition that young Texans would have to be better educated to survive in the future. The reforms started in the early eighties with a new curriculum to bring some standardization throughout the state, and tests for education majors to see if they had learned the skills to be good teachers. These measures were minor compared to House Bill 72, which increased state spending on education by more than $1 billion, required the testing of all 200,000 teachers, and said that if a student did not pass his courses with a 70 percent average, he could not play on a sports team. The bill also said coaches must teach courses and outlawed social promotion (passing kids from one grade to the next out of concern for their psychological well-being). The measure became law after a media blitz by hard-charging Texas entrepreneur H. Ross Perot, but the changes so challenged Texas traditions of low taxes and devotion to sports that the political debates threatened to go on into the 1990s.

The Republicans hated the tax increase—the first in at least a dozen years—necessary to finance the reforms. The teachers' unions hated the testing. And the coaches—beloved and respected figures in many small Texas towns—whipped up a frenzy of resentment against the "no pass, no play" rule.

The reforms all lasted, but Democratic governor Mark White became a casualty in his campaign for re-election in 1986. White had other problems—the bad economy was foremost—but there seems no question that the unwillingness of the teacher unions to endorse a Democratic candidate, and the coaches' opposition, hurt him. In his television ads, former governor William P. Clements, Jr., Texas's first Republican governor since Reconstruction and the man White had defeated in 1982, charged White with "straying from the truth" because, like most Texas politicians, he had promised not to raise taxes. White responded with an ad that recalled Lyndon Johnson's famous 1964 "daisy spot" against Barry Goldwater in which a little girl counts flower petals until her counting is replaced by the countdown for a nuclear blast. In the 1986 version, the girl sang the alphabet, but could not remember it after the letter "Q" and looked helplessly into the camera. "If Clements wants to run for governor to get even, that's his business," the ad concluded. "But if he takes it out on education, that's your business."

Angry Texans did not buy the White campaign and chose Clements. As it turned out, even Clements, with much prodding from Democratic lieutenant governor Bill Hobby—the longtime shadow governor of Texas—ended up agreeing that education had to be the state's number-one priority and signed off on a $333 million spending boost for higher education.

The Texas education department has reported that the reforms have already started to show results in national test scores. A court ruling that the Texas constitution guaranteed equal opportunity to all students assured that the state would have to make up the difference between rich districts and poor. And Texans themselves seemed to have adjusted to the notion that their children will have to take education more seriously; by the late eighties, parents and educators were discussing whether suspension from a sports team and the hope of return would not make a student study more than the threat of permanent expulsion. As Education Commissioner William Kirby put it, "The history of Texas has been written in oil and gas and agriculture, but the future is written in education. In the past, people who dropped out in fifth grade could make a living in the cotton or the oil patch. Those industries may come back, but they won't come back to being employers of the undereducated. In world competition, we're at what I call a starting block disadvantage because all over the world there are people willing to work for less money, for longer hours and harder. The only way to compete is to be more productive. And the only way for our people to be more productive is that they will have to be better educated."

After this public consciousness-raising, it is important to remember that it took all this effort just to raise Texas's educational spending to the national average. Opposition to taxation and big government are still major themes in Texas politics, and the state still faces major educational problems due to the many poor people in the midst of its glittering oil and ranch wealth. One-third of Texas students qualify for the federal government's free-lunch program, and almost one-half of Hispanics drop out before they graduate from high school. By 1990, 50 percent of Texas students will be minorities. If they are not educated, the entire state will suffer, Commissioner Kirby said, pointing out that 85 percent of Texas's huge number of prison inmates are high-school dropouts. "People are survivors," Kirby concluded. "If they can't make a living, they will take it from others."

PLAIN(S) POLITICS: UPENDING TRADITION

The Reagan years have been tough on the Plains political tradition. Republicans continued losing the firm hold they once had on the northern Plains while making inroads into the legendary Democratic voting habits followed by Texans ever since the Civil War.

State by state, the topsy-turvy nature of Plains politics is downright amusing. Minnesota, whose once all-powerful Democratic-Farmer-Labor party had provided the nation both Hubert Humphrey and Eugene McCarthy, was represented by two Republican senators, Rudy Boschwitz and Dave Durenberger.* Minnesota had also elected a Republican governor in 1978, Albert Quie, but he fell victim to a state budget deficit, and Democrat-Farmer-Labor candidate Rudy Perpich was elected in 1982; Perpich was challenged unsuccessfully by fellow Democrat, St. Paul mayor George Latimer, in 1986 on the grounds that the state's economy was falling apart. The supposed Republican bastion of North Dakota ended the Reagan era with only Democrats in top offices—Governor George Sinner, Senators Quentin Burdick and Kent Conrad, and Representative Byron Dorgan. In South Dakota, the 1980 landslide swept Senator George McGovern, the 1972 Democratic presidential candidate, from office. But the reapportionment following the 1980 census took one of South Dakota's House seats for more populous states. When forced to make a choice between their two congressmen, South Dakotans stuck with populist Democratic representative Tom Daschle, who in 1986 went on to defeat James Abdnor, the senator who had defeated McGovern. South Dakota Republicans held onto the governorship vacated by William Janklow, however, electing George S. Mickelson.

In Missouri, Senator Thomas Eagleton, McGovern's 1972 running mate until it was discovered he had undergone electroshock treat-

---

*One figure missing from Plains politics in the eighties was Walter Mondale, the former senator from Minnesota, vice-president of the United States and Democratic presidential candidate in 1984. Mondale moved back to Minnesota in 1987, apparently with plans to challenge Rudy Boschwitz for his Senate seat in 1990. Mondale had precedent on his side since Hubert Humphrey regained a Minnesota Senate seat after he was vice-president and defeated in his 1968 bid for the presidency.

ments, retired in 1986, and former Republican governor Christopher S. (Kit) Bond won the office. Bond had surrendered the governorship in 1984 to another Republican, John Ashcroft, and with Senator John Danforth completed a statewide Republican hold on the Missouri that had sent to Washington such Democratic stalwarts as Harry S. Truman and Stuart Symington.

Iowa seemed to reverse its 1962 to 1974 Democratic dalliance, which had brought Harold Hughes to the governorship and the Senate and John Culver and Dick Clark to the Senate, when it elected the stridently conservative senators Roger Jepsen (in 1978) and Charles Grassley (in 1980). But in the Reagan re-election year of 1984, Iowans threw out Jepsen (perhaps because the staunch moralist had admitted visiting a local massage parlor) in favor of Representative Thomas Harkin, one of the most populist and liberal of congressmen. Grassley proved to have more staying power and was re-elected against weak opposition in 1986. The Republicans also hung on to governorship, moving in 1982 from veteran Robert Ray to the rigidly conservative Terry Branstad.

Nebraska spent most of the eighties represented by two very conservative Democratic senators, Edward Zorinsky and James Exon, and ruled by a very good looking and talented governor, Robert Kerrey—elected at age 39 in 1982. In the governor's office, Kerrey conducted an affair with actress Debra Winger (who had come to Nebraska to film *Terms of Endearment*), which Nebraskans tolerated as his due for his Vietnam War injuries. But after his national acclaim, Kerrey seemed restless in Lincoln and did not seek re-election. State treasurer Kay Orr, a Republican, beat former Lincoln mayor Helen Boosalis in the nation's first governor's race between two women. Then Zorinsky died in office, and it fell to Orr to appoint a Republican, David Karnes. Kerrey, who had considered joining the huge Democratic presidential pack, announced he would seek the Senate seat when it came up for election in 1988.

Kansas upheld the Plains Republican tradition, re-electing veteran senator Robert Dole, who was preparing a 1988 presidential bid; and Nancy Landon Kassebaum, who has risen from her election in 1978 on the reputation of her father Alf (the 1936 Republican presidential candidate) to become a senator independent of Reagan on foreign policy issues. In 1986, the Republicans also recaptured the Kansas governor's mansion, electing Mike Hayden over Thomas R. Docking, the son of a former governor.

Oklahoma, the bridge state between the northern and southern Plains, appropriately sent a senator of each party to Washington, Democrat David L. Boren and Republican Don Nickles. In Nickles's popularity, one could see the change from Oklahoma's old Protestant, populist ways: born in 1948 and a Roman Catholic, Nickles won the nomination partly through his opposition to abortion—which provided him the support of the Moral Majority—and by founding an organization called the Oklahoma Coalition for Peace Through Strength. In 1986, Nickles defeated the respected James R. Jones, even though Jones had frustrated many Democratic liberals with his tightfistedness as chairman of the House Budget Committee. In 1986, the Oklahoma Republicans also recaptured the governorship by re-electing former Governor and Senator Henry Bellmon. Though conservative in his personal life style, Bellmon is not of the "born-again" Republican school that is trying to dominate Oklahoma Republican politics. Bellmon was elected at least partly out of Oklahomans' reverence for his role in bringing his state into modern times in the sixties, but also, one Republican official told me, because of young Nickles's popularity.

Finally, we come to Texas. Reaganism and Texas Republicanism have, for the most part, been a perfect match. The Reaganites could not have been more pleased than when Democrat Phil Gramm (a leader of the "Boll Weevils," Democrats who agreed with Reagan's tax and budget positions) defected from his party and then won a special election for his old House office. Gramm went on in 1984 to win the Senate seat of retiring John G. Tower, who had been elected to Lyndon Johnson's old seat in 1961 as the state's first Republican statewide officeholder since Reconstruction. As chairman of the Senate Armed Services Committee, Tower had been a Reagan ally, but there must have been some consternation in the White House when as the chairman of the commission investigating the Iran-Contra affair, Tower pronounced the president a distant and uninvolved figure in day-to-day decision making.

Gramm turned out to be much more serious about the federal deficit than Reagan. After Reagan walked away from his commitment to control social security increases, Gramm and Senators Warren Rudman of New Hampshire and Ernest F. Hollings of South Carolina introduced their balanced budget act mandating cuts if the Congress did not make decisions about them. Although the act's provisions were restricted by the Supreme Court, Gramm-Rudman-Hollings has had an effect on cutting the deficit.

Texas's senior senator, Lloyd Bentsen, meanwhile, upheld the state's tradition of conservative but Democratic politics and re-emerged as chairman of the Senate Finance Committee when the Democrats took over the Senate again in 1987.

In the politics of regional power through committee chairmanships, Bentsen was the Plains' main man in the Senate. After the Democratic takeover, the only other Plains committee chairman was Senator Quentin Burdick of North Dakota. Burdick seemed to awaken from a nearly career-long deep sleep to take over the Environment and Public Works Committee, and issued the first national press releases of his life to run once again for his seat in 1988 at the age of 80. Polls showed that Representative Byron Dorgan would have beaten him handily in a primary, but Dorgan said he preferred not to split the party.

In the U.S. House, the eighties were also a decade when power shifted southward. After the 1980 census, both Missouri and South Dakota lost a House seat and Texas gained 3, for a net gain of 1 seat in the Plains total of 66. Texas, which already has 27 House districts, is expected to gain 3 or 4 more after the 1990 census and 1992 reapportionment, and Iowa and Kansas are in danger of losing 1 each.

Within the House, Texans were the only men from the Plains to occupy positions of power over their peers in the 100th Congress. At the top was Speaker of the House Jim Wright, who had been majority leader since 1976 and took over with little opposition when Representative Thomas P. (Tip) O'Neill of Massachusetts retired in 1986. Younger, media-minded members who owed their careers to television, considered Wright an improvement over O'Neill, who detested the role of television in modern politics and proved incapable of performing as a counterweight to Reagan's television professionalism. Wright quickly took charge of the House, leading the 1987 override of presidential vetoes on clean water and highway legislation. In late 1987, Wright showed breathtaking political potential when he took the initiative in developing a Central American peace plan, working directly with the presidents of those countries. The Reagan White House was upset, of course, since it considered foreign policy a presidential prerogative, but by that point the administration was in such disarray over other matters that it barely dared to protest.

Below Wright, Texas power on the Hill is held by E. Kika de la Garza, the low-profile chairman of the House Agriculture Committee, and Jack Brooks, chairman of the obscure but powerful Government Operations Committee. As a Democrat, Brooks must have felt the bitterness of the Reagan years, but they have also had a sweet side for him in the end of federal revenue sharing. Ever since its inception in the Nixon administration, Brooks had fought this grant of federal money to states and localities as inefficient, wasteful, and unaccountable. For years, he settled for monitoring the program, but in the Reagan era, it was finally killed off.

SOUTH DAKOTA ELECTS A DEMOCRAT: THE MODERN PLAINS CAMPAIGN

In our impersonal, media-focused age, Americans like to think of the Plains states as the last bastion of personal politics. Rural politicians do hold open, "ask-any-question" forums in towns with populations as small as a few hundred people. Politics is still so clean that even the most minor infraction, such as using a government telephone for personal long-distance calls, is often enough to drive an official from office.

But without much fanfare, television and radio have infiltrated rural politics to a higher degree than they have in the cities. The reasons are rather simple if you stop to think about it. Radio early became a communications lifeline to lonely farmhouses. Today television provides the same function. And because television commercials are cheapest in these small population states, candidates can dominate the airwaves.

So it was that the 1986 South Dakota race between one-term Republican senator James Abdnor and Democratic representative Thomas Daschle became a television classic, and South Dakotans came to see more television commercials for Abdnor and Daschle than for Coca-Cola, Budweiser, or Chrysler. The race could have been a gentlemanly exchange between a grandfather and a choirboy, but it became more immersed in punch-counterpunch television exchanges—and strayed closer to character assassination—than any other in the nation.

Early in the campaign, both candidates' ads—Abdnor's created by Roger Ailes of New York City and Daschle's by Karl Struble's National Voter Contact of Washington, D.C.—tried to capitalize on the legislators' accomplishments in Washington and their record of delivering federal programs and money for the state. In later ads, Daschle attempted to tie Abdnor to the state's distressed farm economy and very lightly raised the issue of Abdnor's competence. Abdnor, trying to shift attention from agriculture, emphasized his own grandfatherly image, and attacked Daschle personally by tying him to actress Jane Fonda, who, Abdnor's ads claimed, was invited instead of a South Dakotan to appear before the House Agriculture Committee.

A poor public speaker, Abdnor's only speaking role was one in which he sat on a front porch explaining that "the only thing I ever dreamed about as a kid was someday to serve my state and my country. . . . God didn't make me a flashy speaker. That's for sure. But we've got a lot of flashy speakers in Congress and if speeches solved problems, we wouldn't have any problem." Abdnor went on to say, "So, I'm not a great speaker. I'm not a great dancer either." But after a crowd cheered and the announcer called Abdnor "a South Dakota institution of integrity," Abdnor took a final shot. "Come to think of it, I'm not a bad dancer."

Daschle's early media humorously reminded South Dakotans that he maintained their values. "Among Washington's BMWs and limos is this," said the announcer as Daschle's 1971 Pontiac sputtered by. "After 15 years and 238,000 miles, Tom Daschle still drives his old car to work," he added. As Daschle's car, rusting and belching exhaust, drove by the White House, the announcer concluded, "Maybe he's sentimental or just cheap . . . it's too bad the rest of Washington doesn't understand that a penny saved is a penny earned."

Then humorous and sentimental appeals to voters gave way to negatives. Abdnor's ads attacked Daschle as weak, ineffective, and captivated by California and New York liberals. "Does Tom Daschle really think the way South Dakotans do?" asked the announcer in one ad over a headline reading "MONEY GIRL. STREISAND SINGS FOR DASCHLE, FIVE OTHER DEMOCRATS." "Or is he the liberal all his Hollywood and New York supporters say he is?," the announcer asked.

Capitalizing on a surprise Agriculture Committee vote Daschle missed, another ad asked "Where was Tom?" as a postcard of a beach in Miami filled the screen and Caribbean music played in the background. "Tom Daschle talks a big story for farmers," said the announcer. "But when the chips are down, Tom's down in Florida."

Daschle's negatives were relatively mild compared with Abdnor's. A mid-campaign Daschle ad featured Abdnor at a farm forum rambling and mumbling a justification for low farm prices. In Daschle's hardest-hitting negative, a door opened to reveal a smoke-filled room full of political consultants chomping on cigars. "We'll distort the farm thing, confuse 'em with Fonda, all the usual liberal stuff," said one as he blows a cloud of cigar smoke. "When we're finished Daschle's mother won't vote for him," laughed another of the consultants. But she did, and Daschle won by 3.2 percent.

PRESIDENTIAL PERSONALITIES:
BUSH, DOLE, AND GEPHARDT

Reigning above all other Texans in the Reagan years was New England transplant Vice-President George Bush. In the 1988 presidential race, he faced two other Plainsmen, Kansas Republican senator Robert Dole and Missouri Democratic representative Richard Gephardt.

In pre–World War II America, Bush would have been considered the ideal candidate for the presidency: son of a white, Anglo-Saxon senator, recipient of the classic prep school and Yale education, military service in World War II, a congressman for two terms, U.S. ambassador to the United Nations, chairman of the Republican National Committee, envoy to the People's Republic of China, and head of the Central Intelligence Agency. Bush had also paid his dues in the emerging America, moving from his native Connecticut to Texas where he made money in oil and helped resuscitate the Texas Republican party before winning his House seat from Houston.

Today the road for a WASP who wants to be president is not so easy, and the oft-forgotten details of Bush's political career bring to mind the moment when one of Lyndon Johnson's associates questioned whether John Kennedy's Harvard-educated aides could win an election in Texas. Those two terms in the House are the only elections Bush has won on his own. Texans distrusted this northeastern Republican whose ancestors by class, if not blood, had controlled their economy and led every liberal social movement from the pre–Civil War abolition of slavery to the modern right to abortion. Bush ran twice for the Senate, but Texans rejected him both times, in 1964 (in favor of populist Ralph Yarborough) and in 1970 (in favor of Lloyd Bentsen). In his own quest for the presidency, starting in 1977, Bush found national resistance from some of the same forces as old-time populists helped create the Republican New Right in response to the national legalization of abortion and the general social liberalization that started in the sixties.

Bush did win the 1980 Iowa Republican caucus, and Reagan wisely picked him to make it easier for eastern, country-club Republicans to vote for a California actor. But in his own campaign to succeed Reagan, Bush faced the same problem as Lyndon Johnson's vice-president Hubert Humphrey and Jimmy Carter's Walter Mondale: how to distinguish himself from his president's policies and reputation, both good and bad. In the Iran-Contra affair, Bush seemed damned if he did admit to knowing about the secret negotiations and left out of things if he didn't. And the comic strip of the baby-boom generation, *Doonesbury*, constantly ridiculed his "manhood."

Bush has tried to walk a fine line between maintaining his New England roots—the only family home the Bushes maintained during the vice-presidency was in Maine, not Texas—and cozying up to New Right leaders such as Jerry Falwell. But Bush has, in fact, shown such a willingness to change his positions that one must question his devotion to any philosophical roots. As a Senate candidate in 1964, Bush ran as a hawkish, right-wing, Goldwater-style conservative promising to vote against Lyndon Johnson's civil rights bill, but after he was elected to the House from an affluent, relatively liberal (frequently northern-born) congressional district, he voted for an open-housing bill. When he was trying to get the Republican presidential nomination himself in 1980, he called opponent Reagan's policies "voodoo economics," but then accepted Reagan's invitation to join him on the ticket.

Bush's intense ambitions make one long for his fellow WASP Nelson Rockefeller, who never made it to the White House, but fought hard for his liberal Republican ideals. For his 1984 debate against Geraldine Ferraro, the first woman to run for the vice-presidency, Bush got mixed reviews, but it may have been his low point. His mannerisms seemed a shadowy copy of Reagan's. His morning-after comment that he had "kicked a little ass" the night before was unseemly for any vice-president, much less an aristocratic one.

Everyone gave Bush high marks in his various appointed positions, but reporters emerging from visits with Bush in the White House had a hard time coming up with quotable or original thoughts. Perhaps it was appropriate that the critical examination of Bush coincided with the Broadway presentations of *The Dining Room* and other plays of A. R. Gurney chronicling the American WASP's loss of hegemony over the ethnic groups seeking a role in today's world. As his campaign started, Bush came off as a kind of empty vessel who was better off carrying out somebody else's policies.

Bush's foremost competitor, Bob Dole—veteran senator from Kansas and the majority leader in 1985 and 1986—seems to be as geographically rooted as Bush is not. Raised in the west Kansas town of Russell, Dole's life has been dominated by disabling wounds to his right shoulder and arm in Italian combat in 1945. A star athlete, Dole returned to the United States on a stretcher and spent three years bedridden in military hospitals before he married an occupational therapist (not his nurse, as is often reported) who took notes for him in law school. Dole still does not have total use of his left arm, and today it can take him 10 or 15 minutes to button his shirt.

Dole channeled all his old athletic competitiveness into politics, winning a seat in the Kansas legislature when he was still in law school and coming to Washington as a congressman in 1961. Dole's Republicanism is rooted in the old Main Street variety, which may be one reason he relishes challenging Bush. In the thirties, Dole's mother moved the family into the basement while renting out their house to oil and gas people, but as Gail Sheehy noted in a *Vanity Fair* profile, "To this day, her son appears to bear a class resentment, but rather than becoming a social reformer, he has followed her pragmatic credo, 'Can't never did anything.' "

Dole's record matches most of the conservative agenda—for Reagan's defense policies, opposed to abortion and gun control, for organized school prayer and a balanced budget—and he has pleased conservatives enough to win their support and anger any liberal. He helped Senator Jesse Helms of North Carolina in his battle for the ranking minority slot on the Foreign Relations Committee, obtained the confirmation of conservative Daniel A. Manion to the federal bench, helped secure Stinger missiles for anti-communist rebels in Angola, and reneged on a dinner honoring Surgeon General C. Everett Koop after conservatives suggested a boycott because of Koop's campaign for sex education to combat AIDS.

But as Kansas (and indeed all the northern Plains states) has evolved, so has Dole. With his farmer constituents in mind, he overcame his Republican free-market attitude to help George McGovern start the Food for Peace program which bought surplus U.S. agricultural products and sent them to poor countries. His biggest break with Republican conservatives was to support food stamps and shepherd the extension of the Voting Rights Act through the Senate. But he also convinced Reagan—over the wishes of Secretary of State George Shultz and the administration's free market economists—to offer the Soviet Union a special deal on wheat before the 1986 congressional elections. With his long years in the Senate, it's easier to pin down Dole's political performance than Bush's. No one questions his intelligence, political skills, or thoroughness on policy. There is no Washington figure who displays a better grasp of the global food situation.

But the Kansan does have his weaknesses, both personal and political. He abandoned his first wife after 23 years of marriage. His early reputation was as a rather mean Republican partisan; and as Gerald Ford's vice-presidential running mate in 1976, Dole embarrassed himself in a debate with Walter Mondale by calling every twentieth-century war a "Democrat war." After the campaign failure, he turned remote and hostile. He also failed in a 1980 presidential bid, but in 1981 he emerged as a "new" Bob Dole; he won the respect of his colleagues by his actions as chairman of the Senate Finance Committee, and became majority leader after Howard Baker's retirement (minority leader after the Democrats won back the Senate). His second marriage to Elizabeth Hanford—the highly regarded Transportation secretary under Reagan—has reportedly given him more social confidence. Elizabeth Hanford Dole is one of his greatest political assets, especially in her native South, although just before her 1987 resignation she was roundly criticized for spending time campaigning for her husband while the public was dismayed by plane crashes and air traffic delays. Dole has also revealed that his presidential failures led him to hire Dorothy Sarnoff, the famed New York image coach who has taught so many executives and politicians how to improve their presence on television. Such training is commonplace and almost a necessity in today's media world, but only the rigors of a presidential campaign—or perhaps the office itself—is likely to reveal whether Dole has really found inner peace, or only presents the image of it.

The Democrats' only Plains entrant into the 1988 presidential race was Missouri's Richard Gephardt, a congressman from St. Louis. An alderman in St. Louis when he was elected to the House in 1976, Gephardt impressed his colleagues with his earnest persistence and seriousness, and they elected him chairman of the Democratic Caucus, a major leadership position for someone who had been in the House less than ten years. He made tax reform his major issue and with Senator Bill Bradley of New Jersey devised the "fair tax" scheme that helped start the intellectual and philosophical debate for the massive reorganization of the tax code passed in 1986.

Gephardt once introduced an amendment to limit abortions, but when he started running for president abandoned this quest because, he said, it was hopeless. He must also have realized that Democratic activists are strongly committed to a woman's right of choice on this issue.

Gephardt's roots in an urban district on the periphery of the Plains were apparent in the strongly protectionist trade position he adopted as the center of his presidential campaign. With their high dependence on exports, most Plains farmers had come to oppose protecting industrial products from cheap imports out of fear of retaliation against U.S. foodstuffs. Gephardt proposed, and got through the House in 1987, an amendment that would require annual surveys of the trade practices of countries that export much more to the United

States than they buy, and required imposition of tariffs and quotas to reduce the countries' trade surpluses by 10 percent a year. The measure received support from organized labor and the auto and steel industries, but horrified the U.S. Chamber of Commerce, the National Association of Manufacturers, and free traders, both Democratic and Republican, who believe that protectionism led to the Great Depression of the 1930s and could bring on another one.

Support for the free-trade position came from President Reagan, who believed that more competition was better, and liberal papers such as the *New York Times* and *The Washington Post*, which argued that misguided Reagan policies such as artificially high valuation of the dollar and toleration of a massive federal deficit were more to blame than the sins of other countries.

Most other politicians were lukewarm at best about Gephardt's obvious targeting of Japanese, South Korean, and Taiwanese industrial goods, but he did bring to the table points the free traders had tried to ignore: that the current relatively free trade system had been developed at a time when the United States was the unquestioned industrial power in the world, that the Japanese were very resistant to allowing the entry of U.S. products, and that U.S. manufacturers have begun making noises that American wages should drop to the level of South Korea's and Taiwan's in order to increase American competitiveness. Gephardt's trade amendment gave him the clear issue for which other candidates still searched, and he tried as early as possible in 1987 to turn the race into a two-man battle with Michael Dukakis, governor of the "economic miracle" state of Massachusetts and a free-trade advocate.

COURTING IN IOWA

In the midst of their economic woes and shift towards two-party, modern media-oriented politics, the Plains states can take heart that first-in-the-nation decision-making about presidential candidates has shifted from New Hampshire's primary to Iowa's caucuses. The decision to hold the caucuses before New Hampshire's primary is, of course, the biggest reason they have become so important to the candidates. The first to make a real breakthrough in Iowa was Jimmy Carter, just a former Georgia governor until he convinced Iowans in 1976 to go to their caucuses and vote for him.

There have been some charges that Iowa politicians and party leaders are shaking down presidential candidates for contributions to their campaigns. Leaders of the big states have also charged that Iowa's population is whiter and more agriculturally oriented that the national average. But with these slight criticisms in mind, Iowa's education-minded citizenry has encouraged more debates than were ever held in New Hampshire. Each campaign season, the number of debates has increased until looking toward 1988, the candidates said "Enough already" and tried to establish some limits. But who wouldn't want to hear what the candidates think about the elderly, education, defense, and, of course, agriculture? Much of the organizational effort behind the debates, it must be admitted, comes from national organizations based in Washington. But the Iowans cooperate fully in these exercises, and for their efforts the nation's political process is ennobled.

THE
GREAT LAKES STATES:
The Tarnished Heartland

I n a bar called Alcock's across the street from the shiny new Midwest Stock Exchange lies the heart and ache of the new Midwest. Alcock's looks like thousands of baby-boom bars around the country. The turn-of-the-century brick walls have been stripped of their paint and covered with posters of cultural icons from Mick Jagger to the Eurythmics. The bar's motto is "We rock." But you would never mistake this establishment for a yuppie bar on Wall Street or a glamor hangout in west L.A.

Alcock's clientele includes the men of the Chicago Board of Trade and the Options Exchange who invented options as a form of industrial investment in 1973. But Alcock's also attracts the financial district's deliverymen and other blue-collar workers, and it is obvious they set the style. The "suits" enter through a small back door in a windowless wall that faces the exchanges, the blue collars through the sunny main entrance looking toward Chicago's once glorious industrial west side. The atmosphere is Chicago masculine to a fault: the men turn their heads purposefully, aggressively, obviously, as a woman walks by, which may be the reason there are only a few in the place. There's no sushi on the menu; the best bet is Chicago's famed Italian beef sandwich. Both the white collars and the blue look like their muscles were forged on the factory floor or farm, not Nautilus. Unlike New York or L.A., with their generations of white-collar dominance, the young Chicago brokers look as though they wonder if it wasn't really much more fun and more manly *making* something.

Chicago today is a city in search of its soul. Gone are its famed stockyards, appliance factories, and steel mills. In their place are acres of rusting buildings and vacant, desolate land—and a new downtown of stock exchanges, law offices, and corporate headquarters. Chicago gained 50,000 jobs between 1984 and 1986, but to the people it's not the same. So many factories have closed that manufacturing, which once employed more than 40 percent of Chicagoans, now provides jobs for under 20 percent of the labor force. As Chicago author and radio personality Studs Turkel puts it in the first paragraph of one of the city's most popular guidebooks: "Ours is a one-syllable town. Its character has been molded by the muscle rather than the word."

The Great Lakes states' loss of economic and political power to other parts of the nation and the world has been so well documented it is in danger of overstatement. These states are not a site of unmitigated economic disaster; despite all the layoffs, the regional per capita income has remained way above the national average. Michigan is not the South after the Civil War, when, as Walter Lord wrote, the cities lay in ashes and "Mississippi seemed but a forest of chimneys." But heavy manufacturing has been at the heart and soul of the Great Lakes states' self-image for three-quarters of a century, and the agony there now is understandable. Mention these states and instantly romantic epithets leap forth: the Heart of the Midwest, the Heart of the Heartland, the Builders of the Nation, the Breadbasket of the World. The people of the Great Lakes states have been taught to think of themselves in grand, physical terms. Finding a new basis for dignity is not easy.

The Reagan years have been crueler to the Great Lakes states than any other region of the country, but the core of the region's economic troubles must be laid to its own complacency about diversification and job creation during generations of industrial prosperity. Reagan administration officials would also argue that their principal economic achievement of wringing inflation out of the economy has benefited the Midwest as much as any other region. But just about every other administration policy has hurt the region. The midwestern farmers who gambled that inflation was a permanent part of the economic landscape discovered the unfortunate results of declining land and commodity prices. The 1981 tax cut, which was designed in part to spur investment in manufacturing through investment credits and accelerated depreciation of plant equipment, was offset by the steady rise in the value of the dollar, which placed many exports off limits and invited a flood of imports. Then, just as the dollar started to head lower on the world currency markets, the 1986 Tax Reform Act eliminated most investment tax credits and limited depreciation on business equipment.

The most damaging Reagan policies were the buildup of a high-tech defense and the curtailment of domestic social spending. Both shifted federal dollars away from the Great Lakes states to other regions of the country. Even if one argues that these policies were necessary for the national good, there is no doubt that the Great Lakes states have fared the worst. "The result," according to Ann Markusen, a professor of management and social policy at Northwestern University, "has been an unstated industrial policy that favors aerospace, communications and related high-tech industries over such traditional Midwest industries as steel, autos, machinery and other kinds of basic manufacturing."

Reagan's commitment to defense spending and opposition to protecting U.S. industries bring up a new question about U.S. policy making. The Great Lakes states long felt safe because they were not dependent on cyclical defense spending. Now defense manufacturing seems the only industry we still believe must be based within our borders. Has the United States established an unconscious policy that the only secure factory jobs are those making missiles and armaments? The Great Lakes' worst drawback in starting new businesses, it turns out, is the lack of "prime" defense contractors who engage in the research and development that lead to new products. Has our economy become so military-oriented that all new invention must come from it?

With little help from Washington, the Great Lakes states have begun to rebuild. They have a firm base on which to begin. Whether they have recognized it or not, these states have always been more than a factory. The superlatives begin with the five Great Lakes themselves—Superior, Michigan, Huron, Erie, and Ontario—a grand expanse of 94,710 square miles and the largest reservoir of fresh water on earth. There are thousands of acres of beautiful forest land and other lakes for recreation, and some of the most productive farmland on the North American continent. These states are still home to some of the greatest U.S. corporations and they have used their wealth to develop some of the nation's largest and best public university systems (Wisconsin's, Michigan's, and Illinois' are leading examples), fine technical schools and private liberal arts colleges (particularly in Ohio), and good suburban and rural public schools. The generations of industrial wealth have also left behind fine museums, symphonies, ballets, and other cultural institutions. Compared with the aborning opera and ballet companies in the Sunbelt, the Midwest is a cultural paradise indeed. The question is whether the people of the Great Lakes will believe it themselves and tell other people.

In every aspect of Great Lakes life—its great city of Chicago, its lakes, its politics and its state governments—there are great strengths, but even an optimist would have to see great weaknesses. The Great Lakes states may, in fact, never recover their glory, but if they do not it will be a fate sure to be repeated in other sections of America in the coming years.

OPTIONS AND ACTORS: CHICAGO, PART ONE

By any standard Chicago is one of the great cities of the world. Its setting on Lake Michigan is magnificent, its history dramatic, and its business base diverse (agriculture, trade, shipping, and bank and corporate headquarters, as well as manufacturing). Its educational institutions, beginning with the University of Chicago and Northwestern, are first rate; and its cultural institutions, from museums to the symphony, are unsurpassed by any city in the country except New York.

Chicago has always had to live in the shadow of New York, but it prefers to ignore the fact that Los Angeles and its metropolitan area are really now the second city in population and national attention. Since the growth of California, there's no denying ours has become a coastal culture. As the East and the West have swirled with every conceivable influence, domestic and foreign, the middle has lost its standing. What interest remains in the interior goes to the sunny South; Sunbelt cities such as Dallas, Houston, and Atlanta have gotten reams of newsprint and thousands of television minutes for their growth alone. But like all truly great cities, Chicago continues to draw on its deep resources and evolve even when it is not at the height of fashion.

There are no more dramatic urban successes in the United States of the seventies or eighties than the creation of the Chicago Board Options Exchange, the growth of Chicago theater, or the city's rise as a center for moviemaking.

The roots of Chicago's new options business go back to 1848, a year that means more in Chicago than Marx and Engels publishing the *Communist Manifesto*. That was the year the first telegram was delivered in Chicago and the first ocean-going ship arrived—and the year that the first wheat arrived in the city by rail and the first steam-powered bulk grain elevator was built.

Most significant to Chicago's long-term development, 1848 was the year the Chicago Board of Trade was founded to overcome the annoyances and inefficiencies of early American agriculture. In those early days, a farmer had to haul grain into Chicago by barge, canal boats, and wagon, and then haul it around the city to merchants, elevator operators, and shippers until he found a buyer. Grades and weights varied so much that violent arguments arose between buyers and sellers. Prices of grains and processed flour and bread fluctuated wildly depending on erratic deliveries, the availability of storage and shipping facilities, and other uncertainties.

The Board of Trade provided a market place with inspectors and standardized weights for the buying and selling of grains, and reduced some of the booms and busts of the commodities markets for farmers, merchants, and, ultimately, consumers. Soon the Board began trading in contracts committing the farmers to deliver a certain quantity of grain at a certain date and the buyers to a previously agreed price. This "futures" system reduced the enormous price fluctuations and stabilized delivery dates. Soon speculators, who were willing to assume more financial risk than either farmers or merchants, began to buy surplus grains at low prices in hopes of selling them later at higher prices. The Board also began to supply contracts for future grain deliveries in hopes that the price would be higher by the time the grain was delivered. Critics of capitalism regarded this system as a form of gambling and perhaps immoral, but farmers, processors, money managers, merchandisers, refiners, exporters, grain elevator operators, manufacturers, and other "hedgers" proved quite willing to sacrifice the opportunity for full profit in order to guarantee a price. The futures market played a big role in establishing Chicago's pre-eminence in the agricultural world: Only 40 years after the Board was founded, the quantity of commodities shipped from Chicago had increased tenfold.

And 125 years later, the Chicago Board of Trade used the same principle to prove that companies and investors would like the same opportunity to reduce or assume risk. The idea of standardizing the trading of stock options started because the grain markets had gone stagnant after the big Russian wheat sales, but the options exchange soon mushroomed into a phenomenal success. Through the Chicago Board Options Exchange (and now other exchanges in other cities), potential investors and holders of stock can make contracts in which the investors pay the shareholders a premium for the right to buy an item (usually 100 shares of stock) at an agreed-upon price at any time within a certain period. If the buyer of the option does not exercise this right by the last day of the period, the option ceases to exist and becomes worthless, and no stock is transferred. If the buyer does exercise the option, he or she gets the stock at a price lower than the market price that day.

"The Board of Trade members tried to sell the idea in New York, and people laughed at them," recalled a gleeful Thomas R. Donovan, the Board's executive director and a former aide to Mayor Richard J. Daley. The Chicago exchanges are constantly innovating and lobbying to avoid transaction taxes which they say would make them uncompetitive. Options trading has been widely touted as an American specialty, but even Donovan is on constant watch for foreign competition from exchanges in London and Tokyo. "The history of futures is that if you get in on the ground floor, it's hard to take it away," Donovan said. "But if they can take it away, it's because their government gives them a leg up. We have to be concerned that our regulators (the Commodity Futures Trading Commission) do not get caught up in internationalism and allow people to do things in foreign markets with less regulation and fewer safeguards than they require us to have. You can't say what a firm in another country can do, but you can say what an American investor can do."

Today options have expanded to U.S. Treasury bonds, metals, petroleum, and foreign currencies as well as hundreds of stocks, from Abbott Laboratories to Dow Chemical to Zenith Electronics Corporation. In addition, the Board of Trade also began around-the-clock trading to compete with Japanese exchanges.

The new stock exchange buildings, law offices, and corporate headquarters and branch offices have replaced muscles as the reality, if not the symbol, of the new Chicago. In the eighties, downtown Chicago has been transformed by a building boom second only to New York City's. According to a Northwestern University study released in 1986, half the city's office space, more than two million square feet annually, had been built in the last seven years. To the west of downtown, decaying industrial neighborhoods are being renovated with art galleries and yuppie boutiques, bars, restaurants, and a gigantic apartment complex called Presidential Towers.

Chicago's 1,000-block core has added $6.8 billion in new construction and renovation since 1979, with another $7.5 billion either under construction or in the planning stages. In addition, after losing thousands of homes and apartments every year since the 1960s, Chicago has actually gained more than 18,000 units—largely downtown housing for young professionals—since 1980. The demand for downtown housing has grown so high, in fact, that developers began eyeing such infamous Chicago downtown public housing projects as Cabrini-Green (which former Mayor Jane M. Byrne once moved into to reduce the crime rate) as the perfect location for new private apartment towers.

Chicago has always been known for its symphony orchestra—perhaps the finest in the country at this writing—but this new wealth and population have also helped the city by the lake emerge as the creative theater capital of the nation. There are 130 theater companies in Chicago, and in the 1985–86 season 2.65 million tickets to more than 1,000 different productions were sold. Actors, directors, and producers are attracted to Chicago by the low costs (most productions are non-union) and a relatively small but loyal theater-going community (70,000 season ticket holders to nonprofit theaters) determined to pay an artist a living wage (though many Chicago performers work for peanuts.) Chicago has produced star playwrights such as David Mamet and actors such as John Malkovich, but its specialty is ensemble companies whose members trade off acting, directing, and set design and nurture each other's creativity. The most famous Chicago ensemble company is Second City, though that is really a commercial comedy club. The most important serious theaters have odd names such as Steppenwolf, Wisdom Bridge, and the Organic Theater (one of the first mid-sized repertory companies to tour overseas). Chicago theater heads claim that their plays are at the cutting edge of American theater today, illustrating modern urban life in mid-America. Chicago theater is young and vibrant with what the Chicago League of Theaters' Carol Thompson calls "an almost California- or Texas-like ethic that it's okay to try something, put it on the stage and if it fails to try again."

"The artists here have taken an inferiority complex and converted it into a kind of rage for excellence," said Robert Falls, director of the Goodman Theatre. "There is an unmistakable 'Chicago style' that harnesses the energy of street theater and combines it with classical traditions." The populist feel of the theater affects even the locations of the buildings themselves; theaters are scattered all over town, and the theater community is constantly pushing Chicagoans to travel to different neighborhoods to attend plays.

American movie-goers have seen more and more of Chicago since the reversal of the late Mayor Daley's policy of reading every script of a movie proposed for filming in the city to make sure he approved of the story and the image it would create of his city. The directors refused to bow to Daley's censorship, but since 1976 major films shot in Chicago include *Looking for Mr. Goodbar, The Blues Brothers, Ordinary People, Pennies from Heaven, National Lampoon's Vacation, Nothing in Common, About Last Night* (on the Chicago-based stage production of David Mamet's *Sexual Perversity in Chicago*), and *Native Son*. One director, John Hughes, has practically adopted Chicago as the setting for his glossy "bratpack" movies that dwell on the trials and tribulations of middle-class teenagers, *Risky Business, Breakfast Club, 16 Candles*, and *Ferris Bueller's Day Off*. Moviemakers apparently like Chicago for its range of middle-class to working-class settings and for the various periods of architecture. But whatever the reason for the directors' fondness for Chicago, an entire generation of movie-goers now see the city in a glamorous light.

All the filming has been enough to develop a new supporting industry that includes service firms from caterers to makeup artists to production companies. Among the television series set in Chicago are "Webster," "Crime Story," and "Jack and Mike." Chicago television lost a national star when Phil Donahue moved to New York after his marriage to Marlo Thomas, but newcomer Oprah Winfrey has more than kept up the city's national prominence in talk.

Chicago is also home to a new generation of extraordinarily creative architects, including "starchitect" Helmut Jahn, who achieved worldwide prominence as an early exponent of postmodernism—the introduction of classical details and ornamentation into modern architecture—but has come under equally enormous criticism for his State of Illinois Center in downtown Chicago.

What can account for this creative surge in the face of regional decline? Chicago is the magnet for thousands of small-town and farm youth who attend the great public universities and private colleges from Ohio to the Dakotas. If they don't come to Chicago immediately upon graduation, they may spend a few years in Minneapolis, Milwaukee, or Detroit before moving on to the big time. There is some indication that the most aggressive now head for national careers on the coasts. "When I graduated from the University of Illinois, the most talented in every field—business, law, politics, photography, the arts—left for New York, Washington or California," said Steve Rabin, a Chicago native who became senior vice-president of Ogilvy & Mather Public Affairs in Washington at age 30. But that still leaves a pool of thousands of highly educated youth each year, an educational distinction that other regions of the country would find hard to match.

Chicago banks and corporations operate on a world scale, and for the first time they are attracting talented young professionals from all parts of the country. Not being from New York is often an advantage in dealing with clients in other parts of the country, said one young Continental Illinois banker: "The only time it's a problem is when a client is determined to prove himself by jousting with a New Yorker."

The rural roots and urban experience in the middle of the country have evolved into a special kind of Chicago charm. Interview a Chicago executive for five minutes, and he will tell you about his rural roots. Ask him or her a question, and the answer is straightforward. The frame of reference is often based on reading rather than travels and other experience, but the answer will be honest. Midwesterners talk about family ad nauseam—and even though the divorce rate there is not much lower than in other parts of the country, there may be something to this midwestern family business. Executives enjoy boasting that Chicago is the best place in the country for both a man and a woman to work and raise a family. In 1987, a *Forbes* magazine poll claimed that Chicago was the best of the major metropolitan areas to raise a family; the low rate of AIDS incidence may indicate that Chicago gays are less promiscuous than those in other parts of the country. Not all is wonderful, however. One Chicago woman, a lawyer who had lived in New York and Europe, complained that "these small town Protestant boys are still uptight. They don't flirt, they're not intellectually playful, and then they go to pornographic movies at lunchtime."

Too few Americans know of Chicago's renaissance. Chicago's convention center, McCormick Place, remains the largest in the country, but the city has little tourism for sheer pleasure compared to the coasts. Europeans love Chicago more than Americans, an indicator that it is not really in tune with modern U.S. times. But as Pierre Collombert, the former French cultural attaché in Chicago and a big fan of the city, put it, "Chicago is a city that thinks it doesn't have to sell itself."

CHICAGO 10 A.D.

Mayor Harold Washington was more than an hour late when he arrived for the candidates' forum at Maria High School, a Catholic institution run by Lithuanian nuns on the city's aging, industrial Southwest Side.

Leaders of the Save Our Neighborhoods/Save Our City Coalition asked the all-white and largely elderly audience to stand, but it greeted the city's first black mayor with a mixture of loud boos and mild applause. The reaction could have been worse, but at the request of the organizers, thirty off-duty Chicago firefighters controlled access to the meeting and ejected several would-be provocateurs. The firefighters carefully eyeballed the crowd and appeared relieved when the mayor finally reached the stage and the audience quieted down.

Washington was alternately conciliatory, vowing to support a program to shore up declining home values in their neighborhoods, but turned belligerent when repeated questions about his commitment registered the audience's distrust. "We lack the spirit to sit down and talk with each other in a civil tone," he admonished after a heated exchange. Some in the crowd jeered.

Before he left, Washington managed to warm up the audience with tales of his days as a high-school hurdler. But his quiet departure could not compete with former Mayor Jane M. Byrne's arrival. The audience came to its feet, and as she attacked Washington for "the tragedies of the last four years," cries of "Get 'em Janie!" filled the hall.

Washington went on to win his 1987 primary, and his victory in a two-way race—attributed to a high turnout and uniform vote by the growing black electorate and low turnout among whites—marked some inching forward in Chicago's transition to late-twentieth-century American city politics. He won the general election easily, against three white opponents.

But the peaceful times lasted only a few months. On November 25, 1987, the heavyset mayor slumped onto his desk in his City Hall office. In the unseemly squabbling that followed his death, a coalition of 21 white and 6 black aldermen elected an old-fashioned black machine regular, Eugene Sawyer, as mayor, until April, 1989.

This is Chicago little more than a decade after the death of the greatest white ethnic machine mayor of them all, Richard J. Daley. The city whose political machine reflexively re-elected Daley for 21 years (1955–76), delivered (perhaps illegally) the winning votes for John F. Kennedy in 1960, and easily jailed antiwar protesters at the 1968 Democratic Convention, is now a case of arrested development.

Daley's Irish-Catholic, ethnic-oriented tight hold on everything in the city held back the rise of blacks, Hispanics, and reform-minded liberals; the unionization of public employees; the emergence of neighborhood organizations; the new-found role of business in civic life; and just plain dissent that other major cities experienced more than a decade ago. When Daley died unexpectedly in 1976, the machine he always preferred to call "the organization" had no successor to fall back on. Corporate lawyer Michael Bilandic took over as mayor, but he was unseated in 1979 by anti-machine candidate Jane Byrne, the city's first woman mayor; and she, in turn, was defeated in a three-way race by then-U.S. representative Washington, who became the city's first black mayor in 1983.

Race dominates Chicago politics today above all other issues, and racial conflict is more open here than in any other major American city. Washington's election was the nearly inevitable product of the city's changing demographics—45 percent black, 35 percent white with 16 percent Hispanic, according to 1987 estimates—and the near-total black unity that resulted from Daley's willingness to use blacks' votes while giving them the least of the city jobs and other spoils. Over the years, many sociological studies have described Chicago housing as the most racially segregated in the country. The largely black and Hispanic public schools are notorious for their poor conditions and low test scores. After the 1983 election, race relations were so bitter that Washington and the white majority opposition bloc on the city council played a game of political brinkmanship that lasted until court-ordered special elections to correct racial gerrymandering in early 1986 gave the mayor a majority on the council. Routine city business proceeded, but major projects languished. Nearly 70 of Washington's appointments to top city posts went unconfirmed. After one lengthy standoff on eliminating Chicago's budget deficit, its bond rating was lowered.

Such shenanigans have made it almost impossible for the city to help create jobs for the city's unemployed youth or its displaced factory workers. For the masses of poor ethnic whites, blacks, and Hispanics who dominate Chicago voting, the busy stock exchanges are more symbolic of an unreachable world than a beacon of hope. "We're afraid of a tale of two cities," said Robert Gannett, co-director of the Chicago Neighborhood Organizing Project, "with a thriving, disconnected lakefront and the rest of the city devastated."

Chicago's face has changed, as population losses have followed the outflow of jobs. From a peak of 3.6 million in 1960, Chicago's population was an estimated 3 million in 1985, with the suburban total exceeding the central city's for the first time. The residents of the city's European ethnic enclaves have grown old and their children have

settled in the suburbs. The old neighborhoods are under constant
encroachment from blacks, Hispanics, and immigrants from Korea,
Pakistan, India, and Thailand—all of whom must battle for service
and construction jobs.

The loss of population and jobs has also changed Chicago's position within its own metropolitan area. While downtown buildings still
house 20 *Fortune* 500 companies, the fast-growing suburbs to the
north, west, and south of the city are home to 19 other *Fortune* 500
firms. New high-tech and service firms are clustered in the office parks
of the "Silicon Prairie" corridors along the interstate highways of Du
Page County to the west of Chicago. "The suburbs used to be a lesser
part of the region," said Lawrence B. Christmas, executive director of
the Northeastern Illinois Planning Commission, but "today they are
dominant."

In the testy racial atmosphere of Chicago, it's hard to find dispas-
sionate analyses of Washington's performance. Leon M. Despres, a
long-time opponent of the machine on the city council and now a
member of the city planning commission, said, "Washington was the
first mayor of Chicago who has put government ahead of patronage,
party and pillage. He eliminated patronage, issued a freedom of information order, promulgated an ethics ordinance [to curb political im-
proprieties] and opened up government to blacks, Hispanics and
women." But Louis Masotti, a Northwestern University professor and
one of the most perceptive analysts of modern-day Chicago politics,
said "Washington was a transitional figure. What we got was quasi-
reform. It was bumbling reform, not really reform and not really black
power. It was a potpourri."

Chicago lacks the essential element of Daley's machine: the patronage employees, who negotiated arrangements, fair and unfair, among
Chicago's many immigrant ethnic groups and controlled every facet
of city and county government through patronage and a general
directive that a precinct committeeman was the easiest source of
everything from a clean street to a building permit. Court orders
reducing the number of politically appointed city workers from 40,000
to about 900 were resisted by Daley and his white successors, but
enforced by Washington. "What made the organization formidable
in its golden era, from 1929 through the death of Daley, was the unity
of politics and government," said Chicago political consultant Don

Rose. "People laughed at the court orders at first but they've taken a horrendous toll on the organization."

But evolution, rather than reform, would be an accurate description of Chicago politics today. The Democratic organization still controls the slating of candidates for many Chicago and Cook County offices. Washington, deprived of the rank-and-file Democratic organization under the control of white ethnic factions, set about creating his own impromptu organization through neighborhood groups financed with city funds. And the city abounds with stories of the new tricks politicians have perfected to keep control of city jobs.

Ten years after Daley's death, Chicagoans longed for the stability of his reign. A *Sun-Times* Gallup Poll found that 73 percent of Chicagoans, including most blacks, still gave the late mayor a "good" or "excellent" performance rating, and even his bitterest political opponents seem to have mellowed somewhat. Chicago's one-man rule under Daley was "a kind of municipal totalitarianism, but he was a very, very skillful political leader," said Despres, who was trailed by Chicago police at Daley's direction. And business leaders have come to recognize that despite his posthumous popularity the machine had died with Daley. "If he were alive today he'd get re-elected," said Thomas Donovan, executive director of the Chicago Board of Trade, who as Daley's administrative assistant oversaw the hiring and firing of nearly 40,000 municipal workers. But, Donovan added, "almost anyone would have a hard time being mayor of a big city today," and noted that in his last years "Daley had momentum, but even then his political base was slipping. He was competing with television and from the 1968 [Democratic] convention on he had lost media support."

Chicago leaders also express a growing awareness that the seeds for much of Chicago's current economic and political turmoil were sown during his regime. "It's ironic the economic decline began under the watch of the great leader," said Donald S. Perkins, former chairman of the Jewel Companies, Inc., and a Commercial Club civic leader. "People were blindsided and were judging the health of the city by the Loop and their own businesses. What we didn't see was this major economic change that had occurred."

Washington's second term could have provided stability to the

Windy City (a term that originated from its politics, not its weather), but politics is only the first of its civic problems. Just as they have few skills to sell the city to outsiders, Chicago's business leaders have few civic skills. Massaged by Daley with millions of dollars in city investment, fast approval of their favored projects, and even settlement of their labor disputes by the mayor, Chicago's businesses today are a disunited and ineffective community. And that community has been decimated by leadership turnovers through a decade of economic transition and corporate takeovers.

A report commissioned by the Chicago Project, a coalition of businesses and civic groups, offered a scathing critique of the state of the city's civic life. "Common ground is hard to discover in Chicago," the report said. "Fragmentation and confusion frustrate its civic endeavors . . . there is conflict within the business community and between business and government . . . instead of working on an agenda that reflects the diversity of the city, each faction pursues its own game plan."

The city's business leadership did very little to quiet the political posturing during Washington's first term. Thomas Donovan has seen with each new mayor a greater and greater detachment between City Hall and the business community. "Republican leaders who lived in the city had a great liking for Daley because he wanted to help the city," said Donovan. "Bilandic had some of this and Byrne had a little less. When Washington came in, it was very easy for people who didn't know him to make the break. It was a chance for people to sit back and not feel an obligation."

Chicago's premier business group, the Commercial Club (sponsor of the turn-of-the-century Burnham Plan, which determined much of Chicago's twentieth-century growth), has made some moves towards reinvolvement, issuing a report with recommendations on the city's finances. Most of its efforts, however, are concentrated on the very real problems in the "Chicagoland" metropolitan area's ability to compete with other parts of the country. Ronald Gidwitz, president and chief executive officer of Helene Curtis Industries, Inc., and a Republican appointed by Washington to chair the Chicago Economic Development Commission, said, "What bothers me is that we have so few people who are active, period. We have participatory government

today. If we don't assume a role, someone else will do it for us and
that's what's happened historically. If the city worked so good, how
come the schools are so lousy?"

The collapse of Chicago's plan to host a 1992 World's Fair—
a popular event in the generation of Daley and important in Chicago's physical and cultural development on several occasions in the
past—reveals the depth of the troubles confronting contemporary
Chicago.

In 1980, Chicago, competing with Miami and Los Angeles, won
the international rights to host a 1992 fair, marking the 500th anniversary of the discovery of the New World. It would have been the first
"universal exposition," the most prestigious fair sanctioned by the
Paris-based Bureau of International Expositions, in the United States
since 1939. Then, neighborhood groups fought to stop the event,
claiming it would drain funds from them and cause displacement.
Vying political factions quarreled over its location. Chicago's new
mayor supported it, but only lukewarmly according to many. The
business community split into opposing camps. Fights developed over
financing, and, finally, without Chicago's unified backing, the fair
died quietly in the state capitol in Springfield.

John D. Kramer, who headed the World's Fair Authority and is
now a developer in Chicago, charged that the Chicago neighborhood
groups and others "that claim credit for killing the fair are vastly
overstating their role. The Chicago fair failed because of the inertia
of the system and the lack of willingness on the part of the political
leaders of the city to come together."

City leaders are still split over whether the fair could have helped
the city overcome its international "Al Capone" reputation or its loss
of "Second City" status to Los Angeles. Many still argue that it would
simply have benefited a few developers at the expense of taxpayers
and neighborhoods. Chicago, Kramer noted, has never sunk to the
depths of Cleveland, Indianapolis, or Pittsburgh, which have since
formed sustained public-private partnerships and rebounded. "No one
learned a lesson from the fair, even though I'd like to think they did,"
he concluded. "The politicians who did not unify over the fair are still
fighting over other things. They're still concerned over who will control the government in the next five years, not what Chicago will look
like in the 21st Century."

Paying a Price

It was a poignant moment at his 1987 state-of-the-state speech at the capitol of Indianapolis when Governor Robert Orr of Indiana delivered copies of *The Reckoning*, David Halberstam's work on the American auto industry and its competition from Japan. "Be forewarned, don't get caught," seemed to be Orr's message to the legislators.

That Orr would deliver Halberstam's book and the message was odd indeed since there is no region of the country in which the political culture so failed its people as in the Great Lakes states. And even stranger, neither of the two very different political cultures in this region understood the coming economic challenge.

The southern tier of states bordering on the Ohio River—Illinois, Indiana, and Ohio—have had strong two-party competition for more than a century. But these states saw politics in terms of jobs and spoils rather than as a vehicle to improve people's lives. While other states created programs, these states saw government as something to protect people from. They minimized taxes and the services taxes could provide. Federal environmental standards, civil rights legislation, worker safety rules (especially in the coal mines in the southern parts of the three states), social-welfare and highway-building programs were all resisted in the early days by Illinoisans, Indianians, and Ohioans.

To the north, in Michigan and Wisconsin, one-party politics (Republican) was the primary political milieu, at least up until the Great Depression. Then, strong Democratic parties emerged, oriented to issues, not the rewards political office has to bestow. These two states taxed heavily, but the taxpayers' return on their dollar was visible in the superior levels of schools, parks, social services, and the quality of life and the environment in general.

History explains much of the difference between the two tiers of Great Lakes states. Illinois, Indiana, and Ohio welcomed large contingents of southerners before the Civil War and harbored spirited Copperhead sentiments during that conflict; the result was a pronounced Democratic legacy in numerous rural counties near the Ohio River, a sentiment which the dominant Republicans in the states associated with rebellion and treason. To this day, the great- and

great-great grandchildren of those steadfast Democrats often support
the party of their ancestors, although contemporary television, universal education, and easy mobility have eroded some of the once lop-
sided majorities. When the New Deal arrived, big-city ethnic
Europeans and later the newly arrived blacks from the South joined
traditional Democrats to swing the balance of power, at least occasionally. Opposed to them were the more Republican descendants of New
England and Middle Atlantic Yankees, deeply imbued with the Protestant work ethic and proud of the fact they had climbed to positions
of wealth or stature, or both, through their own sweat and blood. After
World War II, Republicans remained fairly unified, but the Democrats in the three states were afflicted by recurring divisions between
their old-line rural (and usually conservative) followers and the increasingly numerous urbanites. The disadvantaged blacks and the
ethnic city dwellers took on the conservative trappings of middle-class
America. In all three states, one still found no small amount of bipartisan collusion for corrupt ends, a practice with wide acceptance but
carried to its fullest flower in Illinois and only slightly less so in
Indiana.

The heritage of the two northern Great Lakes states is almost
diametrically different. No large number of southerners made their
way here, except for the late-arriving blacks who trekked to the cities
directly before and after World War II. Michigan and Wisconsin
fought wholeheartedly on the side of the Union during the Civil War,
afterwards leaving no Democratic party worth the name. In these
states, the Scandinavian and German immigrants worked with the
Republican Yankees who had preceded them, and laid the foundation for a tradition of high-quality public education through the
university level. When agrarian protest rose late in the nineteenth
century, and still later when the Progressive movement to clean up
and open up government gained momentum, the dissent was concentrated within the Republican party. Immediately after World War II,
there was reason to think the northern tier might return to their
traditional Republican moorings. In Wisconsin, Progressive senator
Robert LaFollette, Jr. (son of the turn-of-the-century Progressive
champion) was defeated in the 1946 Republican primary, impelling
his more liberal followers into the then-moribund Democratic party.
Across the lake in Michigan, organized labor decided to join the

Democrats, providing the crucial enthusiasm and organizational talents to revive the party there. There already was an institutional base for an issue-oriented Democratic party in both states—the LaFollette Progressive movement in Wisconsin and the politically attuned United Auto Workers under the impetuous Walter Reuther in Michigan. It was relatively simple for these liberal elements to move in and assume control of the weak shell that then passed for the Democratic party in both states. With strong civil service traditions which encouraged political participation for public policy reasons, not jobs, it was not long before newcomers were in control, pushing aggressively for their socially oriented government programs.

From World War II until the early 1960s, the Great Lakes industrial behemoth sped along, a seemingly inevitable result of a location close to major markets and midway between the iron ore of the Mesabi Range and the coal of the Appalachians. The only serious economic question Great Lakes politicians faced was how much to tax and what to spend the money on. Liberal Michigan and Wisconsin and middle-of-the-road Illinois concentrated on spending tax money while Ohio and Indiana kept wealth in private hands. Neither political tradition, unfortunately, turned out to be capable of foreseeing the challenge that the Sunbelt states, Japan, and other foreign countries would present, much less responding to it.

The cost of doing business in the Great Lakes states—in labor, taxes, and energy—was often higher than in the Sunbelt or other parts of the world, but it was not worse than in New England, which began to blossom in the 1970s. The Great Lakes' worst problems, it now appears, were the fruits of prosperity: complacency on the part of both labor and management, bitter labor-management relations, lethargy in modernizing old factories, and an unsupportive atmosphere for small business. Financial institutions continued to lend money to the auto makers and other manufacturers with which they had long-term relationships. Heavy industry continued to grab the most promising engineering talent; few young people went to the trouble to form their own companies, and those so inclined often headed for the South and the West, regions which provided both the financial and psychological support to encourage new companies and new industries.

Even the structure of the Great Lakes' aging industries caused problems. Unlike publicly held companies, observed Representative

David R. Obey, (D.-Wisconsin), the heads of Milwaukee's family-held corporations were unwilling to try new ideas. The Milwaukee corporations became complacent, Obey said, because executives "only had to satisfy their in-laws instead of dealing with 6,000 hell-raising executives."

Until the early 1980s, whatever economic development strategies the Great Lakes states had in place seemed part and parcel of a heavy-industry economy and lacked orientation to emerging technologies. The acknowledged pioneer of midwestern industrial raiding techniques was James A. Rhodes, four times elected governor of Ohio (1962, 1966, 1974, and 1978). Rhodes set out on one of the biggest smokestack-chasing hunts in American history, focusing on neighboring Michigan and Indiana. Under his administrations, Ohio also handed out tax abatements that allowed some businesses to avoid all property taxes for as many as 20 years. Economic development officials said the exemptions proved highly successful in luring new companies, but they forgave so many tax liabilities and left local governments with so little money that government services did not keep up with the rest of the country. Ohio closed more schools than any other state in the country.

Most of the jobs Ohio attracted were in heavy manufacturing. The ultimate effect of the Rhodes strategy and its counterparts across the region was to inaugurate a backbiting competition that blind-sided them to fast-approaching economic challenges.

In the eighties, the governors and legislators of the Great Lakes states have become more intimately involved in their economies than those of any other region of the country. The goal is economic diversification through entrepreneurship, small-business growth, development of high-technology and service industries, and modernization of old manufacturing plants. Michigan and Indiana were the first to retool their economic development strategies, but the other states, including Ohio since Democrat Richard F. Celeste succeeded Rhodes in 1983, have followed suit. Key assistance has come in the form of state-run venture-capital funds. The very thought of Great Lakes states' businesses needing venture capital from state governments seems laughable since the steel and auto industries had made the region rich for generations. But the old, wealthy people of the Great Lakes states preferred to invest their money in other regions and countries where the opportunities for profits were higher and taxes lower. Michigan and Indiana pioneered the state venture-capital concept in the region. Michigan allowed five percent of its public employee retirement funds to be invested as venture capital in small businesses. Michigan also sought to become the nation's center for robotics production, creating the Industrial Technology Institute in Ann Arbor to study manufacturing techniques and the Molecular Biology Institute in East Lansing to specialize in agricultural and forest technology.

Midwesterners remain somewhat suspicious of high tech, however, and perhaps rightly so. Regional experts caution that a complete restructuring will not come quickly, since about 50 years elapsed between the flight of older industries from New England and their replacement by high-technology companies. "Detroit or Flint in the 1980s is not Boston in the 1960s," said Nina Klarich, vice-president and chief regional economist of the First National Bank of Chicago.

A DEFENSELESS ECONOMY?

The effects of low levels of defense spending in the Great Lakes states go deeper than just missing out on this decade's premier financial bonanza. The high-tech business development process, noted Stanley Pratt, editor of *Venture Capital Journal*, "is driven by entrepreneurs, not by venture capitalists." That means ideas, the kind of ideas which come from the federal research and development monies flowing to "prime" defense contractors. Ann Arbor, for all its allure as a scientific and engineering center, suffers a major drawback. It has no defense industry.

Federal expenditures on a per capita basis for research and development, including defense, show the Great Lakes states faring poorly, with only Ohio near the national average. The Midwest's share of federal research and development money is three times less than its share of the population. The defense spending story is the same, with Illinois, Iowa, and Michigan among the bottom 10 states in terms of per capita defense spending.

If subcontracting—the money that the big defense contractors spend on purchases from other companies—is taken into consideration, the picture is somewhat better. Ohio moves from eleventh to seventh, Illinois from eighteenth to eighth. Heavily industrialized Michigan still does not make it into the top ten, but it does move from seventeenth to eleventh. As a group, Illinois, Indiana, Michigan, Ohio, and Wisconsin rank eighth in defense spending, the lowest of all U.S. regions, at $1,407 per capita. Once again, however, the huge populations of these states indicate a fairly heavy flow of funds, and in addition to the traditionally weak position of Wisconsin in both bases and defense plants pulls down the region's ranking.

Industrial and agricultural states "are being sucked dry" by defense spending, charges Marion Anderson, head of the Lansing, Michigan, based Economic Research Associates. Anderson, a Quaker, argues that all but a handful of states send more tax dollars to Washington to pay for the defense budget than they receive in defense spending. Among the big losers, according to the firm's calculations, are Illinois, which sent $10 billion more to the government than it received in defense spending, and Michigan, which posted a $6.6 billion loss.

Anderson's answer to this problem is not to fight for more defense money for these states, but to shift the money from defense to other federal programs, especially repairing the nation's roads, bridges, and water systems. Military spending, the firm's report concluded, "guarantees depletion and deprivation for large areas of the country, and provides a parasitic stimulus for areas in which military contractors and installations are located."

But her own state seems to be taking the opposite approach: if you can't beat 'em, join in. To bolster its auto-dependent economy, Michigan has mounted what appears to be the most aggressive state effort to get defense dollars. Michigan has hired a Washington defense consultant, who also represents defense contractors, to steer Pentagon business to the state. Back home it set up 17 local procurement offices to link local businesses looking for subcontracts with prime contractors. The Michigan Department of Commerce claims its efforts have landed an additional $300 million in prime contracts since 1984 and created 3,500 jobs per year, at an annual cost of $1.25 million. The state's total share of prime defense contracts nearly doubled from $1.45 billion in 1982 to $2.78 billion in 1985.

Whatever role high technology plays in the economies of the Great

Lakes states, many believe that traditional manufacturing industries will remain the lifeblood of the region. And for the Midwest's manufacturing base to thrive, massive investments are needed over the next two decades. A study by the SRI International consulting firm concluded that without as much as an extra $20 billion annually in new investments over the next 15 years, the Midwest runs the risk of turning into "a second-class supplier" region.

Modernizing and managing its traditional industries may be the toughest job for the Great Lakes states. It does not take very long in this part of the country to realize how resistant the people—managers and workers alike—are to change. Within minutes the outsider talking to midwestern businessmen and unionists knows how badly the old times are missed, how good they were, and how much everyone wants them to come back. They cannot come back, of course, unless management designs and builds products that can compete with those of foreigners and unless workers can produce them efficiently. The federal intervention to save the great Chrysler Motor Corporation set a protectionist precedent that exists to this day. In the eighties, Chrysler, General Motors, Ford, and American were once again making money. But millions of Americans still preferred Japanese cars and were turning toward even cheaper imports from Korea. Whether all the automakers in Detroit could stand the long-term international competition—and continue to provide the high-paying jobs that made auto workers the envy of other workers worldwide—remained the Great Lakes' most agonizing question.

THE WASHINGTON POLYGLOT

The Great Lakes states may have overcome their shortsightedness and backwardness in business development, but their national voices remain muted by partisan divisions and parochial fragmentation. Such behavior is common to populous, prosperous places (California and New York are the same way), but turns into a very expensive luxury when the economy goes awry.

Consider these electoral contradictions: Wisconsin and Ohio both voted for Jimmy Carter in 1976 and then joined Michigan, Indiana, and Illinois to vote Republican in 1980 and 1984. But the Great Lakes' unhappiness with the Reagan administration was registered in 1982, when three governorships—Michigan, Ohio, and Wisconsin—shifted to the Democrats and Jim Thompson barely held Illinois for the Republicans. In 1986, the Wisconsin governorship shifted back to a Republican, Tommy Thompson.

The regional congressional delegation was evenly split as Reagan took office, but shifted to a Democratic majority in 1982, despite redistricting based on population losses in strongly Democratic areas during the 1970s. By 1986, the region's 80 House members—5 fewer than before the 1980 census—consisted of 46 Democrats and 34 Republicans, and the 10 Senate seats were split between 6 Democrats and 4 Republicans.

Great Lakes powerhouses on the Potomac begin with the obscure Michigan representative John Dingell, chairman of the Energy and Commerce Committee, whose jurisdiction over the securities industry will give him a major role in cleaning up the problems revealed by the Black Monday crash.

If the Great Lakes states ever decide they really want to put their eggs in the military basket, they have Representative Les Aspin (D.-Wisconsin), chairman of the House Armed Services Committee.

In the convoluted and uncooperative political culture of the Great Lakes, it's unlikely Aspin would ever be called upon to make such a scenario come true, but it's unknown what he would do should he be asked. Aspin rose to the committee leadership by defeating another midwesterner, the aging Representative Mel Price of Illinois, who deferred to the various branches of the military rather than promote his region. Aspin's election thrilled Pentagon critics: because Wisconsin receives one of the lowest levels of defense spending per capita and the congressman is himself a product of Wisconsin's postwar liberal questioning of defense spending, those critics hoped Aspin would help break up the defense pork barrel.

As head of the committee, Aspin has pushed for greater congressional scrutiny of weapons systems in light of overall military strategy, but has tiptoed his way between other defense questions, supporting both the nuclear freeze and the MX missile. His support for the MX, plus his decision to vote with the Reagan administration in favor of aid to the Nicaraguan Contras, nearly cost Aspin his chairmanship;

liberal Democrats, angered by his arrogance, were willing to vote for a more conservative chairman until Aspin worked very hard to mend fences.

On the pork-barrel issue, Aspin seems of two minds. His constituent newsletters proudly reprint articles with headlines such as "State firms benefit from Aspin's clout." In 1987, he told the *Wisconsin State Journal* that Wisconsin businesses would "win more than our share" of federal contracts. "Everyone needs the Armed Services Committee chairman." Ultimately, Aspin's schizophrenia reflects his own region's general political chaos.

If anyone from the Great Lakes states could have helped the region during the Reagan years, it was Michigan Republican David A. Stockman, who resigned his House seat to become Reagan's powerful director of the Office of Management and Budget. But Stockman, who had voted against the Chrysler bailout, was the most determined of all Reagan's aides to reduce government favoritism to anyone or any region. In his memoirs, *The Triumph of Politics: Why the Reagan Revolution Failed* (Harper & Row, 1986), Stockman traced his political roots to his family's Michigan farm, but his behavior was that of the pure intellectual, transformed from a church-going Republican youth into a Vietnam-era leftist and by the Reagan period into a neoconservative supply-side "radical ideologue." Of Stockman's intelligence there is no question; his greatest power may have lain in his presentation of "the numbers" to members of Congress and their staffs. Ambitious staff members, especially, loved the idea that someone from their ranks (Stockman had worked for former Representative John Anderson) could achieve White House power and push his purist, numbers-based positions with such energy and authority. "I couldn't help but be impressed as he took out one computer printout and then another when I said the first budget proposal was unacceptable," said a House staff member who was Stockman's ideological opposite.

Stockman was, of course, subjected to continual political considerations by the very public-opinion-minded Reagan White House. In his memoirs, Stockman blamed the failure of the Reagan revolution and the huge budget deficits that the administration left not only on Congress, but on Reagan himself, who "proved to be too kind, gentle, and sentimental. . . . He sees the plight of real people before anything else. Despite his right-wing image, [Reagan's] ideology and philoso-phy always take a back seat when he learns that some individual human being might be hurt." To that, we might say Thank God.

Stockman eventually came to the realization that "politicians can be a menace. . . . Their social uplift and pork barrel is wasteful; it reduces our collective efficiency." But, he added, "there is only one thing worse, and that is ideological hubris. It is the assumption that the world can be made better by being remade overnight. It is the false belief that in a capitalist democracy we can peer deep into the veil of the future and chain the ship of state to an exacting blueprint. It can't be done. It shouldn't have been tried."

Stockman's frank assessment of his own performance is endearing, but leaves the impression that this naive man, so inexperienced with human need and frailty, so downright immature, used one of the most powerful positions in the land as a training ground. When Stockman left the government, he did not return to Michigan or even Chicago, of course; he moved where roots and other inconvenient complications don't matter—a job on Wall Street and a home in the executive suburbs of Connecticut.

While Stockman hated deals, Dan Rostenkowski—product of the old Chicago machine, congressman from the eighth district of Illinois, and chairman of the House Ways and Means Committee—used the Reagan years to perfect his deal-making skills, eventually drawing up the 1986 tax reform act. Rostenkowski is pure Chicago. He is proud of his Polish background, but divides his time between his district and the golf courses which he frequents with the corporate executives and lobbyists who are so strongly affected by the tax legislation his com-mittee passes. Like many Chicago politicians, his ethics have often been questioned; one of his investments reportedly turned $200 into a profit estimated between $20,000 and $60,000.

Rostenkowski loves to win in the tangle of congressional politics. After Reagan's 1981 tax bill was passed over his committee's objec-tion, he was determined this would never happen again. Rostenkow-ski has been a major player in virtually all important fiscal legislation since 1983, including the social security bailout, the budget battle and tax bills of 1984, and most of all the 1986 tax reform. Rostenkowski proved so willing to accommodate fellow committee members' requests for favored treatment of specific industries that many charged the final bill was far from the reform that had been promised. Rostenkowski and his Senate counterpart, Bob Packwood, countered that the bill had closed many loopholes and simplified the system, but their greatest accomplishment of all was that it passed. Rostenkowski differs with traditional Democratic politicians including House Speaker Jim Wright in his resistance to high government spending.

Two midwestern House Republicans stood out during the Reagan years. One is Bob Michel of Illinois, the House minority leader. Known for his personal decency and good fellowship, Michel has rallied his party since he assumed the job in 1980. He took to the floor to back Republican issues such as support for the Nicaraguan Contras and the Strategic Defense Initiative, but shocked Reagan by voting to override the President's veto of the 1987 highway bill. The other midwestern House Republican whose name will not be forgotten by political trivia buffs is Delbert "Del" Latta, who has been in the House for 30 years, but has risen from anonymity only twice: in 1974, when after filling a vacancy on the House Judiciary Committee he became a "no-holds-barred" supporter of Richard Nixon during that year's impeachment hearings; and in 1981, when his Gramm-Latta substitute budget passed the House. His fight against higher taxes is so intense that he voted against the 1982 tax increase even after it had been endorsed by the president.

Indiana's Richard Lugar turned out to the midwest's shining Senate light while the Republicans controlled the body from 1981 to 1986. Lugar brought impressive credentials to Washington; he had been elected mayor of Indianapolis in 1967 at the age of 35 and was responsible for merging the city and county into the nationally noted Unigov. He had also won the dubious accolade of being Richard Nixon's favorite mayor. Elected to the Senate in 1976, Lugar stepped into the chairmanship of the Senate Foreign Relations Committee and into history after Senator Charles Percy of Illinois was defeated in 1984. On a trip to the Philippines to observe the 1986 elections that international pressure had forced on dictator Ferdinand Marcos, Lugar broke with long-time Republican support for Marcos to declare the "victory" a sham, a position which helped convince Reagan that

Marcos's days were over and that it was time to support Corazon Aquino. Lugar is no consistent liberal—he has been a strong proponent of aiding the Nicaraguan Contras—but he led the fight among Senate Republicans for strict sanctions against South Africa and publicly criticized Reagan for vetoing the measures the Senate had passed. When the Democrats won back control of the Senate, the Senate Republican Caucus denied him the ranking minority position on foreign relations in favor of Senator Jesse Helms of North Carolina. Lugar fought hard to prevent the hardline conservative from becoming the Republican party's chief foreign policy spokesperson, but even Republican liberals such as Senator Lowell Weicker of Connecticut voted for Helms in order to prevent a breakdown in the Senate's traditional seniority rules.

The Democratic takeover of the Senate also brought Wisconsin's William Proxmire back to the chairmanship of the Senate Banking, Housing and Urban Affairs Committee. Proxmire first came to the Senate in 1957, filling the seat left open by the death of Joseph R. McCarthy. He is best known as the body's resident spending skeptic, opposing a variety of budget initiatives, and giving out his monthly award, the "Golden Fleece," for "ridiculous" or "ironic" waste of taxpayers' dollars. In 1987 he announced in an almost one-sentence news conference that he would not run for re-election in 1988. Bigger news than the retirement of a septuagenarian was Proxmire's decision to support the diversification of commercial banks into stock brokerage and other financial services. For years, Proxmire had sided with the small-town bankers who fear that more diversified big city banks will put them out of business.

The Great Lakes' second most prominent Democratic senator is Ohio Democrat John Glenn, the brilliant fighter pilot in World War II and Korea, and the first American to orbit the earth. Glenn has made nuclear proliferation the centerpiece of his legislative agenda and is the author of several key laws which make it more difficult for other countries to acquire the technology to make atomic weapons. Glenn came into sharp conflict with the Reagan administration when he proposed cutting aid to Pakistan if Reagan couldn't confirm that Pakistan wasn't attempting to develop nuclear weapons. The measure lost, but only after intense pressure was brought to bear by the administration. Glenn also voted against the SALT II treaty, but has since become a more vocal supporter of arms control issues. Glenn made a 1984 bid for the Democratic nomination, but it bombed after embarrassing losses in Iowa and New Hampshire. The aborted campaign left Glenn with a $2-million-plus debt and rare questions about his integrity. Several Ohio banks which had made loans to the campaign had received "letters of comfort" from rich Ohioans despite the fact that federal campaign finance laws prohibit guarantees of debt to political candidates.

The Great Lakes politician who decided to run for president in 1988 was not one of the region's distinguished senior senators but Illinois freshman Paul Simon. An Oregon native who entered public life as the editor of the *Troy Tribune* in southern Illinois, crusading against vice and political corruption, Simon was elected to the state legislature at 25 and went on to the state senate and the lieutenant governorship. He served five terms in the U.S. House before bucking the Reagan coattails in 1984 to defeat Republican Charles Percy. It would be hard to find a senator with a greater reputation for decency, thoughtfulness, or traditional Democratic values. Simon won his Senate seat partly by promoting such ideas while the incumbent Percy was associated with Reaganomics. But Simon also won because Percy was hurt by his liberal ways as chairman of the Senate Foreign Relations Committee, which offended conservative Republicans; by his sympathy for the Palestinian cause, which offended Jews; and by his support of a Republican for mayor of Chicago, which offended Chicago blacks who had veered from their normal Democratic ways to support him.

Simon does not buy the technocratic, free-market approaches of many younger Democrats; his agenda is the old-fashioned idea of guaranteeing a job for every American who wants to work. In his book, *Let's Put America Back to Work* (Bonus Books, 1987), Simon called for paying unemployed people the minimum wage to do government-sponsored work rather than paying them welfare or workmen's compensation. He likens it to FDR's Works Progress Administration (WPA), which he claims provided 2.6 million jobs to the unemployed in its first seven months of existence in 1935. It is the most far-reaching jobs proposal since the 1970s' Humphrey-Hawkins Full Employment Act. As Simon put it when he announced his candidacy, "I'm not a neo-anything. I'm a Democrat."

WATER, WATER EVERYWHERE

In these troubled times, the region's plentiful water is the greatest comfort to the leaders of the Great Lakes states. Water logically defines the Great Lakes region. With the exception of 100 miles on Ohio's eastern border and 50 miles on Wisconsin's northwestern boundary, the Great Lakes states are entirely separated by water from surrounding states. These natural boundaries comprise three of the greatest waterway systems in the country and give the five states a role as major exporters of both agricultural and industrial products, notwithstanding their landlocked location. Winding its way along the southern borders of Ohio, Indiana, and Illinois is the 981-mile Ohio River. In pioneer days, the Ohio was the interstate system of its era, bringing settlers by raft to homestead in the new lands of the Northwest Territory; today it is a commercial artery of the first rank, its traffic slowed only by the annual spring floods and the occasional winter freezes. Along the western edges of Illinois and Wisconsin is almost half of the mighty Mississippi River, the grand-daddy of North American rivers at 2,348 miles from its headwaters in Minnesota to the deltas of Louisiana. From east to west along the northern tier are the Great Lakes themselves, aptly called the fresh-water Mediterranean of the Western Hemisphere. With their 2,342 miles of connecting waterways, the lakes form the largest inland water transportation system on earth.

As a transportation system, a source of water and recreation, and, one must admit, a garbage dump, the lakes have been integral to the economic and cultural development of the Great Lakes region. What the Atlantic and Pacific oceans are to life, commerce, and culture on the East and West coasts, the Great Lakes and the St. Lawrence Seaway are to the heartland Megalopolis: a window to the sea and to the world at large.

Great Lakes leaders hold out the hope that the lakes will be their salvation. That may happen one day, but so far the talk is so vague and idealistic that there's more point in concentrating on the problems that remain.

The first is the environment. The one great difference between the coastal ports and those of the Great Lakes is the oceans themselves. By virtue of their salinity and sheer magnitude, the oceans still seem relatively inviolate to the pollution of man, notwithstanding the coastal degradation and occasional oil spills. The same cannot be said of the Great Lakes. In the 1960s, the Great Lakes, especially Lake Erie, were on the verge of an ecological death, choked and smothered by the thousands of tons of insidious wastes poured into them daily. But the tidal wave of environmental concern, fostered by the likes of Wisconsin senator Gaylord Nelson, led to a federally forced cleanup and the expenditure of billions of dollars for treatment facilities. By the 1980s no self-respecting ecologist would yet pronounce the Great Lakes cured of all their ingested ailments, but there had been enough success stories to show that concerted anti-pollution campaigns can make a crucial difference. After $15 billion in anti-pollution expenditures and a limit on phosphorous detergent pollutants, Lake Erie—occasionally referred to as America's Dead Sea—has become a fisherman's paradise. But the degree and type of pollution in the Great Lakes and the surrounding lands is much greater than anyone initially realized (or better known than in other places, some state officials like to say, because of stricter monitoring). Both the states and Canada have tried valiantly to reach agreements so that polluters cannot pit one state against another: today when a permit renewal for a polluting plant comes up, another state can at least register an official objection. But getting at the source of the pollution is tough. Officials pointed out that one-third of the pollution in Lake Superior, for instance, comes from acid rain, rather than local industry.

The message from the eight-state Great Lakes Commission and others was clear: while much has been done, much more remained if all the lake shore beaches were to fill with children again, if the fish were to spawn and thrive, if the water was to cease to be a health hazard and a cesspool.

The St. Lawrence Seaway, completed as a joint project with Canada in 1959, linked Lake Superior with the Atlantic Ocean and created a "fourth American seacoast" in the midst of the heartland. But the dreams of the inland shipping potential, of transforming cities like Cleveland and Chicago into New Yorks and Rotterdams of world trade, raised hopes far beyond what has ever been realized. The Seaway can handle ships of up to 29,000 tons and 730 feet. Foreign vessels venturing as far as Duluth, Minnesota, rise almost 600 feet above the Atlantic through an intricate series of locks not only in the St. Lawrence River but among connecting lakes as well. The Seaway's problems started with the legislative horse-trading needed to overcome opposition by eastern interests and the railroads. To win approval, the Seaway was required not only to cover its operating expenses but also to repay its construction costs and bond interest through its tolls—a provision omitted, oddly enough, for similar projects such as the Houston Ship Canal. As a result, the cost to each freighter passing up and down the passage has been higher than anticipated, and overall ship traffic has been lower than was once hoped.

By the late 1980s, the Seaway needed repairs and maintenance, and there were conflicts with Canada over user fees and tolls. Intra-lake shipping had dropped significantly since the auto industry required less raw material and grain shipping had run into problems with railroad deregulation. Added to that, the federal government's Food for Peace program that shipped food overseas required that up to three-fourths of the cargo travel on American ships using eastern or southern ports.

In their wildest moments, Great Lakes politicians like to talk about the Southwest as the "parch belt," and debate whether they should sell water to that region (usually an unpopular idea) or wait until industry gets tired of the dry Southwest and comes back to them. For now, ironically, the problem may be too much water. The lakes have risen as they have not since white settlers arrived. And while Great Lakes officials argued about whether the lakes were indeed at their highest water levels ever, homes along Indiana's sand dunes slid into Lake Michigan, beaches and docks disappeared under feet of water, and waves rivaling those on the Atlantic Ocean crashed over Chicago's famed Lakeshore Drive and swamped the luxury condominiums and apartment buildings lining the lake.

Officials pointed fingers, donned raingear and boots to help bail out flooded buildings, and blamed each other for the onslaught. Michigan tried incentives to get people to move their homes further in from the water and to get towns to build dikes. It was left to Chicago, its entire East Side fronting on Lake Michigan, to ponder erecting the biggest dike of them all: dozens of artificial barrier islands to protect virtually its entire shoreline. In Chicago and Indiana and the other Great Lakes states and cities it was becoming clear that unless nature lowered the lakes, it would cost tens of billions of dollars to stop the rising waters.

A RURAL DIVERSION

One of the more extraordinary news photos of the Reagan years was of the president of France, François Mitterrand, holding a pig on the Illinois farm of Reagan's first Agriculture secretary, John Block. "When he arrived he had on a black cashmere topcoat, but he quickly peeled that off and put on a light blue jacket that had 'Block Farms' written across the back and 'Mr. President' over the lapel," Block later recalled. Then, he quickly climbed on the tractor with me. As we started out, I was driving and I asked him if he wanted to steer the tractor. He said, 'no,' but then he reached out and took the steering wheel and started steering the tractor. And, before I knew it, I was moving off to the side and he was running the tractor alone. Except for one thing: I had my hand on the throttle. I had it going very, very slowly. All the photographers were backing up in front of us, taking pictures. But President Mitterrand was saying, 'faster, go faster.' And I said, 'We might run over one of the photographers and cause an international incident.' Then we looked at the little pigs, and I handed him a pig and he appreciated that very much."

The level of the urbane French president's appreciation will never be known, but the moment was clearly a high point for the rural Great Lakes areas, which can rarely compete for attention with the region's industrial cities or the farm states to the west. In reality, geographically, economically, and culturally, this area of America is more like four subregions than five states, and three of those subregions are rural. First there is the southern hill country, second the fertile farm belt to the north of it. Inserted in the farm belt as it nears the Great Lakes are the immense urban and industrial centers; finally comes the North-woods, where the winters are long, the people scarce, and the scenery superb. The southern hill country falls roughly south of the Old

National Road, later U.S. Highway 40 and, in contemporary times, Interstate 70. The Old National Road, the first great highway building venture of the federal government, was constructed in the early 1880s, moving out from Cumberland, Maryland, and bisecting such cities as Columbus in Ohio, Indianapolis in Indiana, and Vandalia in Illinois (with a later extension, built by Illinois, to reach St. Louis). Here, in the southern hill country, can be found people every bit as poor and poverty-ridden as the destitute in Appalachia or the Ozarks, where many of the people have their roots. Indeed, the countryscape closely resembles the foothills of the Appalachians and the Ozarks, contoured with endless ridges and hollows that have a rustic attractiveness of their own, except where the scars of the coal mines have been left without restoration. The first settlers were hardy southerners, Virginians and Kentuckians for the most part. Vestiges of the original culture persist, especially when it comes to race relations.

Just to the north is the farm belt, extending like a giant wedge across central and northern Ohio, Indiana, and Illinois to the Mississippi River. This is the land in which Ronald Reagan spent his childhood, in the northern Illinois towns of Tampico and Dixon, dependent on farming and the Mississippi River trade.

The farm belt's northern perimeter is more ill-defined, interrupted by the urban industrial masses along the lakes, but it does extend northward to include the orchards of Michigan and the dairy farms of Wisconsin. When other Americans think of the Midwest, this is the flatland they picture. Here is where 42 percent of the nation's corn is grown, 26 percent of the hogs are raised, and 11 percent of both cattle and wheat are produced. In 1800, the government sold the land of the farm belt at two dollars an acre to induce settlers to homestead. Even with today's lower land values it can cost more than $1 million just to buy an average-sized farm in Illinois, where the rich soil is made even more fertile by modern productive technology. Since pioneer days the family farm has been the primary stabilizer of the farm-belt economy, but the pressures of technology, escalating costs, and an aging rural population are taking their toll, leaving the land more and more to the bigger, more efficient operators, be they individuals or corporations.

In northern Michigan and Wisconsin lie the Northwoods, an area sorely depressed economically since World War II but now showing significant signs of development. Like the southern hill country, the Northwoods' population seems to be in inverse proportion to the number of pines and hardwoods that cover its surface (even as new people move in, portions of the land are cleared, prompting environmentalists to question if the newfound growth will be worth the price paid). Poverty exists here too, but not in the concentrated form of the cities or even the southern hill country. In addition to Michigan's Upper Peninsula, still largely a forsaken area, the Northwoods includes the northern third of Michigan's lower peninsula plus most of the upper half of Wisconsin. Once rich in resources, first from the pelts of fur-bearing animals, then from timber, later from copper and iron ore, parts of the Northwoods resemble ghost towns. Since the 1970s, however, professionals, retirees, and people to serve them have begun migrating north with or without jobs, sometimes retreating in fear and frustration from the urban scene, usually seeking some kind of quality of life lacking in their previous homes.

The men and values from the rural Great Lakes states have held great power during the Reagan era. First, the president himself was raised in Illinois' northern farm country, and those basic American values he always talked about were honed there. Second, there was Secretary of Agriculture Block. And third, and even more powerful, was rural Michigan's David Stockman, whose conservative ideology set the basic tone for the administration's opposition to domestic social programs. Stockman antagonized farmers in his famed *Atlantic Monthly* interview by saying that he intended to cut back on federal farm programs by pitting one agricultural sector against another. Congress didn't agree, of course, and the Reagan administration ended up increasing farm spending faster than defense.

The great power in Great Lakes agriculture lies in the dairy industry, whose regional cooperatives—Associated Milk Producers, Inc.; Mid-American Dairymen, Inc.; and Dairymen, Inc.—together overshadow all other agricultural groups in political donations. Dairy industry officials attribute their high level of contributions to their head start in forming PACs and to a more efficient system of collecting money. The industry's organization into business cooperatives allows dairy co-ops to deduct a voluntary PAC contribution from payments to farmers. The three top dairy PACs all make bigger contributions than either the Chicago Mercantile Exchange or the Chicago Board of Trade. Other farmers have been reluctant to contribute to PACs because of tradition, anti-government sentiment, lack of experience, and the memory of unfavorable publicity generated by the dairy lobbies' questionable financial relations with the 1972 re-election committee of President Nixon. But the tactics of the dairy industry have been adopted over time by other farm groups, including the American Agricultural Movement (AAM), the anti-establishment group whose members drove their tractors onto the Mall in Washington in 1979 to protest the Carter administration's farm policies.

The world may view the rural Great Lakes as tediously unchanging or as a refuge of stability, but the dairy industry is undeniably dynamic. As the nineties dawn, the dairy industry is in a political quandary over the safety and economic implications of bovine growth hormones, a biotechnology innovation to make cows produce more milk. At a time when the world is awash with excess milk and Washington is paying farmers to send their herds to slaughter, the last thing America needs is the ability to produce more milk. "It would just destroy the dairy program as we know it today," said Representative Steve Gunderson, (R.-Wisconsin). But the Monsanto Corporation insisted on marketing this "progressive" product, and political economist Larry G. Hamm of Michigan State University predicted, "This is just the first wave. There's a lot more coming."

Toledo, Ohio: The Museum as Metaphor

As romantic as one may like to get about rural life, it is more appropriate to leave the Great Lakes states on an urban note, for cities are where the most of the region's people live and where its twentieth-century character has been set. No other part of the country is—or has been—so rich in big and medium-sized industrial cities.

Hugging the shores of Lake Erie and Lake Michigan are the great metropolises: Chicago and its sinewy suburbs, Detroit, Cleveland, and Milwaukee. Here too are Youngstown, Akron, and Toledo; Flint and Grand Rapids; Gary, Hammond, and East Chicago; Racine and Kenosha. Half of the region's people, more than 20 million of them, live in the metropolitan areas in this 200-mile wide band. These cities,

once the New World havens for thousands of European immigrants—
the Irish, the Poles, the Slavs, and the Germans, seeking steady work
in the auto plants, steel mills, and meat-packing factories—have all
but ceased to grow, their central cities actually declining precipitously.
But not all Great Lakes cities are in this shape. Indianapolis and
Columbus are two of the most economically vigorous cities outside the
Sunbelt and Cleveland is undergoing a revival.

Scattered throughout the farm belt are the medium-sized cities,
some within the northern megalopolis, some without, often seemingly
like concrete extensions of the cornfields. Rockford, Moline, Cham-
paign, Terre Haute, Muncie, Ft. Wayne, Green Bay, Lansing, Pontiac, Battle Creek, Warren, Lima, Zanesville: they differ greatly in size
but all retain common qualities. John Gunther rather unkindly described the middle cities of the Midwest in 1947 as "the ugliest, least
attractive phenomena in the United States. They represent more
bluntly than anything else in the country the worst American characteristics—covetousness, ignorance, tolerance of slums, absence of aes-
thetic values, get-rich-quickism, bluster, lack of vision, lack of civic
spirit, excessive standardization, and immature and undisciplined social behaviour."

Forty years later, these cities have lost some of their reputation for
stubborn provincialism. Their biggest boost may have come from the
1984 publication of *And Ladies of the Club*, an account of the Waynes-
boro, Ohio, women's club from 1868 to 1929. The story of the book's
publication was itself a heartwarming midwestern tale since the author, Helen Hooven Santmyer, was in a nursing home by the time her
novel reached a national audience. But more importantly the book
served to remind readers that not all midwesterners were as venal and
narrow-minded as those Sinclair Lewis had depicted in his novels.
Social critics, horrified by the materialistic "me generation" values of
the seventies and eighties, have also lauded the region for its sense of
family and its penchant for paying bills on time. But even as they
began to look more attractive to outsiders and some of their own
youth, the lesser cities of the Great Lakes states fared the worst in the
economic turbulence of the 1980s. First they lost their factories to the
Sunbelt and overseas, then their corporate headquarters as companies
making such mundane items such as tires sought to "reposition"

themselves as diversified multinationals. A good example was Fire-
stone Tire & Rubber's decision to leave its 87-year-old base in the
Rubber City of Akron, Ohio, for Chicago to become a "retailer of
automotive services."

To get a sense of the trials and tribulations of these cities today, I
spent a weekend in Toledo as the guest of my friend Marcy Kaptur,
the city's remarkable congresswoman. Kaptur is the kind of person a
home town is proud to call its own: of Polish-American roots, graduate
of the local Catholic schools, winner of a scholarship to the University
of Wisconsin, national activist in the neighborhood movement of the
1970s, aide in the Carter White House and a Ph.D. candidate at MIT
in 1982 when she entered the House race because the "logical" male
candidates decided a Democrat couldn't win election to the House
that year.

Marcy, as many of her constituents call her, was holding her annual
bake sale, which raises several thousand dollars for her campaign. The
elderly constituents who bake the breads and cookies are what Kaptur
calls "her people" because their loyalty is unquestioned. To do her
job these days, Kaptur spends much of her time in the company of
businessmen, trying to forge strategies to keep jobs in the city and
create new ones. Fully half of the local economy is tied to the auto
industry; Toledo's biggest employer is the AMC Jeep plant, which
was owned by the French firm of Renault until Chrysler bought it in
1987. The Jeep plant employed 8,000 people, including most of the
city's black middle class, but Toledoans were worried sick that its
antiquated state meant management might close it. They also worried
about losing the headquarters of Owens Corning. But they had used
federal funds to fix up the harbor overlooking Lake Erie, attracted a
Sofitel hotel (another French connection), and built a small festival
market place on the order of Boston's Faneuil Hall and Baltimore's
Harbor Place.

When I asked a group of small businessmen about their problems,
they complained that local banks require unreasonably high collat-
eral. The banks deny such a charge, but it would be hard to refute
one small businessman's observation that his competitors in California
had been able to raise capital by taking advantage of increases in
home values which never hit Toledo. When I spoke with Toledo
businessmen, large and small, most gave the usual midwestern reason

for staying around: family. When you asked them about excitement, most mentioned other places, primarily California.

The odd thing was that Toledo was quite the place to be that weekend. The PGA golf championship was in progress, and John Block, an executive with his family-owned *Toledo Blade*, told me that 10 major golf tournaments are played in Ohio and half of them in Toledo. Block is a sophisticated local booster. His family was rich enough for him to spend his childhood summers on Lake Geneva in Switzerland, and he contends that "the Maumee River is comparable." Block also praises Toledo for its openness compared with the East: "My father came out here from New York in 1935," he said, "and the first thing we noticed was how friendly people were."

The most fascinating institution in Toledo is its extraordinary Museum of Art. The museum was opened in 1901 by glass magnate Edward Drummond Libbey. Ranging from ancient Egyptian sculpture to twentieth-century American paintings, with a natural specialization in glassware, the collection is breathtaking, and unexpected in a city so far off the tourist track. It's impossible to rate art museums, but museum officials say it compares with those in much larger Kansas City, St. Louis, Minneapolis, Indianapolis, and Cincinnati; I could not help but think of all the glittery, glowing Sunbelt cities which have no collections to rival Toledo's. While the Sunbelt shouts the establishment of each fledgling cultural institution, a very high quality of life simply goes on year after year in Toledo and other Great Lakes cities.

And yet the history of Toledo's Museum of Art illustrates the challenges of a midwestern city today. When Mr. Libbey founded the museum in the days before income tax, he had so much money he did not have to try to raise funds; he and a few friends bought art and invited the public to view it. Since 1960, the museum has had a membership program, but people in the community still seem to be afraid of it. All Toledoans go to the museum as students (the institution's children's program is its pride and joy), but after that it is largely the province of the upper classes and the junior executives who are fewer in number in Toledo than in cities with more corporate headquarters. An unpretentious couple who had moved to Toledo from the South told me at Kaptur's bake sale that they had tried in vain to get their neighbors to go with them to the museum.

Toledo's great museum proves it is a city of distinction, and well-established ballet and opera companies and symphony orchestras are distinguishing marks of the other Great Lakes cities. But wide participation is a hallmark of modern American life in both culture and business. With a little loosening up, a little shaking free of their old, rigidities, Toledo and the rest of the Great Lakes cities could compete with and even prevail over other regions into the twenty-first century.

THE SOUTH:
Divided and Conquered?

Miami; the Mississippi Delta; McLean, Virginia; Boone County, West Virginia; Hilton Head Island, South Carolina; Lake Charles, Louisiana. Jesse Helms and Jesse Jackson. Paula Hawkins and Chuck Robb. Can such diverse places and personalities really add up to a region today?

Yes, according to the white, male, conservative Democratic politicians who organized 1988's Super Tuesday, the nation's first regional presidential primary. Maybe, if you listened to Bert Lance, famed as President Carter's ousted director of the Office of Management and Budget and later chairman of the Georgia Democratic party, who has been quick to point out that the South's diversity in modern times is often overlooked. And probably not, if you examined the growing differences among the South's 12 states from Virginia to Florida and west to Arkansas and Louisiana, between its prospering cities and depressed rural areas, and between its white fundamentalist conservatives and newly enfranchised blacks.

Forged by war, that most unifying of experiences, the South's continuing sense of regionalism cannot be denied. "The war" still comes up in southern conversation. Before the war and after the war. Even in the 1980s, you always know which war, and it's not the Vietnam War, World War II, or even World War I. "Which side were your people on in the war?," the attendant asked when I stopped at the visitor center of the Vicksburg National Military Park in Mississippi. "Neither side. They were still in Europe," I replied. "Oh, dear," she sighed. "Well, I guess you can just relax and enjoy the cemetery." A friend who moved to Colorado in the seventies told his Tennessee father that "out west" they don't talk much about the war. "They weren't invaded, son," was the father's reply.

But the South has lost most of what C. Vann Woodward, the region's distinguished historian, described as the "indisputable fact that the South was different—the one-horse farmer, one-crop agriculture, one-party politics, the sharecropper, the poll tax, the white primary, the Jim Crow car, the lynching bee." It would, he added, "take a blind sentimentalist to mourn that passing" of monuments to regional distinctiveness.

Never again, it appears, will the South be the national economic stepchild it was during its "Civil War century," when a dreary cotton economy reigned, when textile mills exploited semiliterate workers, when "southerness" seemed to other Americans synonymous with backwardness.

On a lighter note, the battle between southern gentility and modernism continues, though today gentility must defend itself to outsiders. In the mid-1980s, as a guest in a governor's mansion in the South, I thoughtlessly extended my hand to a woman guest who laughed nervously and extended her fingertips. Seeing my embarrassment, another woman came over and told me, "I know men and women shake hands in business in the North, but a properly raised southern lady just doesn't shake hands with a strange gentleman."

The long tradition of conservative Democratic politics that grew out of the Civil War has seen hard times ever since the national Democratic party seriously took up the cause of blacks, beginning in the 1940s, and Republicans promised to go slow on integration in the mid-1960s. The organizers of Super Tuesday publicly set out to reassert the southern Democratic voice in selecting the party's nominee and influencing the party's platform. But can a majority of southern voters still present a unified front that would make any separate statement to the nation? So many states scheduled primaries for March 8, 1988, including neighboring Texas (a Confederate state which has changed so extraordinarily it can longer be considered in the same league with the rest of the South) and others outside the South that the idea of a strictly southern event lost all meaning. South Carolina and West Virginia declined to participate.

Many southerners argued with some justification that the rest of the country, disenchanted with social change and especially its speed, has joined the South. There was certainly strong polling evidence that white males nationwide had left the Democratic party in droves as the party was perceived as the representative of minorities, women, and special causes such as the handicapped and homosexuals. But the first southern candidate to declare for the 1988 Democratic presidential nomination was the South Carolina–born Reverend Jesse Jackson, who was expected to have no trouble winning the votes of the black 17 percent of the electorate.

Shock of all shocks, the Republicans saw the advent of Super Tuesday as one more opportunity to make headway in the South. In the open primary states, they hoped that many Democrats forced to choose among liberal Democrats would feel sufficiently alienated to vote in the Republican primary. And after Vice-President George Bush, who is still regarded as a New Englander despite his long Texas residency, the first southern Republican to throw his hat in the ring was the Reverend Pat Robertson, an evangelical Christian feared almost as much by the Republican mainstream as Jackson was by the Democrats.

"The South is evolving toward a full-fledged two-party system," said Hastings Wyman, Jr., editor of the *Southern Political Report*. "Every two to four years, people discover the Republican party is growing down there."

But growing Republicanism is only one of several competing political trends in the South. Chaos, unpredictability—and excitement—mark the politics of the once "Solid South." Every group of southern voters is in the process of evolution. Whites are becoming middle class and urbanized, losing their poverty and their roots in the rural Democratic establishment. The new urbanites are joining small-town white business owners and their families in voting Republican in presidential elections while remaining tied to the Democrats for lesser, especially local, offices. The formerly disenfranchised blacks are registering and voting (almost always Democratic) in record numbers and demanding a role in the Democratic party leadership. The swing voters today are religious blue-collar whites and small farmers torn between Democratic promises of economic relief and that party's commitments to racial equality, freedom of choice on abortion, and other liberal social values. There is also enough of a new-generation mentality to have allowed Colorado senator Gary Hart to win the 1984 Florida Democratic primary and to do well in Georgia.

In the midst of this political stew, the southerners' determination to establish the first and biggest regional primary may have had more to do with assuring themselves a big role on the national scene than with establishing a distinct, recognizable, southern agenda. A super primary guaranteed the kind of national attention southerners still love, in order to make up for the feeling that they are often ignored. "The people in the South need to know that they are important," Lance once told me. "We want the candidates to understand that they've got to campaign in the South."

As great an accomplishment as it was for the South to establish its primary, presidential candidates undergoing litmus tests on defense, abortion, school prayer, creationism, and civil rights are far less interesting than the changes that have transpired in the region. The real story of the South in the eighties is the saga of a region not yet freed from its crippling racism and century of economic depression, but filled for the first time with the real possibility of entering the American mainstream.

REAGAN'S SOUTH

The South has been good to Ronald Reagan. But has Reagan been good for the South?

The willingness of every southern state except Georgia to reject their own President Carter in favor of Reagan was a key to his 1980 victory. Reagan's free-market, pro-business economic policies would seem a perfect fit with the South. But beginning with the recession of 1982–83, the South's unemployment situation was so bad that

politicians such as Arkansas's Democratic governor Bill Clinton felt
free to say that the popular president must take at least some of the
blame for the region's problems, particularly in the rural areas. The
Reagan-era phenomena of tight money, tax cuts, growing budget
deficits, and expanded government borrowing, Clinton said, struck
hard at agriculture and industries subject to foreign competition, both
disproportionately represented in the rural South.

Reagan inherited a South that had glittered like a precious economic jewel throughout much of the 1970s. While the nation's northern industrial heartland came upon the winter of its economic
discontent, the southern states prided themselves on growing, growing, growing in jobs, income, and wealth. The southern states remained at the bottom of the nation's state-by-state income statistics,
but there was real growth in the number of jobs and the level of wealth
throughout the region. Southern per capita income, once far below
the national average, had risen to 86 percent of the average by 1981.
There was even a reversal of the great 50-year tide of blacks moving
out of Dixie in search of better treatment and better work in the cities
of the North and West.

"In the mid-'70s, we were in a euphoria in the South. We had a
Georgia President. Energy was up. Agriculture was OK. Plants were
locating here. But then the bottom fell out," said former governor of
Mississippi William F. Winter, who has chaired two blue-ribbon
southern leadership panels. "Almost without warning we saw international markets dry up with the high-priced dollar. Low-wage, em-
ployee-intensive industries started to go offshore. Agriculture hit a
decline; then energy sagged. Federal support constricted. Revenues
began to drop sharply. We've been fighting the battle since 1980 and
we still haven't recovered."

In stark contrast with the 1970s, when the South rode high and the
Northeast and Midwest were in deep recession and had the highest
unemployment, the tables have been turned in the 1980s. In 1986,
unemployment in nine of the southern states ran above the national
average of 6.7 percent. During the eighties, the nation's highest rate
of unemployment shifted within the region from West Virginia to
Louisiana to Mississippi. Manufacturing jobs, which rose throughout
the region in the 1970s (17 percent compared with 5 percent nationally), declined in 10 southern states during the eighties because of

declines in the refining, petrochemical, shipbuilding, textile, and steel industries.

Jesse White, executive director of the Southern Growth Policies Board, citing the region's deep losses in textile and shoe plants, concluded that "the South is undergoing an industrial restructuring just as profound as what was happening in the Rustbelt."

The Winter panel, in its 1986 report, "Shadows in the Sunbelt," issued under the auspices of the North Carolina–based research group, MDC, Inc., emphasized that the region's recent economic downturn was not a universal phenomenon. The same theme was echoed in a report by the Southern Growth Policies Board's Commission on the Future of the South, also chaired by Winter: "The sunshine on the Sunbelt has proved to be a narrow beam of light brightening futures along the Atlantic Seaboard and in large cities but skipping over many small towns and rural areas."

Southern officials, to be sure, did not all agree with these notes of alarm. The South's problems are "basically short-term, less than five years," as the region undergoes a transition related to changed international markets, insisted Keith Henderson of the Sunbelt Institute, an advocacy and research group working with southern members of Congress. In Tennessee, the envy of most other southern states because of its capture of massive Nissan and Saturn auto plants, Democratic representative Jim Cooper noted that the problem was chiefly how to spread "the boom" among more of his state's counties. "Tennessee prospects have never looked brighter," he said. "Every politician in America is jealous of the Sunbelt."

On a statewide basis, strong job gains were posted in most southern states during the latter Reagan years. The region's population continued to expand faster than the national average (though Florida absorbed most of the migrants). At least for the short run, the high number of families that had recently migrated from the North boosted the South's retail sales, school construction, and teaching positions and provided a ready pool of entry-level labor. But there were fears that the aging of the baby-boom generation would sharply reduce the ranks of Americans prone to migration. Southern leaders can be justifiably bullish about the metropolitanization of their region—the economic diversification, service economy growth, low jobless figures, and even labor shortages reported from Richmond to Charlotte to

Atlanta. Large medical, banking, legal, entertainment, distribution, and service industries, often tied into major academic centers, thrived in the cities and their expanding suburbs. "In Nashville," Cooper said, "even your dog can get a job."

But in vast stretches of the rural South the story is different. The worst headache isn't recruiting new plants and new jobs, it's holding on to the plants and jobs southerners thought would always be there. More than 95,000 jobs in the textile industry and 16,000 in the apparel industry have been lost in the Southeast since 1980. American apparel workers who average $6.52 an hour, the Winter report noted, can scarcely compete with their counterparts in South Korea and Taiwan who earn $1 and $1.43, or with Chinese workers who receive about 26 cents.

By 1987, the worst shakeout may have been over in areas such as textiles, shoes, and apparel, but the unraveling of the old low-skill job base has already hurt doubly because two-thirds of the total income that the South's besieged farm families generate comes from such off-farm earnings. The 1980s have been a disaster for the region's agriculture, which has been hit by plummeting prices and foreign competition. In North Carolina alone, 13,000 farms went out of business from 1980 to 1985, a 14 percent decline. Cotton prices finally started upward in 1987, but there were fears that the farm credit crisis which hit the Midwest in the mid eighties had yet to hit the South with its full force.

There are a few bright spots: hope for expansion of specialized fruits and vegetables tied to local processing, for example. Some southern farm output—the big poultry industry, catfish farming—is relatively immune to foreign competition and thus doing well. And a substantial number of southern rural counties have avoided the pain by becoming retirement havens and tourist attractions. But that economy is open only to the lucky few counties that are beautiful, warm, and well located.

Clinton argued that to allow the rural South to go into permanent decline is a totally unacceptable scenario. Rural America "is an important part of our whole culture; it can't be left to die on the vine." Other politicians have pointed out that if southern cities become engulfed by poor, ill-trained migrants from the hinterland, the cities too will suffer.

Clinton insisted that the traditionally minimalist, low-tax southern state governments must pick up some of the federal slack through education spending, job-training programs, and business recruitment. But he also believes that the federal government should pick up welfare and Medicaid, and establish national standards for program eligibility which "would make all the difference in the world" for the rural South.

Who is right? The South is now so divided between its prospering metropolises and its poor countryside that it is impossible to reach a single conclusion about the effects of Reagan policies in the region. Low inflation, low oil prices, and a free-trade attitude have undoubtedly helped southern urbanites as they have other Americans. But as always in the South, the contrasts are clearer, the differences starker than in the richer parts of the country. All of rural America has suffered during the Reagan years, but in the South the problem is worse because Dixie has the nation's highest percentage of rural residents—38 percent—and just as it has since the Civil War, the rural South has stayed the nation's poorest area, with the lowest income, the lowest educational level, the lowest wages, and an unemployment rate in 1986 that was 37 percent worse than the national average. For rural southerners, Ronald Reagan's America is Darwinian indeed.

A MILITARY ASIDE

Reagan's economic effect on the South may be mixed, but there is damning evidence that the region has not gotten a return on the massive Reagan defense buildup proportionate to the kneejerk support its members of Congress gave to its passage.

Virginia, Florida, and Georgia have benefited disproportionately; the rest of the southern states have ended up just as they do in all other statistical state rankings: in the last quarter. The reason, of course, is that Reagan has used most of the new money to buy weapons and for high-tech research. Most of the southern states simply lack the university research departments, the educated work force, and the military contractors to play today's high-tech game. While New England and California get high-paying weapons factories, most of the South gets bases built on cheap land and staffed by low-paid recruits.

Florida, home of Cape Canaveral, and Virginia, home of the Pentagon, are the southern defense stars. In 1985, Florida ranked 5th in total defense spending, receiving $18.3 billion, with Virginia close behind in 6th place at $18 billion. From there on, it's downhill to Georgia at 17th place. Virginia is also the most defense-dependent state in the country, with Pentagon dollars responsible for 11.6 percent of the net state product in 1985. But after Virginia, the only other southern state in which defense spending is a major economic factor is perenially poverty-stricken Mississippi, which ranked only 30th in defense receipts, but 9th in the importance of defense to its economy.

Clearly it is time for southerners—politicians and citizens alike—to re-examine the role of the military in their lives. Reagan could not have gone forward with his plans if were not for the strong support he has gotten from southern members of Congress. Southerners have always supported military spending, partly out of ideology and partly because the military played a big role in modernizing the South during World War II. For many years, southern politicians were masters at bringing home the defense bacon. One of the most famous characters in southern politics was the late House Armed Services Committee chairman L. Mendel Rivers, who was an unabashed enthusiast for every request the military made. Rivers so loaded his South Carolina district with military installations that his predecessor as chairman, Carl Vinson of Georgia, was moved to remark "You put anything else down there in your district, Mendel, and it's gonna sink." Rivers—who used the campaign slogan "Rivers Delivers"—brought a higher level of prosperity to his impoverished constituents, but the American mainstream is a moving target, and bases will not do the job today. The South would appear to have two choices in the matter: question the levels of defense spending or help build up the region to share in the defense cornucopia.

THE NEW SOUTHERN AGENDA

While the Reagan administration and many southern members of Congress were preoccupied with free-market economics and with increasing the nation's weapons systems, southern governors and state legislatures were attacking two of the most stubborn and questionable of the South's traditions: its poor educational systems and its tax-break, "smokestack-chasing" system of economic development. A few were even trying to figure out what their states could do to help out their worst-off rural areas.

These developments coincide with seismic shifts in southern politics. The 1960s saw the defeat of the last old-line segregationist governors. The 1970s witnessed the election of moderates of the brand of Jimmy Carter in Georgia and Reubin O'D. Askew in Florida, who modernized state bureaucracies. In the eighties, southern governors seemed even more committed to using the state to improve the lot of their people. "State government is not the problem," said former Tennessee Republican governor Lamar Alexander. Rather, state government "is the primary catalyst that southern states have to take care of their biggest problem—low family income."

Dixie's educational systems have trailed the national norm throughout the nation's history, first as a consequence of antebellum traditions of private education for the few (the first public school systems in many southern communities were introduced during Reconstruction), secondly as a result of generations of low spending. When the 1980 census was taken, the South still had the country's lowest incidence of college graduates (13.8 percent) and highest percentage of adults who never made it to the eighth grade (23.9 percent). The bright side is that older southerners pull down the average. Today, 80 percent of young adults in the South are high-school graduates, including 70 percent of blacks; in 1950, less than half of southerners—and only 20 percent of blacks—had graduated from high school.

The southern education movement started in the 1970s when parents and business leaders, alarmed by declining test scores and fearing for their communities' economic future, began demanding teacher competency testing and minimum graduation requirements. Democratic governor James B. Hunt, Jr., of North Carolina became chairman of the Education Commission of the States and leader of a major study on educational reforms by the Task Force on Education for Economic Growth. In Tennessee, Lamar Alexander pushed a "master teacher" plan. Led by such governors as Winter, Clinton, Alexander, Richard W. Riley (D.-South Carolina), and Robert Graham (D.-Florida), the first half of the eighties saw passage of major school reform packages incorporating tougher graduation standards, competency standards for teachers, and increased money for elementary and secondary education.

The argument for major new investment in the schools didn't become politically salable until the 1980s brought a sudden departure of low-skill southern factories and growing fears that the southern work force would be unable to match the Japanese or other competitors in either flexibility or intellectual competence. There is widespread hope that higher education levels can improve the South's poor position and fashion a recovery based on technological innovation—as happened in the Northeast in a parallel economic downturn in the 1970s. Most southern states lag well behind the national averages on such future growth indicators as business incorporations, numbers of patents issued, and high-technology (engineering and physical science) doctorates. Only Georgia at 2.9 incorporations per 1,000 residents in 1985 and Florida at 4.1 were above the national average of 2.8. But the most shocking statistics are in education, the very lifeblood of innovation and new business today: In high-tech doctorates, the U.S. average was 30 per million residents in 1983, but Arkansas and Kentucky had only 6 per million, Alabama and Mississippi 9, West Virginia 8, Florida 10, Georgia 16, Louisiana 13, and South Carolina 19. Only Virginia at 25 and North Carolina at 26 even approached the national average.

Educational reforms could not have come soon enough for the nation's interest since the South has become home to a greater percentage of the nation's youth. In the 1970s, while national elementary- and secondary-school enrollments dropped by 9.4 percent, the decline in the South was only 1.1 percent, and Florida's enrollment rose by 11.4 percent. The South's (including Texas's) share of students rose from 20.9 percent to 23.1 percent, and in 20 years, this generation could give the region a new level of momentum—if it is properly educated. But it will be a decade or more before today's children, however well educated, begin to strengthen the southern work force.

It is still tough to raise taxes to finance education the way most of the nation does, however. Virtually no southern state taxes its population, relative to wealth, as heavily as the national average. And even if the political will for increased spending exists, some of the southern states simply lack the taxable wealth to bring their spending levels close to those of their northern and western competitors. "Education spending is definitely an obstacle," said one southern economist. "But it's a function of income. As a proportion of total personal income, some of the southern states—and some of the poorer southern states— are spending as much on a percentage basis as are other states in the nation."

Progressive southern politicians have had to push harder to over- turn the South's time-honored methods to boost economic develop- ment and employment: glittery advertising pitches, low wages, low taxes, taxpayer-subsidized facilities, and the absence of unionization. These "smokestack-chasing" methods, reinforced by rare but cele- brated hits such as Tennessee's Saturn plant, still dominate attitudes in the region. But the departure of so many textile plants for even cheaper overseas labor, and the appearance of national studies show- ing that small business creates more jobs than big business, finally produced at least a questioning of the old ways of promoting business.

The Winter report likened smokestack chasing to the buffalo hunts of the nineteenth century: "The stampede of plants to the South is definitely over—especially for the rural areas that lack a skilled work force, transportation, infrastructure and cultural amenities. Yet the hunters continue in their pursuit, hoping to bag one of the remaining hides."

But some political leaders remained wedded to the smokestack- chasing model. Tennessee's Representative Cooper argued that Tennessee's "low-tax stance is a primary appeal in recruiting industry. It would kill us to raise taxes." Georgia Democratic governor Joe Frank Harris, in taking aim at the Winter report, said: "We're going to continue to be competitive. Everything is fair in love and war and competition, so we're going after it."

Even in its heyday, smokestack chasing achieved only limited goals. After all the South's courting of business, the region remains overwhelmingly a land of branch plants and small businesses. Big business headquarters are still mostly elsewhere. In 1987, *Fortune* found only 54 of the nation's top 500 industrial companies in the 12 states of the South, compared with 138 in the Mid-Atlantic states, 125 in the Great Lakes states and 55 in little New England. And the jobs they did attract to the Sunbelt never paid as well as those in other states.

LEST WE FORGET

When the 20th anniversary of Martin Luther King's march on Washington was celebrated in 1983, black parents around the nation found themselves shocked at how little their children knew of conditions in the American South before the civil rights "revolution" of the 1960s. Many black children simply found it hard to believe that only 20 years earlier they could not have gotten a drink of water from any public fountain in many southern towns. Even many adults have forgotten that it was in 1965—less than 25 years ago—that three young civil rights leaders from the North—one black, two white—were abducted and murdered in Mississippi for trying to investigate the burning of a black church. Mississippi's barbarity at that late date was extreme, but similar violence had dominated the region as the federal government enforced integration.

The ease with which Americans have forgotten the racial conditions in the South is an indication of how much the region has changed in a short time. But it also serves to remind us that we cannot understand this region or appreciate the difficulty of its changes without recalling that in culture and economics as well as race, the South was very different from the rest of the United States.

In the beginning, the Border states—Virginia, North Carolina, West Virginia, Tennessee, and Kentucky—*were* America: the first permanent European settlement on the continent occurred at Jamestown in 1607, and Virginia provided the chief architects of American independence and four of the first five presidents, dominating the national scene clear down to the 1820s; then the nation-building impulse shifted over the mountains to Kentucky and Tennessee, the Golden West of the time, providing creators of the national destiny of the caliber of Andrew Jackson and Henry Clay.

Even in their golden age of leadership, the Border states never had a golden economic age, at least not for their common people. In the coastal plains of Virginia and North Carolina, the plantation mental-

ity held on tenaciously as whites and blacks toiled through the years
for the most meager return. The Piedmont, the next strip of land
westward, would wait generations to develop first its textile mills and
then the "urban corridor" stretching from the northern Virginia suburbs of Washington, D.C., to Richmond and to the North Carolina
cities of Charlotte, Raleigh, and Winston-Salem. And then there was
Appalachia, the mountainous "outback" of eastern America, one of
the most physically and culturally isolated regions of the United
States. Here the hardy frontiersmen who had fought so hard in the
Revolution eked out an existence. The tobacco-producing midlands
of central Kentucky and Tennessee, to the west of the mountains,
and the Mississippi River plantation lands and their city of Memphis completed the Border South's economic regions. The people
of every Border state were severely divided between the Union and
the Confederacy, and the conflict threw these states into a deep
spiritual and economic depression from which they did not begin to
emerge until after World War II pulled the reign into modern
times.

The history of the Deep South began with early colonization by the
Spanish and French, and later transference of colonies to the United
States. But despite the glories of cities such as Charleston, Savannah,
and New Orleans, much of the pre–Civil War Deep South—Louisiana, Arkansas, Mississippi, Alabama, Georgia, South Carolina, and
Florida—was a rough area. The dirt-poor white farmers far outnum-
bered the plantation gentility who would later be enshrined in southern lore. Large tracts of the South were subjected to incredible
devastation during the Civil War, and afterwards the ruling classes
effected their own return to affluence through exploitation of both
poor whites and blacks. The one-crop cotton economy, marked by
high risks and low returns, created a huge sharecropper and tenant-
farmer population and exhausted the soil. Whatever industry there
was—cotton mills and logging operations—was of the most decimat-
ing kind. Wages were rock bottom and profits went into the hands of
a narrow few. The virgin timber stands of the South were destroyed
to feed the sawmills in what one expert described as "the most ruthless
destruction of forests known in history."

Despite a few spots of major industry such as steel mills in Birmingham, the Deep South remained overwhelmingly rural and bound to

the land during the very decades that the rest of the United States was industrializing and urbanizing. In 1930, the vast majority of the Deep South's people lived on farms or in little villages—in Mississippi, the most rural of all, the figure was 83 percent. And the per capita income of the region was only half that of the country as a whole. During the 1920s, the boll weevil ravaged southern cotton crops, and then the Great Depression struck the region like a sledge hammer.

The historians may never fully agree on whether the South's destitution up to World War II was primarily its own fault or that of the North. Physically, there was nothing to prevent development of diversified agriculture and industry in the South. But the federal government did virtually nothing to encourage southern economic recovery after the Civil War, and even if it had tried, the plantation owners cared little about diversification. It was true that discriminatory freight rates and low wages paid by northern-owned mills helped to keep the region in a kind of semicolonial status, but even when southerners accumulated some capital, they were reluctant to invest it in new industrial efforts in their own part of the country—except, perhaps, for cotton mills. There was a professed belief in diversified industry on the part of Atlanta editor Henry Grady and the other apostles of a "New South" in the late 1800s, but the cotton mentality was still dominant.

The roots of the South's modern-day economic revival lie in the New Deal and such phenomena as the Tennessee Valley Authority, approved soon after Franklin D. Roosevelt became president. Suddenly there was a prospect of cheap power and industrial development in dirt-poor, flood-ravaged areas. New Deal agencies pumped huge amounts of money into the region. The 1938 federal report that identified the South as "the nation's No. 1 economic problem" also said it could be a region of great economic opportunity if its chronic waste of human and material resources was halted and a serious program of development undertaken.

But it was World War II—with its multi-billion dollar spending for military bases and the chemical, ammunition, and shipbuilding industries in the South—that provided the greatest catalyst for economic expansion. By 1950, southern manufacturing wages were 55 percent higher (after inflation) than before Pearl Harbor. Even the almost warlike conditions during the civil rights marches and demonstrations did not hold back southern economic development. By the 1960s, after national civil rights laws gave the southern states new national respectability, they found themselves on a spectacular economic roll. Pulp and paper mills, aluminum plants, petrochemical factories, aircraft plants, shipyards, steel mills, and tourist attractions were all part of the New South.

While the white southern establishment was promoting economic diversification, its leaders rarely exhibited much concern about the millions of poor blacks in their midst. And whatever improvements did come to the blacks took a back seat to the terrible, institutionalized racism that was a cornerstone of southern economic and social life.

From Reconstruction until the 1960s, southern blacks had to suffer in an inferior caste status in their work, their recreation, their associations, their schools, and the places they could eat and sleep and even get a drink of water. In fact, southern whites viewed legally enforced segregation as morally right—a hangover of the earlier belief that slavery was right. The fear of black uprisings, the notion of miscegenation, the concern for inviolate white Southern womanhood all came down directly from antebellum days. And if the black man, as the codes of slavery had indicated, was something less than human, then even the most refined classes could look in the other direction when 2,441 lynchings were recorded in the South between 1883 and 1959. A group of southern women did organize to fight lynchings in the 1920s, but southern senators and representatives fought tooth and nail to block national anti-lynching legislation, just as they would fight anti-poll-tax legislation, voting-rights legislation, and the desegregation of public accommodations, schools, and housing.

In the 1960s, the momentous changes in the life of southern blacks finally took place. But behind them were all the elements that had become what was known as the Movement: the litigation of the NAACP Legal Defense and Education Fund and the American Civil Liberties Union, the decisions by the Supreme Court that culminated in the 1954 *Brown* school case ruling that schools could not be "separate, but equal," the push forward of Lyndon Johnson's administration with a cooperative Congress, and the Freedom Riders and other civil rights activists who risked and sometimes lost their lives in "massive resistance." But most of all there were black southerners who put their jobs, homes, and lives on the line, protesting in Montgomery and Albany and St. Augustine and Birmingham and Selma, marching on Washington, and participating in much less heralded confrontations at bus stops, water fountains, and hundreds of voting registrars' offices. Finally, there was the Movement's great leader, Martin Luther King, Jr., a Southern Christian preacher in the noblest sense of the term.

SOUTHERN POLITICS:
RACISM VERSUS POPULISM?

After the Reconstruction era, southern politics were so monolithically Democratic for a century that every Republican victory was worthy of attention. When Republicans won four southern Senate seats on Ronald Reagan's coattails in 1980, national party leaders were jubilant. It was the party's greatest advance in the region since Barry Goldwater broke through the southern Democratic tradition in 1964. Not only were the four new senators—Alabama's Jeremiah Denton, North Carolina's John P. East, Florida's Paula Hawkins, and Georgia's Mack Mattingly—Republican, they were also a dream come true for the New Right social conservatives who opposed abortion, homosexuality, and feminism, and who wanted to restore prayer and the teaching of creationism to the public schools. Six years later, the rise of the New Right proved short-lived as Denton, Hawkins, and Mattingly were vigorously attacked by Democrats as incompetent. All three went down to defeat as did the appointed successor to East, who had committed suicide over health problems.

Even after the Senate losses, the Reagan years had modestly benefited the Republican cause in the South. When the 100th Congress took their seats in 1987, the 12 southeastern states had 2 more Republican senators than in 1977 for a total of 6, and had gained 6 more Republican U.S. House members for a total of 32. In 1987, the Republicans also held 1 more governorship than in 1977 for a total of 4. The long-term gains are even more dramatic when one remembers that in 1962, the Republicans held only 13 southern House seats, 2 Senate seats (both in Kentucky), and no governorships.

In 1986, while 4 southern Republican senators lost their seats, Republican candidates took all three of the retiring Democratic governor's offices in the South. In Florida, the GOP captured the governor's seat for only the second time with Hispanic former Tampa mayor and ex-Democrat Bob Martinez. Martinez was initially seen as the national symbol of the Republicans' efforts to move beyond their white, suburban base. In 1986, the GOP also won the Alabama governorship for the first time in 112 years when little-known Guy Hunt, who garnered only 26 percent of the vote in a 1978 bid for governor, swept aside Lieutenant Governor William J. Baxley, whose campaign had been poisoned by a long nomination battle. After a long, closely-fought campaign, Republican representative Carroll A. Campbell, Jr., narrowly defeated Democratic lieutenant governor Michael R. Daniel in South Carolina, only the second time the GOP has won the office in modern times. GOP strategists considered that race essential to their future prospects in the South. "In the Deep South, Campbell's victory is very significant because it is the first win not based on Democratic disarray," said University of South Carolina political scientist Earl Black.

On the Democratic side, the biggest breakthroughs of the Reagan era were the 1986 elections of two blacks to the U.S. House: Mike Espy from the near-majority-black Mississippi Delta region, and a veteran of the civil rights movement, John Lewis, to Andrew Young's old seat in Atlanta. Espy and Lewis joined Harold Ford (D.-Tennessee) to make up a southeastern black "caucus" of three in the House, but this advance was marred by corruption charges against Ford. Virginia also elected a black lieutenant governor, Douglas Wilder, in 1985 when Democrat Gerald Baliles succeeded Chuck Robb.

The Democratic senators elected were Representative Richard Shelby over Jeremiah Denton in Alabama, Representative Wyche Fowler over Mack Mattingly in Georgia and Representative John Breaux in Louisiana, replacing retiring Democratic senator Russell Long. In Florida, Democratic governor Bob Graham unseated Senator Paula Hawkins, and in North Carolina former Democratic governor Terry Sanford defeated James Broyhill. The new Democratic Senate class had one liberal (Fowler), two conservatives (Breaux and Shelby), and two moderates (Graham and Sanford). Black turnout as high as 85 percent in Alabama, Georgia, Louisiana, and North Carolina was credited with assuring the election of all four of these Democratic, though not necessarily liberal, senators.

By and large, Republicans have had the most successes in the border states of Tennessee and Kentucky where they've elected governors intermittently throughout the century, and in Virginia where they elected three in a row beginning in 1969. In Arkansas, the Republicans also won three gubernatorial races since 1966. But in Louisiana the GOP has elected only one governor in this century, and in Georgia and Mississippi, the Republicans have not elected a governor since Reconstruction. In Arkansas, the modern-day Republicans have yet to elect a senator.

In the U.S. House, the Republicans have done the best in fast-changing, growing Virginia, in which they controlled half of the 10 seats in the 100th Congress, and in Florida, in which they held 7 of the 19 seats. In all the other southern states, the Democrats made up way over half the House delegation, and in poverty-stricken West Virginia they held all 4. The Democratic hold on southern legislatures is still overwhelming, despite the fact that the Republicans continue to inch forward by a few seats per year—except in Mississippi, Alabama, and West Virginia where Democratic dominance is extreme—and have gained more than 100 state house seats since 1980 and more than 30 state senate seats. The national Republican party has tried to help Republicans win legislative races because the legislatures are in charge of redistricting after each census, but the Democrats continue to capitalize on a far-superior party organization and in many local races there is not even a Republican candidate. A major reason the Republican efforts have found so little response is that the divisive national issues—taxes and spending, national defense, foreign policy—on which the Republicans appeal to conservative southern Democrats have little relevance in state races. That argument "is absolutely not relevant" in these contests, said the former governor of Tennessee, Republican Lamar Alexander. And many rural southerners still vote "the way their daddy shot" in the Civil War—as a look at history reveals.

No region of the United States has had politics as complex and perplexing as those of the South. Before the Civil War, there was a fairly clear division—the planter-merchant classes, gathered in the Whig party, who defended slavery with the most fervor, and the rugged white yeomen of the Dixie uplands, whose political loyalties had been formed by the great champion of the plain man on the frontier, Andrew Jackson, and who had little personal stake in the system of slavery. After the war, it would have been logical for the Bourbon Democrats, as most of the old Whig classes came to be known, to form one party and for the poor agrarian masses (white and black alike) to form another. And at times there were indications that might happen. The early Populists wanted to form an alliance of the dispossessed of both races, a vision held together by Georgia's Tom Watson in the early 1890s: "You are made to hate each other because upon hatred is rested the keystone of the arch of financial despotism which enslaves you both. You are deceived and blinded that you may not see how this race antagonism perpetuates a money system which beggars you both." But it was not to be, because the Bourbon land-owners intimidated their black sharecroppers or paid them to vote the way the landowners wanted. Watson and many of the other Populists grew angry at the blacks' inability or unwillingness to join them in opposing the Bourbons at the ballot box and began to believe the blacks were incapable or unworthy of participating in democracy.

Since it was unthinkable (except in a few hill counties which had resisted Confederate conscription the most vigorously) to join the hated Republicans, all the energies and competition were channeled into one party—the Democratic. The South developed a one-party (or really no-party) politics on the state and local level, a kind of stultify-ing experience in which the voters rarely comprehended the essential issues before them, elections centered on personalities and voting for friends and neighbors, and the have-nots ended up with the short end of the stick.

But the South (except on race) was never as monolithically conserv-ative as its reputation. From the hard times in the Depression, south-erners welcomed the TVA, the agricultural reforms, and all the federal programs that poured money into the area. The liberal trend came to halt only when presidents starting with Harry S. Truman and north-ern senators such as Hubert H. Humphrey of Minnesota took an active interest in the plight of blacks. In a region that had habitually given astronomical percentages to Democratic presidential candi-dates, the 1948 Dixiecrat movement led by South Carolina's Strom Thurmond presaged the political demise of progressive southern leaders like Senator Claude Pepper of Florida (later to reemerge as a congressman and spokesman for the elderly) and Alabama's James Folsom.

For the Republicans, the erstwhile pariahs of southern politics, the moment of golden opportunity seemed to have arrived, but Eisenhower failed to win the Deep South except Louisiana in 1956. It was after this that the Republicans first adopted their famed "southern strategy." Abandoning civil rights in the name of states rights, Barry Goldwater in 1964 got virtually unanimous support from Dixie's delegations to that year's Republican National Convention, and then went on to sweep Louisiana, Mississippi, Alabama, Georgia, and South Carolina. The election underscored the deep division between the Deep South and the rest of the country since the only other state Goldwater won was Arizona.

Forced school desegregation and northern working-class anger over the liberalizing social values in the sixties opened the way for Alabama governor George Wallace's 1968 presidential campaign. In 1968, Wallace carried every state of the Deep South except South Carolina and Florida, but that was also the year that Richard Nixon met in an Atlanta motel with Strom Thurmond (who had abandoned the Democratic party) and other Republicans to refine the "southern strategy" in a successful attempt to win the nomination away from Ronald Reagan. To the extent that Nixon and his attorney general, John Mitchell, felt they could get away with it, enforcement of the civil rights laws and federal court desegregation orders was hamstrung. Ironically, sweeping school desegregation went forward, but the courts were chiefly responsible, and the president certainly wanted to take no credit for it. Nixon carried the South again in 1972.

After the Watergate debacle and the Democratic nomination of the Georgian Jimmy Carter in 1976, every southern state but Virginia diverged from the southern trend to vote Republican in presidential races. But in 1980, every southern state except Georgia went Republican.

There is no question that the Republicans' southern strategy worked, at least to some extent. As blacks became more outspoken members and reliable voters in southern Democratic parties, large numbers of white southerners shifted their allegiances to the GOP. In 1952, more than 78 percent of white southerners considered themselves Democrats, and only 19 percent Republicans, according to University of Michigan researchers. By 1984, in the rush of Reagan's second landslide re-election, the GOP had reached virtual parity, trailing the Democrats only 46 to 43 percent for the allegiance of white southerners.

Initial analyses of the growth of Republicanism in the South attributed the phenomenon to the migration of northerners as its economy improved in the 1950s and later. But more sophisticated studies have shown that the conversion of southern whites is responsible for most gains; northern migrants tend to be independents and actually reduce the Republican percentage. It also appears that the GOP has time working in its favor. The Republican advance in the South is based on an urban-suburban vote—and the region's metropolitan-area population has been growing faster than its rural population. Even the most moderate, popular Democrats have trouble winning white suburban votes. "Democrats are basically fighting a rearguard action against the creation of an urban middle class," said Black. "I believe the trend is irreversible," said Mitchell E. Daniels, Jr., who was an assistant to Reagan for political affairs, "unless the Democrats undergo some sort of epiphany."

That doesn't mean the Republican road will be smooth, however. In their fervent desire for growth, the Republican party has sought out large numbers of evangelical white southerners who want to make abortion illegal, restore prayer to the public schools, discourage gay rights, and encourage women to stay at home to raise their children. In previous generations, many of these evangelical Christians voted Democratic out of tradition and economic need or didn't vote at all. Although liberals have been shocked at their rise and attributed it to television preachers such as Jerry Falwell, it was not surprising given the speed with which the country's social mores have changed since the 1960s. The Republican establishment has welcomed their voluntarism and votes, but their life style and economic differences with the party's country-club leadership only begin with the fact that evangelicals do not serve cocktails at fundraisers. Republican leaders, both southern and national, have discounted questions about the party's ability to keep this coalition together by pointing out that for 50 years the Democrats managed to keep together every group from southern racists to labor unions to northern civil rights activists.

Ronald Reagan's nomination and his platform opposing the Equal Rights Amendment as well as abortion was a real triumph for southern evangelicals, but their agenda made little headway and their leaders developed strong fears that they were being used. "Republican establishment leaders want us to sleep with them on election night, but they won't respect us in the morning," said Gary Jarmin, political consultant to Christian Voice, a grass-roots conservative religious lobby. "I'm becoming increasingly pessimistic that the integration of evangelicals into the party is going to have a happy ending."

The strongest sign of the business-evangelical split was the Reverend Pat Robertson's candidacy. The son of a U.S. senator from Virginia and a graduate of Yale Law School, Robertson's origins are more upper class than most evangelical Christians, but as a young lawyer he was "born again" and started his highly successful religious broadcasting empire. Robertson had no political record to put before the public, but in fundraising speeches, he touted the conservative line. "All of the liberties we have enjoyed presuppose the existence of God," he said. "I'm not sure we're one people anymore. There are deep divisions in this country." He warned that "if our families fall apart then society will fall apart." On the threat of communism, he said, "It makes no sense to adopt a policy of containment. The only intelligent policy for the United States is the total elimination of communism."

Robertson faced the problem that for all their publicity, evangelical Christians are a distinct minority in the United States—and one distrusted by others who believe that preachers, including broadcasters like Robertson, bilk people out of their money. The flagrancy of Jim and Tammy Faye Bakker caused a sensation in the late 1980s, but such stories go back to Sinclair Lewis's *Elmer Gantry*. Robertson's own candidacy and reputation were not helped when he revealed that his son was born only 10 weeks after he got married. Robertson noted that this happened before he found religion, but for all but his most devout followers the revelation of premarital sex put him in league with the rest of the tainted evangelists. It's also possible to overestimate the evangelicals' religious orientation in picking a candidate. "Even among committed evangelicals, when they vote for president, they look for competence on economic, foreign policy, and leadership issues just like other voters," said Houston pollster Frank N. Newport.

Black America and
Its Southern President

"We changed the U.S. Senate, but there's no sign of it," the Reverend Jesse Jackson said frequently after blacks delivered the margin of victory that won Republican-held Senate seats in Alabama, Georgia, and North Carolina and kept the Senate seat in Louisiana in 1986. "There's no massive thank you parties, no letters of thanks, as if they assume that . . . [we] will continue to work for no wages." But in late 1987, Jackson and other blacks finally got a signal when every southern Democratic senator except South Carolina's Ernest F. Hollings opposed the Supreme Court nomination of Robert H. Bork due to their dependence on black votes to get re-elected.

Whether they like Jackson or not, the white southern establishment do need to heed Jackson's words. Black dominance in northern cities has attracted a lot of attention, but it is still in the South where the black presence is the largest on a statewide basis. Black kids in housing projects in Boston and "buppy" lawyers in California may support Jackson's candidacy, but it is in the southeastern states, where blacks make up 20 percent of the population—double the percentage nationally—that his base lies.

West Virginia is the only southern state with a minuscule black population (3.3 percent), and Kentucky is only 7.1 percent black. But the black percentages in the other southeastern states would be compelling to any politician: Alabama, 25.6 percent; Arkansas, 16.3 percent; Florida, 13.8 percent; Georgia, 26.8 percent; Louisiana, 29.4 percent; Mississippi, 35.2 percent; North Carolina, 22.4 percent; South Carolina, 30.4 percent; Tennessee, 15.8 percent; and Virginia, 18.9 percent.

The figures would be even higher if it had not been for the movement of blacks to the North. In 1900, the population of the Deep South states was 47.3 percent "Negro;" by 1970, it was only 24.5 percent. Starting with a trickle around the time of World War I, accelerating during World War II, and then in a mighty flood, blacks left the Deep South's poverty and overt racial discrimination. About

1.3 million went north during the 1940s, 1.2 million in the 1950s, and 1.1 million in the 1960s.

The 1980 census proved that this great population movement had ended. Between 1975 and 1980, only 220,000 blacks left the South, and nearly twice as many (415,000) moved in from other parts of the country. The North's essential attractions—jobs and a more liberal social atmosphere—had given way to the South's own economic development and second reconstruction. Most blacks who move south, demographers say, are between 25 and 35 and have above-average educations. There is also a smaller movement of retired blacks back to their southern roots. Liberal political activists are, in fact, most excited about the idea of black people in small towns with income not tied to the local economy bringing ideas and opinions which they developed in the North and the Midwest.

Economically, however, most southern blacks are far from being able to enjoy retirement homes. Blacks earn only 66 percent of the white median income in Kentucky, 63 percent in North Carolina and Florida, only 49 percent in Mississippi. Even in Virginia, where the black median family income is highest in the South, it was only 54 percent of the white in 1980. Just as the black population percentages give a unique tone to southern politics, these figures have direct implications for southerners' well-known concern with building a modern image. The economic standing of many southern states will stay firmly below national norms unless ways are found to bring blacks into the economic mainstream.

Black activists charge that the South's boom of the 1970s bypassed heavily black areas. Studies by the Federal Reserve Bank of Atlanta have confirmed that high-growth counties had small black populations. In the rural South, America's worst-off region, blacks are the worst off of all. Per capita income for rural southern blacks is only 30 percent of the U.S. average. Racism is compounded by industrial scouts' belief that blacks, with their civil rights movement background, are more attracted to labor unionization than are whites, said George B. Autry, Jr., president of the MDC research group. And black farmers, whose operations are often small and marginal, have been leaving the land two and a half times faster than white farmers—a problem made worse, the Atlanta-based Emergency Land Fund has charged, by discriminatory lending practices.

Even in the fast-growing metropolitan areas, older central cities with large black populations have benefited less than the middle-class white periphery. Atlanta, which has a 66.5 percent black population, lost more than 21 percent of its middle-income families during the 1970s. While Atlanta's downtown remains vital, computer companies have been locating in the suburban office parks located close to the white work force, the superhighways, and the airport.

Aided by the Voting Rights Act of 1965 and its extension, blacks are becoming an established and courted part of the southern political world. Even formerly segregationist politicians such as Senator Strom Thurmond, (R.-South Carolina), now gear their campaigns to appeal to blacks. Mississippi Republican senator Thad Cochran's campaign commercials feature black constituents relating his office's efficiency in tracking down government checks. Southern Republicans don't get many black votes, but attention to blacks makes moderate whites more comfortable voting Republican and it decreases the likelihood that black voters will organize against Republican candidates and programs.

The entry of blacks into the southern political process was, of course, one of the most hard-fought victories of the civil rights movement. Between 1889 and 1902, all the states of the old Confederacy had adopted new statutes or constitutions including such devices as the poll tax, increased residency requirements, literacy tests, and the famed "grandfather" clause that permitted Civil War veterans to avoid them all. The intent and effect of all was the same—to keep blacks away from the polls, insuring the continuance of an apartheid society.

Until the Supreme Court invalidated the white primary in 1944, there was not a single state in the Deep South in which as many as 10 percent of the voting-age blacks were registered to vote. After that, blacks began to register in some numbers, especially in urban areas. But countless legal impediments remained, and in the rural country-side economic threats and physical violence were enough to hold the black vote to pitifully low levels. In 1958, the U.S. Commission on Civil Rights found 44 Deep South counties in which not a single black person was registered. Almost invariably, these were also the counties in which blacks formed a majority of the population and their vote was feared the most by the white establishments. In 1960, only 5.2 percent of the voting-age blacks were registered in Mississippi, 13.7 percent in Alabama, and 15.6 percent in South Carolina. The highest figure was 38.9 percent in Florida. The percentage of black registrants gradually increased, but it took the historic Voting Rights Act of 1965, which made literacy tests illegal and authorized federal voting examiners to order the registration of blacks, to snap the spine of the old system.

The South's wall of official resistance to black voting has largely fallen before court decisions and the Voting Rights Act passed in 1965 and extended in 1982 under the direction of Senator Howard Baker of Tennessee. The Justice Department still sends federal observers to the South on Election Day, and the private Voter Education Project in Atlanta still receives occasional reports of counties and cities that purge voter roles frequently or place registration booths in remote areas to discourage black participation. From the smallest rural towns, where paper ballots are still used, they also receive complaints against county commissioners who threaten to delay the delivery of social security and welfare checks to recipients who have voted against the local establishment. The 1982 extension allows complaints on the basis of the discriminatory effect of an election practice whether discrimination was intentional or not, which civil rights lawyers say had an "immediate and dramatic impact."

The number of southern black state and local officials has increased more than a hundredfold since 1962, when there were only 25 elected blacks in the entire region. The Joint Center for Political Studies found 2,870 southern blacks in state and local offices in 1986. Cities with black mayors include the metropolises of Atlanta and New Orleans. But only 4.4 percent of all elected officials in the South are black, according to the Voter Education Project. The most common techniques to keep blacks from elective office are at-large county and city election systems, which dilute the power of the black vote, but court orders and political pressure have largely ended multi-member state legislative districts.

An even worse problem, civil rights activists say, is racial gerrymandering to avoid districts with black majorities. Georgia's Andrew Young became the first black southerner to go to Congress in 1972.

But after Young was named U.S. Ambassador to the United Nations in 1977, Harold E. Ford, a Democrat of Memphis, remained as the lone black U.S. House member from the South until 1986 when Mike Espy was elected from the Mississippi Delta and John Lewis was elected from Young's old Atlanta district.

While black southerners have had few opportunities for "one of their own" for Congress, they have had a presidential candidate, the Reverend Jesse L. Jackson. Jackson's adult home has been Chicago, and he would say his campaign is national, his Rainbow Coalition's appeal multiracial. But Jackson was born the illegitimate son of a 17-year-old girl in Greenville, South Carolina, on October 8, 1941, and both his religious and political roots are in the South. The only big difference, in fact, between a Jesse Jackson campaign rally and a white evangelical revival meeting is race. The elements are the same in both: emotional religion, the deep hurt that comes from centuries of poverty, and self-confidence-raising "I Am Somebody" speeches.

Jackson left home to attend the University of Illinois on a football scholarship, but left after his freshman year frustrated by the racial hatred he thought he had left behind. After graduating from North Carolina A&T, he went back north to attend the Chicago Theological Seminary and was ordained a Baptist minister in 1968. Jackson entered the national spotlight with his 1967 appointment by Martin Luther King, Jr., to head Operation Breadbasket, the economic branch of the Southern Christian Leadership Conference. In 1971 he founded PUSH (People United to Serve Humanity), a Chicago-based civil rights and economic development organization.

Early on, Jackson appeared more personally ambitious than the other black leaders who seemed to share the national leadership after King's assassination. In 1984, without money, organization, or support from what conservatives call the "civil rights aristocracy," Jackson mounted a presidential candidacy.

Jackson's Rainbow Coalition called on the downtrodden and liberal of all races to demand their fair share of the pot of gold. White America did not know what to make of this black man who had never held public office and yet had the audacity to run for president. When he characterized New York City as "Hymietown," (revealed by a black reporter, Milton Coleman of the *Washington Post*), all fears of a blatant, separatist appeal were confirmed. Jackson had already put the traditionally strong black-Jewish coalition under a strain when he embraced Yasir Arafat, the leader of the Palestinian Liberation Organization, and the openly anti-Semitic Louis Farrakhan, head of the Nation of Islam. Just before the Democratic convention he did pull back from Farrakhan, and he used his convention speech to apologize for his anti-Semitic remark.

Jackson won his place on the convention program by finishing third behind Walter Mondale and Gary Hart. But his fabulous success was based on his winning 88 percent of the black vote; his white vote was minuscule. In interviews, Jackson has recalled relishing going head-to-head with the white candidates in the television debates. One was Senator Ernest F. "Fritz" Hollings, who as governor of South Carolina had defended segregation while Jackson was in college leading sit-ins in whites-only theaters and restaurants. That summer, long after Hollings had been eliminated, Jackson was addressing the convention on prime-time national television.

Among black Americans Jackson is revered for both strongarming American business to hire and give business partnerships to more blacks and appearing at schools throughout the nation to urge black children to take more responsibility for their own development. But all America knows him for his astounding success in being received by foreign leaders. He persuaded President Assad of Syria to release captured Navy pilot Robert O. Goodman, Jr., embarrassing President Reagan; he has been received by the Pope; and he once pressed Soviet leader Mikhail Gorbachev on the plight of Soviet Jews, surprising and scoring points with many Jews back home. In Latin America, he met Castro in Cuba, and later, after noting that he had convinced the Cuban leader to attend church for the first time in 20 years, quipped, "If I had stayed a week longer, I could have gotten him to shave."

Except for his meeting with the Pope, most of Jackson's forays overseas have been visits to severe critics of U.S. policy. Whether these men truly admire Jackson or have used him as a thorn in the Reagan administration's side, his effort is as traditional and as radical as the Gospel he preached. Jackson may meet with communists and other leftists, but his rhetoric is biblical, a moral vision, his supporters say, that affirms the rights of those who are oppressed and unfortunate.

As he approached the 1988 campaign, Jackson tried a multiracial populist appeal. He opened up an exploratory committee office in Greenfield, Iowa (state of the first caucuses), spoke to the National Farmers Organization, and addressed a group of United Auto Workers. After serious racial incidents in Howard Beach, New York, and Forsyth County, Georgia, Jackson spoke with a tone of conciliation, not confrontation. "The real fight is at the farm foreclosures, the plant closings, the missile sites, and the shipyards where foreign goods that put our workers out of jobs enter the country," he said. Jackson seemed to be trying to forge the same kind of populist coalition Georgian Tom Watson wanted before he grew disenchanted with the manipulated black vote and turned racist.

As a national political strategy, however, the populist approach of uniting the urban and rural have-nots against the economic and political establishments did not work in the 1890s when the variation in income was much greater. Outside the South and the northeastern cities, Americans have never felt very strong class identities, and the likelihood of forging a presidential campaign on economic inequality seemed questionable indeed. Jackson's registering of 2.5 million black voters seemed like a much stronger strategy than his populism.

The *Washington Post Magazine*'s Walt Harrington, who followed Jackson to Mozambique to attend the funeral services of President Machel, has called Jackson the "President of Black America." It is a term Jackson rejects in his quest to become president of all the people. Black journalists close to Jackson have also said that he really believes he will one day be president. It is a tough goal not only because of the color of his skin, but the anti-establishment tone of his ideology. But it also thoroughly southern and thoroughly American. Across the United States including the prospering metropolitan South, much more moderate blacks have been elected to office; Jackson is a rarity in his continuing emphasis on the poor. Yet where else but in America could a Jesse Jackson say "Nineteen years ago, we were fighting for dues checkoffs for garbage workers. Today we are planning with a measure of assurance to win the Democratic presidential nomination."?

SOUTHERN LEADERSHIP TODAY

The Democratic takeover of the Senate in 1986 restored the South to one of its classic roles in American history: running Congress. In the first two-thirds of the twentieth century, southern Democrats—reelected in good years and bad, outlasting their colleagues from more fickle northern constituencies, and absolute masters of their legislative specialties—rose to control a majority of all the committee chairmanships in Congress, thereby imposing their views on the laws of the nation. Into the 1970s, the names of many southerners were etched into this century's history. Running the Senate committees were Georgia's Richard Russell and Herman Talmadge, Alabama's John Sparkman, Arkansas's John L. McClellan and J. W. Fulbright, Mississippi's James O. Eastland, and Virginia's Harry F. Byrd. Powerful southerners in the House, among others, were Mississippi's William M. Colmer on Rules, Louisiana's F. Edward Hebert on Armed Services, and Arkansas' Wilbur Mills on Ways and Means. Congress, said Washington wags, was the only place the South had not lost the Civil War.

Two of this "magnificent breed" survived into the late 1980s, the chairmen of the Senate and House Appropriations committees, Senator John C. Stennis, who was first elected in 1947, and Representative Jamie Whitten, first elected in 1941. Both are, appropriately enough, from Mississippi, the slowest-changing state in the region. The rest of the southern delegation is at least a generation younger, but they still had enough seniority and stature to chair 7 of the 16 committees in the Senate and 5 of 20 in the House in the 100th Congress. Besides the octogenarian Stennis, southerners chairing Senate committees were Georgia's Sam Nunn (Armed Services), Florida's Lawton Chiles (Budget), South Carolina's Ernest F. Hollings (Commerce, Science and Transportation), Louisiana's J. Bennett Johnston, Jr. (Energy and Natural Resources), Kentucky's Wendell H. Ford (Rules and Administration), and Arkansas's Dale Bumpers (Small Business).

In the old days, the agendas of the southern Democratic powerhouses were fairly simple and uniform: a big federal pork barrel to bring water projects and other modernizations to their impoverished states, a strong national defense, and absolute opposition to every civil rights bill from the anti-lynching bills of the 1940s to the climactic statutes of the 1960s. A number of these giants were patricians of great and wide vision on national and international issues, but even the greatest of them, Georgia's Richard Russell, opposed equal rights for blacks with a cunning ferociousness.

Southern Democrats today still fit the populist image—conservative on social issues (often opposing abortion, school busing, gun control, and favoring the death penalty) and on foreign and defense policy (favoring aid to the Nicaraguan Contras and financing the Strategic Defense Initiative), but liberal on economic issues (favoring water projects, aid to the domestic energy companies, and mixed on free trade). The result, according to *National Journal*'s survey of key votes in the 99th Congress, is an overall centrist southern Democratic profile in both the Senate and the House.

In 1981 and 1982 some of the southern House Democrats defied their party leadership, formed the Conservative Democratic Forum, and voted for President Reagan's domestic spending cuts, but fewer than half joined the so-called boll weevil movement. As the years went on, many came under increasing pressure from the leadership to change their ways. Southern Republicans, meanwhile, have been so influenced by the region's poverty that their votes favoring programs to bolster the South's economy have kept them from the top ranks of congressional conservatives. In the Senate, however, Jesse Helms of North Carolina and Strom Thurmond of South Carolina were among the ten most conservative.

As personalities, the current southern chairmen have a tough reputation to live up to. None of them walks around the Capitol today in a pure white planter's suit as some did in the days before air conditioning.

At the top of the list of southern senators in Washington must come Robert H. Byrd of West Virginia, the majority leader the Democrats returned to power and the minority leader during the years Republicans controlled the body. Known for his grasp of details, especially schedules, Byrd is far from a national inspirational or even ideological leader. After Byrd comes Stennis, the elderly, gentlemanly Mississippian who has had a cancerous leg amputated, forcing him to appear in the chamber in a wheelchair. Stennis is the dean of the Senate, and with the Democratic takeover of the body after the 1986 elections he became the President Pro Tempore as well as chairman of Appropriations. In his old age, Stennis's top priority has been projects, such as the Tennessee Tombigbee Waterway, to help his impoverished state. He gave up his ranking spot on Armed Services in favor of Appropriations. Stennis has announced that he will not seek re-election in 1988.

The most powerful and nationally respected southerner in the Senate today is unquestionably Sam Nunn of Georgia. Democrats from other parts of the country still find Nunn very conservative because of his social stands supporting prayer in the public schools and opposing abortion. They also didn't like his success in pressuring President Carter into increasing defense spending, but it was on this very issue that Nunn emerged during the Reagan years as the most credible Democrat in Congress. Nunn is acknowledged by politicians of all political stripes as a serious man of military affairs who does not jerk his knee toward either the right or left. During the Reagan years, Nunn went so far as to characterize Caspar Weinberger's reign over the Defense Department as amounting to a "Department of Procurement, not a Department of Defense."

Along with Arizona's Barry Goldwater, Nunn criticized the Reagan Defense Department for placing far too much emphasis on fancy technological gimmickery instead of on war-preparedness. He was basically cold to the building and deployment of the MX missile, but then ended up a major player in several deals linking more vigorous pursuit of arms control with the Russians to congressional support of the MX. Later in 1985, when the missile was coming under increased attack, he helped broker a compromise to deploy only 50 MXs. Nunn has also supported a return to the draft, arguing that the all-volunteer army could not win a protracted conflict. The strongest hope of conservative Democrats in the 1988 presidential race, he disappointed his supporters by refusing to run.

South Carolina's Ernest "Fritz" Hollings made his contribution to the Reagan years by sponsoring the Gramm-Rudman-Hollings deficit reduction act passed by Congress in 1985, and diverged from the southern defense bent to argue for scrapping the B-1 bomber and to oppose the MX missile. Hollings also displays an old-fashioned southern distrust of big industry and is a leading critic of the deregulation of trucking and railroads. His presidential ambitions seem to have ceased since he dropped an initial 1988 bid.

J. Bennett Johnston of Louisiana is chairman of the Energy and Natural Resources Committee, the biggest political plum a senator from oil-dependent Louisiana could want. Johnston has led the fight to ensure that big oil companies spend their resources on oil discovery and production rather than on corporate mergers, but he has favored an oil import fee.

None of these chairmen was as visibly ambitious as Albert Gore, Jr. of Tennessee, who announced in early 1987 that he was running for the presidency after only two years in the Senate and eight years in the House. At the age of 39, Gore was also the first member of the baby-boom generation to enter presidential politics. Gore's candidacy was greeted by immediate discussion of his patrician background: the son of a senator, born in Washington, D.C., and educated at expensive private schools and Harvard. Gore entered the race after receiving the backing of Democratic business contributors, but when he spoke of "the shifting of the tectonic plates of economic history . . . the greenhouse effect," some politicos wondered if he could have anything to say to ordinary people. Gore told me he got more of his inspiration from his constituents than most Washingtonians saw, however, holding more than 1,000 town meetings throughout his House district and taking his political cues from what people asked him about. The subjects were not what one might expect from rural Tennessee: the nuclear arms race, the connection between diet and disease, and the effects of biotechnology on cattle ranches. "People really want somebody representing them who's willing to roll up his sleeves and dig into issues that are complicated that they don't have the time to dig into," he said. "They want you to check back with them and tell them what you found and in terms that are understandable." As a presidential candidate, Gore tried to distance himself from the pack by questioning the Democrats' liberal foreign and defense policies.

Only two southern Republicans had enough seniority to chair committees while the Republicans controlled the Senate from 1981 to 1986. But Reagan could not have found two men more rightward in their thinking: Strom Thurmond of South Carolina, one of the architects of the Republicans' southern strategy, and Jesse Helms of North Carolina, the New Right's greatest fundraiser, who chaired the Agriculture Committee.

Thurmond was an arch segregationist in the 1960s who once even wrestled Senator Ralph Yarborough of Texas to the floor as Yarborough tried to get him to make up a quorum for a civil rights vote. Perhaps due to age, Thurmond had mellowed considerably by the time he became a chairman, and surprised his colleagues with his easygoing charm and his ability to work with liberals like Ted Kennedy. Under Thurmond, the Judiciary Committee was the focal point for the New Right's social agenda. The panel approved constitutional amendments requiring a balanced federal budget, restricting abortion, and allowing organized prayer in schools, along with legislation to revive the death penalty for some federal crimes. All failed in the full Senate. Thurmond abolished the anti-trust subcommittee in 1981 primarily to keep Senator Charles Mathias of Maryland, the Senate's most liberal Republican, from chairing it, removing a possible obstacle to huge corporate takeovers.

Helms, who comes out of the broadcasting world, is anything but the old southern gentleman, but he has restored the South's reputation for sending characters to the Senate. A hero to the true believers in the New Right, Helms can always be counted on to take the farthest right position imaginable on everything from voting against the national holiday honoring the birthday of Martin Luther King, Jr. (saying that King espoused "action-oriented Marxism") to trying to purge the State Department of liberals. Helms even went to the right of the Reagan administration when he supported Roberto d'Aubuisson, who had been linked to the Salvadoran military death squads, in the presidential elections in El Salvador. After the election, Helms charged that the CIA had covertly assisted Jose Napoleon Duarte's efforts—and got himself criticized for revealing classified information. Occasionally even the dictators offend Helms, however; he has made a considerable effort trying to remove Panama's Jose Manuel Noriega because of his alleged connections with drug dealing. As Agriculture chairman Helms fought against farm subsidies, arguing for a free-market approach, but made an exception, of course, for tobacco, one of North Carolina's principal products.

North Carolina Democrats put their best possible candidate against Helms in 1984, when they ran Governor Jim Hunt, but the campaign became so nasty that the voters finally saw they had a choice between two evils, and stuck with the one they knew. Helms spent $16.5 million on the race, raised through his own political action committee, the National Congressional Club, then one of the best organizations in the country at raising money for right-wing candidates.

Claude Pepper, the representative from Florida, is chairman of one of the most powerful committees in Congress, the House Rules Committee, through which nearly every bill of any importance must go before it makes it to the floor. But Pepper's chairmanship gets lost in comparison with his national role as the spokesman for senior citizens—an appropriate one considering both his Miami district and his own age (he was born in 1900). Pepper's House career is his second in Congress. He was a U.S. senator from Florida in 1950 when he was labeled "Red Pepper" by an opponent; that was enough to beat him during the McCarthyism of the time.

Senior citizens are Pepper's first priority. He once called Reagan's proposed cuts in social security "a wholesale assault on the economic security of America's elderly population." But his liberalism is not limited to the elderly. He also helped lead the effort against allowing religious groups to hold meetings in public schools.

No congressman could be happier to head the House Foreign Affairs Committee than its current chairman, Dante B. Fascell. In many districts in the interior of the country, Foreign Affairs, however glamorous, is a questionable assignment, but in Miami it's local politics. As might be expected, Fascell sides with his Cuban constituents in vehemently opposing normalizing relations with Castro's Cuba, but beyond that he is not easy to pin down ideologically. He favored aiding the government of El Salvador, and he was willing to do so even if aid was not linked to improvements in human rights. But he helped write the War Powers Act, which limits the president's ability to conduct undeclared wars, and he fought the Reagan administration on the MX missile, nerve gas weapons, and the Strategic Defense Initiative.

Old-fashioned southern support for the military lives on in G. V. "Sonny" Montgomery of Mississippi, an arch-conservative who often goes against the wishes of the party's liberal leadership. As chairman of the Veterans Affairs Committee, Montgomery has maintained a lonely interest in the American role in Vietnam long after his less committed colleagues have moved on to more fashionable topics. In the 1970s, he headed a committee to determine whether American soldiers listed as missing-in-action in Vietnam were still being held prisoner by the North Vietnamese. It reported sadly that there wasn't much evidence prisoners were still being held. In 1984, Montgomery traveled to Vietnam to investigate the long-term effects of Agent Orange, learn more about the fate of American sympathizers, and negotiate the release of children of American servicemen. Even when he votes more conservatively than the majority, his colleagues respect him for his Vietnam commitment.

SOUTH BY SOUTHEAST:
A SOCIO-ECONOMIC TOUR

If the South wanted to consider itself one economic region, it would be impossible. Even state lines do not tell the story. The South today consists of four subregions, and we shall complete our tour by treating each one separately. First, there is Florida, a megastate finally reaching its maturity; second, the industrializing "New South" of Virginia, North Carolina, South Carolina, and Georgia; third, the "Slower South" of Alabama, Mississippi, Arkansas, Louisiana, and parts of Tennessee and Kentucky; and finally, coal-based Appalachia, including West Virginia, western Virginia, and the eastern sections of Kentucky and Tennessee.

Out of the way and plagued by hurricanes, malaria, and scorpions, Florida was long the least likely of the southern states to achieve any sort of greatness. After achieving statehood in 1845 and joining the Confederate side in the Civil War, and even after its first rush of northern winter visitors in the 1880s, no one would have predicted its barely comprehensible growth since World War II: from 2 million people in 1950 to 9.7 million in 1980 to 12 million in 1987.

Migration is obviously the key factor in the Florida economy, but as time has gone on, retirees have become only one of many elements in Florida's massive change. Florida still grows more citrus than any other state, although many farms are now endangered by juice makers' purchases of land in Central America and Brazil where the weather is more dependable and land is cheaper. Landowners are finding salvation in turning the groves into residential tracts and industrial parks. Tourism, from Key West to Miami Beach to the new

Disney Epcot Center in Orlando, ranks first in dollars earned and people employed. While manufacturing represents only 12 percent of Florida's economy (compared with 21 percent nationwide), from the first space launches of the 1950s that gave Cape Canaveral global fame through the Reagan military buildup (and the sad loss of *Challenger*), the state has been among the top recipients of aerospace and weapons contracts. In south Florida, the 1959 migration of Cuban businessmen shortly after the revolution started Miami on its way to becoming the economic capital of Latin America.

The most exciting news of the eighties, however, is that for the first time Florida—controlled longer and more deeply by land developers than any other state—is beginning to act like the populous, diverse, and increasingly wealthy state it is. The only real question is whether the change of heart is too little, too late: high-rises have gone up on wetlands, beaches have been turned into hotel back yards; zoning has been derided as akin to communism; and the state has been "saved" from an income tax, which might have discouraged some of the more selfish northerners from buying lavish homes (in order to establish full-time Florida residence).

As Florida became the fourth most populous state in the country and threatened to surpass even Texas by the year 2000, its leaders finally began coming to terms with the fact that its tumultuous population growth has come close to ruining the state. The *Orlando Sentinel* sent a team of reporters across the state in 1985, and they returned to write that "After a three-week, 3,000 mile journey through Florida, a traveler's overwhelming feeling is that the state has become a changeless, grimy highway, replete with obnoxious billboards, blinking trailer signs, traffic jams, shopping centers, branch banks and rotting roadside garbage." Florida's state legislature, which was the first to allow its sessions to be televised, has turned into a debating society focused on land-use and growth issues. The leader of Florida's newborn civic consciousness was House Speaker Jon Mills, a young dynamo with an academic background. In 1985, under the leadership of Mills and Governor Robert Graham, the state for the first time moved to contain unnecessary sprawl, protect its wetlands, and make developers pick up some of the cost for new growth. The armies of sun-seeking northerners have already damaged much of delicate, natural Florida beyond repair, and developers were expected to use every weapon at their disposal to render state land-use planning ineffective, but still Florida became the first Sunbelt state to pass a meaningful land-use act.

In 1987, Florida moved even higher up the list of innovative states when it became the first megastate to slap a sales tax on services, the expanding sector of the U.S. economy that is now largely tax-exempt. By hitting such activities as newspaper, radio, and television advertising, real estate, legal services, computer services, and contracting, Florida hoped to find the money to meet the pressures to build schools, prisons, and highways. Mills supported the measure, of course, but the surprise supporters were newly elected Governor Bob Martinez, the Hispanic, ex-Democratic mayor of Tampa who had campaigned on a limited-government platform, and Senate President John Vogt, a conservative. Florida repealed it after advertisers threatened boycotts of Florida conventions and lawyers threatened to sue, but state government specialists expected the tax to catch on in other states.

After Florida, the South's most diversified economies and generally lowest unemployment rates are in the "New South" states of Virginia, North Carolina, and Georgia.

Virginia has benefited handsomely from its proximity to Washington, D.C., and enjoys the highest per capita income and lowest unemployment rate of the South. Hundreds of thousands of federal employees have settled since World War II in the northern Virginia suburbs, enjoying salaries that increased steadily (at least until the Reagan era) plus relative job security and generous pensions. Government offices and consulting and high-tech firms spread out in a great arc from Washington, and an array of military bases and shipbuilding facilities in the Hampton Roads area of southern Virginia added a welcome measure of stability. From its former rural base, Virginia capitalized on its low unionization rate to become a major manufacturing state. It was one of the first states to open a European trade and investment office.

It is still hard for the rest of the state to compete with the action in the northern Virginia suburbs that are really the southern end of the great northeastern megalopolis. In 1987, northern Virginia's already booming economy got another boost when Mobil Oil announced it would move its world headquarters from New York City to Fairfax County. But while Mobil's move got the publicity, it was the accumulated needs of thousands of other branch offices and small businesses as developers marched farther and farther west from downtown Washington in search of cheaper land and large, undeveloped parcels that threatened to suffocate northern Virginia.

On the drawing boards for Loudoun County, just to the north of Washington's Dulles International Airport, in the old aristocratic hunt country, were a half-dozen major office and industrial parks along with several huge residential developments. Each of the half-dozen office projects would double the total amount of office space in the county. Potomac Park, a mammoth project being developed by Xerox, including headquarters for more than a dozen major corporations, housing, hotels, and a conference center, would bring 30,000 jobs to the county—equal to nearly half of Loudoun's population. One residential development adjoining the Xerox project will be home to more than 13,000 new residents. And none of that includes the impact of expansions at Dulles Airport, which could attract up to 50,000 new passengers per year—and fuel the area's service economy by $100 million annually—or the planned Center for Innovative Technology, which will add even more jobs and residents.

Residents who fled to Loudoun to escape congestion in neighboring Fairfax County viewed the future with a single emotion: dread. One of the few things those residents could count on was traffic. Anti-growth groups began to arise, making very unsouthern demands that the pace of development be curtailed and that developers pay at least part of the cost for new roads and services. Said the county's director of economic development and chief sales person: "It absolutely scares me to death when I see the amount of residential growth coming on."

North Carolina has been spending the eighties basking in the glow of having become America's newest megastate when it vaulted past Indiana and Massachusetts to become the country's 10th-largest in population. North Carolina's economic profile has long been unique, and it seems even more solitary now that it must be compared with states such as New York and Ohio. Industrialized since the post–Civil War years, when textile mills sprang up to take advantage of its cheap labor, inexpensive water power, and easily available cotton, North Carolina now gets its image from Research Triangle Park, the high-tech industrial area that joins Duke, the University of North Carolina, and North Carolina State. But most North Carolinians work in facto-

ries—34.2 percent, higher than any other state—at wages that have
been dead last for industrial workers in the country. Employment
remained heavily skewed to textiles, tobacco processing, and furniture
making—as long as the factories stayed open. Between Research Triangle Park, with its high-tech high pay for a limited number of
well-educated people, and the decrepit, closing textile plants that
couldn't compete with still lower wages in the Third World, North
Carolina displays the differences between the South's past and future
more vividly than any other state.

Now more than ever, Georgia's prosperity and progress can be
summed up in one word: Atlanta. Since the state legislature decided
in the 1830s to build a rail line connecting the sea with the opening
American interior and chose Atlanta as the terminus, it has been the
South's prime distribution center. In the late eighties, Atlanta's huge
Hartsfield International Airport surpassed Chicago's O'Hare as the
busiest in the country—as air travelers who experienced its many
delays could attest. Atlanta's recession-resistant services—finance, insurance, retail and wholesale trade, and government—always keep
Georgia in better shape than the rest of the South, and in the eighties
it became the refuge for Texas developers looking for places to build
after the bust in the oil economy. But Georgia's economy outside
Atlanta—a mixture of carpet mills, apparel plants, poultry farms,
forest products, shipping, cotton, peanuts, and small grains—has not
performed as well. The rural economy has continued to diversify, but
Georgia's farmers remain some of the most debt-ridden in the South.

Tennessee became the envy of most other southern states because
of its capture of massive Nissan and Saturn auto plants near Nashville
and the decision of American Airlines to make Nashville a hub.
Tennessee has every reason to prosper: immense reserves of coal, millions of acres in productive forests, a mighty river system, relatively
cheap power provided by the TVA, and one of the South's more
broad-based economies—diversified agriculture and contrasting
specialities ranging from banking to insurance and country music in
Nashville to the corporate headquarters of constantly expanding Holiday Inns, Inc., and Federal Express Corporation in Memphis. But the
Federal Express story is the exception rather than the rule in Memphis, an old city which owes its economic origins to the cotton trade
and has experienced many plant closings and little development in the

eighties. Adding to the usual southern rural problems, Tennessee's unemployment has remained above the national average.

ARKANSAS: YUPPIE YOGURT AND CATFISH FARMS

After eight years of Reagan's rule, the "Slower South" states—Louisiana, Alabama, Arkansas, and Mississippi—are in the same place they've always been: dead last or close to it. As we have learned, the South is no longer a monolith. But Arkansas as much as any displays the internal contradictions of a southern state today so I decided to spend a few days there.

Little Rock, Arkansas, is near the end of the string of southern cities that have come to dominate the region. Compared with Atlanta, Raleigh-Durham, and New Orleans, Little Rock is obscure indeed. Nevertheless, the eighties have not forgotten Little Rock. Its Stevens, Inc., has become famous as the largest investment banking house off Wall Street, giving birth to a whole generation of nouveau riche "bond daddies" that would thrill the retailers in any city. Better known to the nation is TCBY—This Can't Be Yogurt—a kind of dairy MacDonald's that seems to be opening stores everywhere.

As a state capital, Little Rock watched Bill Clinton, its youthful governor and his wife, a Yale-educated lawyer, fight hard (and successfully) to improve education; Clinton also rose to head the National Governors' Association at the age of 40 and considered running for president in 1988. And 30 years after Governor Orval Faubus tried to defy the U.S. Supreme Court's order to integrate the Little Rock public schools by ordering the Arkansas National Guard to bar the entry of black students, Little Rock has a black woman mayor who is intensely loyal to her city. "I would feel like one of the happiest persons around if I could leave the city of Little Rock or the borders of this state and not have people feel that we were still in 1957," said Mayor Lottie Shackelford.

An hour and a half southeast of Little Rock, in the cotton town of Dumas, everything looks pretty, but underneath there is despair. In the eighties, as China and other countries began producing cotton, and the strong dollar made U.S. products ultra-expensive, Dumas plunged into a depression. "Driving through here, you'd think this is the most prosperous country in the world," said Clifton Meador, the state agriculture commissioner. "But I'll guarantee you most of these farmers are in debt up to their ears." Meador knows. He got into so much debt himself that he had to sell off some of his land to keep the rest. And Meador is lucky; as a well-traveled, well-educated man, he could find a job in the urban world. It's much worse for the poor blacks who live on "their side" of Dumas. In their run-down little trailer houses and wooden houses that would be called shacks in other parts of the country, they are a reminder that not all blacks moved north or even to the urban South. Most of the year these people can be forgotten—except on Election Day, when they are changing the face of southern politics.

Not every farm in Dumas is suffering. A few miles from town Kelly Farms cannot grow enough catfish in its 85 ponds to please the food processors across the state line in Mississippi. Kelly has installed a "raceway," a kind of fish swimming pool with a waterfall that aerates the water and allows the pond to be stocked so densely you can't see between the fish. Still, the Kelly story is definitely the exception to the rule. This is the South in the eighties where the cities prosper and the rural areas sing the blues.

APPALACHIA TODAY

While the agricultural, rural South found itself in difficult straits because of low world crop prices, the eighties were the meanest to Appalachia, the "outback" of eastern America that runs through the heart of West Virginia, eastern Tennessee, and Kentucky, the western parts of Virginia, North Carolina, and South Carolina, and northern Georgia, Alabama, and Mississippi.

Physically and culturally one of the most isolated regions of the United States, these highlands are peopled by proudly independent, poverty-afflicted mountain folk. Living on coal-rich hills cruelly controlled by outside corporations, the Appalachian people have always had to "make do with very little." Ignored as backward "hillbillies" in the early part of this century, they were romanticized in the sixties for their dulcimer music, quilts, and wood carvings.

The romantic view of the Appalachian people coincided with their rise in national consciousness after John Kennedy campaigned in the 1960 West Virginia presidential primary and became the first national politician since Franklin Roosevelt to take note of the incredible hardships which had befallen the mountain people. After a great flood in 1963, Kennedy created a President's Appalachian Regional Commission. Kennedy died that same autumn, but early in 1965, President Johnson was able to sign, as the first piece of "Great Society" legislation sent him by Congress, the bill creating a statutory Appalachian Regional Commission. In the next 20 years Congress poured in hundreds of millions of dollars to improve the region's highways and build sewers, hospitals, and schools. Black-lung benefits made life easier for disabled coal miners.

The goal of the government programs was to bring Appalachia up to national standards and diversify the economy, but no matter how much money was spent coal remained the lifeblood of the region. Appalachia enjoyed unprecedented prosperity in the seventies, when coal prices were high, and suffered mightily in the eighties as the price went down, competition from other countries and the strong dollar hurt Appalachia's export markets in Asia, and the mine mechanization that started in the fifties continued. In 1987, West Virginia Democratic representative Bob Wise told me, Appalachia produced the same amount of coal as ten years before, but with half the number of miners.

It didn't help that Reagan's budget cutters took a meat ax to the Appalachian Regional Commission; only the persistence of the region's congressional delegation and a measure of national shame saved the commission from being totally dismantled. With such odds, it was no wonder that West Virginia's joblessness in February 1983 reached 21 percent, the highest recorded for any state since the federal government began collecting unemployment statistics in 1940; the rate went down as some people found jobs and others left the state, but only when the oil bust hit Louisiana did West Virginia lose its worst-in-the-nation distinction.

Even before Reagan, critics had expressed disappointment in the small and slow benefits of all the federal money, so I went with Wise to watch him deliver the 1987 graduation address to Sherman High School in Boone County, West Virginia, and see if Appalachia had changed over the years. The result of government spending was clear in the modern school building. The people looked like they could be anywhere in the country in their fashionable spring clothes. But when I talked with school officials, a very different piece of America began to emerge. Of the 121-member class, only 15 percent were headed for college. Another 15 percent had signed up for the military, so many in fact that the Army recruiter attended the graduation. That left 75 people to look for jobs; with the factories in Detroit and Cincinnati no longer hiring, the best jobs were now "working construction" at $5 to $7 per hour in North Carolina and the Washington, D.C., suburbs. But these graduation figures didn't account for the even more astounding 25 percent of the county's youth who had already dropped out of school.

Most upset about the migration was James J. MacCallum, president of the Boone County Board of Education. A lawyer in his 30s who had returned home from California in the affluent seventies, MacCallum noted that he had won a seat on the school board at such a young age because "in the '50s, our graduates left and went to the Northeast and Ohio. What I found here in Boone County was a missing generation of leadership. Now that's happening again."

Wise has resisted pressure to run for governor, a friend said, because the state's resources are so strapped he does more good fighting for funds in Washington. When I asked Wise what would improve Appalachia's situation, he replied "a serious energy policy keeping the commitments that Nixon and Carter made," and a federal effort to develop methanol, a coal-based fuel. But Wise seemed less excited about those ideas than Boone County's project to identify potential school dropouts in the fourth grade and about his series of town meetings to convince distrustful West Virginians to vote for statewide school bonds and other educational funding they have turned down in the past. The theme, unthinkable for a southern state in the earlier decades of the twentieth century: "Don't expect any federal hand to scoop us up."

THE
MID-ATLANTIC STATES:
Still the Power Axis

E very morning, as they have for generations, the pin-striped, trench-coated commuters stream into New York's Grand Central Station and head further downtown to Wall Street. They seem to move faster these days and with good reason. For East Coast stockbrokers, investment bankers, lawyers, and accountants, there's never been a greater opportunity to make money than in the free-wheeling, deal-making, money-conscious eighties. But in fact they may be just as motivated to avoid the bag ladies, the Vietnam veterans, and other homeless people who perch on the sides of steps and lie along the walls in Grand Central's lobby.

This is Mid-Atlantic America—New York, New Jersey, Pennsylvania, Delaware, Maryland, and the District of Columbia—where life is a set of extremes: the greatest concentration of economic, political, and cultural power in the country equalled by some of its worst social problems.

Compared with the rest of the country—and with the 1970s, when they suffered a massive manufacturing decline and high unemployment—the Mid-Atlantic states had to think of the eighties as good times. The new wealth helped New York City recover from its near-bankruptcy in the seventies, and the *New York Times* reported in 1987 that even the South Bronx, believed to be the worst ghetto in the country when President Carter visited it in 1977, was experiencing the beginnings of renewal. New Jersey rose to become the region's star, emerging from the shadows of New York and Pennsylvania to come into its own.

It is the deepest of ironies that Ronald Reagan, who rose from the West to challenge the "liberal" eastern wing of the Republican party, should end up helping this region so munificently. But when the theme of government is survival of the fittest, then the fittest are in the best position to survive—and thrive.

In the pro-business, defense-building Reagan era, the Mid-Atlantic states had all the elements for success. The rest of the country competes with the East more than ever, but these five states and the District of Columbia remained home to more than one-fourth of the *Fortune* 500 industrial corporations, more of the largest life insurance companies and banks than any other region, the biggest stock exchanges, and the national capital in Washington. Nowhere did the Reagan-era culture of unfettered free enterprise and unregulated capitalism bloom more wildly than on Wall Street. With more research laboratories and defense plants than Americans usually realize, the Mid-Atlantic states also benefited from Reagan's high-tech-oriented defense buildup. New York, Pennsylvania, and New Jersey ranked third, fourth, and tenth, respectively, among the states in total defense spending in 1985. Best of all, the Mid-Atlantic states have such diversified economies that they were able to take the defense dollars without becoming heavily dependent on this variable industry; less than 6 percent of the New York and New Jersey economies were defense-dependent. If a post-Reagan administration should be less enamored of defense, this region would be less likely to suffer than California, where nearly 10 percent of the state economy depends on the war machine.

Yet the story is not quite so simple. In this golden age of Wall Street, New York gained 200,000 service jobs at such high skill levels that they paid an average of $590 weekly. But at the same time it lost some 131,000 manufacturing jobs that paid an average of $431 a week. Such developments led Samuel M. Ehrenhalt, the commissioner of the Bureau of Labor Statistics in New York, to warn in 1987 that the state was losing manufacturing jobs so fast it was putting too many of its eggs in the service basket. And a report by the Regional Plan Association in New York said that these better-paying new service jobs require skills that poor people don't have. "More than anywhere else in the country, we are creating a two-tier society of the haves and have-nots," said William S. Woodside, chairman of American Can Co. and of the planning group.

Midway through the Reagan era, freewheeling Wall Street was hit by a series of scandals that prompted the strongest debate over business ethics since the age of the robber barons. The East's greatest cities—New York, Philadelphia, and Washington—were beset with City Hall scandals and poverty of which the homeless were only the most visible signs. And back in the suburbs, old-timers saw drastic changes in their peaceful life styles as office parks went up, new housing construction took place at an unprecedented rate, and little country lanes were overwhelmed by traffic.

In the most nationally significant symbol of the Mid-Atlantic region's continuing economic supremacy over the nation, these states were the hatching ground for the most significant legislation of the Reagan presidency, the tax cut of 1981 and the Tax Reform Act of 1986. The 1981 cuts are known in shorthand as Kemp-Roth, for New York Republican representative Jack Kemp and Delaware senator William V. Roth, Jr. The 1986 tax reforms cutting out many business and personal deductions in exchange for lower tax rates in a supposedly simpler system were developed by New Jersey Democratic senator Bill Bradley and sold to Republican conservatives by his 1978 Republican opponent Jeffrey Bell.

But for post-Reagan presidential politics, the region's possibilities were mixed. After his electrifying speech to the 1984 Democratic convention, Governor Mario Cuomo of New York dominated the speculation, but he refused to become a declared candidate. Delaware Democratic senator Joe Biden's campaign faltered early. That left Republicans Pierre (Pete) du Pont IV, the former governor of Delaware, and Jack Kemp, a representative from upstate New York, to scramble with candidates from other regions for their party's nomination.

The Decade of Delight:
Wall Street in the Eighties

In the lobby of Dun and Bradstreet's office building near Wall Street stands a larger-than-life bronze statue of a frontiersman and a factory worker with their arms linked. "Credit," the inscription reads. "Man's Confidence in Man."

Those words must—or at least should—cause shudders to go down the spines of some of the business executives who go through D&B's doors to get their bonds rated. After enjoying and profiting from the Reagan administration's deregulatory, free-market ideology, Wall Street appeared ready to end the eighties with its reputation shattered by insider-trading scandals, a major crash, and Congress incensed both by the scandals and by the chaos of constant corporate takeovers that had become a staple of economic news. The nation, meanwhile, sat meekly wondering how to tame the monster in an increasingly international economy.

A relatively staid place in the decades after the crash of 1929, Wall Street in the eighties hummed with divestments, acquisitions, mergers, and corporate borrowing. People across the country watched in awe and horror as the biggest oil companies, the biggest airlines, and the biggest television networks were taken over by former competitors. The value of mergers and acquisitions affecting firms listed on the New York Stock Exchange rose from an annual average of about $2 billion in the first half of the 1970s to $20 billion in 1980 and $95 billion in 1985, according to data compiled by Stanford University economist John B. Shoven. The takeover business bred a new type of millionaire, the young hot-shot investment banker who made his money moving money around and altering the ownership of corporations rather than worrying about anything so mundane as making a product that the world wanted. Michael Milken, the 40-year-old innovator of the junk bond as a takeover weapon, was reportedly worth a half billion dollars by 1986.

Corporate raiders defended the takeovers as a way to cleanse and renew a business community more interested in protecting management positions and perks than companies and shareholders. "Only a few chief executives have ever made any money on their own," wrote

T. Boone Pickens in his autobiography, *Boone*. "In fact most of them haven't made much money for their stockholders either; they just aren't money-makers. They are bureaucrats, caretakers. They have learned to move up through the bureaucracy with a minimum of personal risk."

Some analysts claim the whole takeover situation is the logical result of the maturing of certain industries and the inefficiencies of big bureaucratic corporations. But the scale of this revolution was made possible by the "junk bond," the low-rated financial instrument Drexel Burnham Lambert first used to help one company raise huge amounts of cash to take over another whether the takeover was welcome or not. The process varied slightly from case to case, but the raider's basic strategy was this: secretly buy stock in a company until you owned so much the law demanded a public announcement, then put up enough capital to take over the company, an offer which is hard to refuse because it increases the value of the stock.

Such activity requires a great deal of money, of course, and Drexel's Milken found a way to raise the capital that was needed. The junk bond takeover strategy started when Milken noticed that while the risk of "speculative grade" bonds—those issued by weaker companies—was much higher than other issues, only a very small portion of the firms issuing the bonds failed to make an interest or principal payment on time in any given year. Even the bonds which defaulted lost only part of their value. If investors subtracted expected losses from defaults, the return from junk bonds would still be much higher than from lower-risk investments. Milken and other investment bankers took the risky bonds one step further, however, issuing the bonds on the financial position of both the company raising the cash and the value of the company to be taken over. Because the bonds were still low rated, the continued to be known as junk. But based on Drexel's success, other aggressive Wall Street firms quickly moved into the junk bond market.

The huge amounts of capital junk bonds could generate meant that any company was susceptible to a takeover no matter what its size or whether its management wanted to be taken over. Into this scene came other money men, called risk arbitragers, to buy, independently of the raiders (at least theoretically), shares in companies whose stock prices they believe are low because their assets—land and office buildings, for example—make them more valuable than has been recognized. The risk arbitrager holds his stock long enough to make a profit on the difference between its pre-takeover and post-takeover value. A variation on this theme is "greenmail," a scheme in which a corporate raider accumulates a large block of stock and then sells it back to a firm at an above-market price in exchange for agreeing not to try to take it over.

Management, of course, tried to hold onto their jobs. In desperate efforts to fight off would-be buyers, companies swallowed legal "poison pills," bought unprofitable companies as subsidiaries, or took on enormous debt to make themselves less attractive to raiders, but also reducing their value to their regular stockholders. They restructured their corporate operations. Other managers chose not to fight and took the "golden parachute" compensation packages they had negotiated when they took their jobs. The whole enterprise horrified many traditionalists inside and outside the business world. American corporations have been "pushed into subordinating everything (even such long-range considerations as a company's market standing, its technology, indeed, its basic wealth-producing capacity) to immediate earnings and next week's stock price," wrote business guru Peter Drucker in the *Wall Street Journal*. "In America," complained Robert Reich, a lecturer at Harvard's Kennedy School of Government, "industry has become a plaything of finance." Even as his own firm participated in the game, Felix Rohatyn, a partner in the distinguished international investment firm of Lazard Freres, lamented "Now the whole world is a casino. Las Vegas, at least, closes at 5 A.M. This thing does not." Added to this was the sadness and anger in communities around the country which saw corporate headquarters, executive jobs, and commitments to charities, the arts, colleges, and local governments depart in this financial frenzy.

The Reagan administration did not, of course, play any role in encouraging these activities. That would not have been in keeping with its ideological commitment to get government out of business. But, also in sticking to its ideology, the administration did nothing to stop them. The mergers promoted economic efficiency, benefited consumers, and were the only way to discipline badly run companies, administration officials and economists argued. Before departing for Wall Street himself, Deputy Treasury Secretary Richard Darman attacked "corpocracies" as "bloated, risk averse, inefficient and un-imaginative." Remarking that "some high-priced private managers seem to spend less time developing R and D [research and development] budgets than they spend reviewing golf scores," Darman went on to describe corporate raiders "as a new kind of populist folk hero, taking on not only big corporations but the phenomenon of corpocracy itself."

The administration backed up such statements by showing little interest in enforcing the Sherman Antitrust Act. In 1986, the Federal Trade Commission received 2,400 merger requests, twice as many as in 1981. The commission chose to challenge only six, and that was the largest number of challenges since 1979. Six others were abandoned after the agency began its initial reviews. Some Democratic members of Congress were boiling mad, but the only serious challenge to the free-market orthodoxy came from states where the attorneys general claimed the anti-competitive impacts could be felt locally. By 1987 the National Association of Attorneys General issued merger guidelines to help their members change state law and take companies to court. The Reaganites dismissed the attorneys general as ambitious politicians (their organization is sometimes called the National Association of Aspiring Governors) creating potentially inconsistent state laws that would threaten the national economy. But the attorneys general stood firm. "If the federal government is not going to enforce the law, somebody else should," said California attorney general John K. Van de Kamp. And as one attorney put it, the free-market defenders in the administration and academia seemed to have forgotten that "antitrust started off as a sort of populist reaction to perceived abuses by the trusts."

Abuses by Wall Street there were. By the late 1980s, the legal, if controversial, corporate raids had taken a back seat to revelations that some of the biggest deals had been based, not on "pure" free-market deal making, but on inside information. One of the earliest and most spectacular cases was the arrest of *Wall Street Journal* "Heard on the Street" columnist R. Foster Winans for providing advance copies of articles to his roommate David Carpenter and stockbroker Kenneth Felis. Winans was charged by the Securities and Exchange Commission with trading on misappropriated or stolen inside information. The arrest proved particularly embarrassing to the financial community's newspaper of record, which was criticized by the editors of other publications for putting a young and poorly paid staff member in such a powerful position. In his autobiography, Winans confessed that in the Wall Street of the eighties it was very annoying to realize that others were making millions off his articles while he was being paid a starting journalist's salary.

But arrests within the securities firms themselves proved even more damaging. Dennis Levine of Drexel Burnham Lambert was charged in 1986 by the Securities and Exchange Commission with making $12.6 million on insider trading. Arrested the following day for obstructing justice by attempting to destroy records, he pleaded guilty to four felony charges and agreed to pay $11.6 million to settle civil insider-trading charges. Two months later Litton Industries, Inc., sued Shearson Lehman as well as Levine for $30 million, charging that Litton had paid more than necessary in its takeover of Itek Corporation because of the insider trading. Arrests of other investment bankers and takeover lawyers followed, and so did their guilty pleas.

Wall Street pundits at first tried to dismiss insider trading as limited to a small number of overly ambitious yuppies, who weren't mature enough to handle Wall Street. Then in November 1986, Ivan Boesky, the corporate takeover artist who'd published a book extolling the benefits of risk arbitrage for the public good and intimating that he possessed special powers of stock divination, agreed to pay a $100 million fine for insider trading. Boesky was too old to be considered a yuppie, but he was still dismissed as someone outside Wall Street's traditional club.

Some on Wall Street blamed the decline in ethics on the demise of Wall Street's old clublike policies that kept investment banking in all-WASP and all-Jewish firms in which the ethical contours were governed by religious and ethnic heritage. In this rather small town atmosphere, the supposed price of ethical deviation was to be run out of town. "For all the oligarchy's snobbish exclusivity, it did promote a measure of probity and honor," wrote Myron Magnet in *Fortune*. "The recruits that investment banking has attracted to its new meritocracy truly are the talented. But what they often lack is the ethic that belonged not to the business but to the class that once ran it." Magnet could have mentioned, however, that a president of the New York Stock Exchange during the 1930s was jailed for embezzlement.

And in the winter of 1987 arrests of more senior Wall Street executives began.

The Reaganites turned a deaf ear to charges that their anti-regulatory, go-go attitudes contributed to this unhealthy situation. But clearly that is the case. In congressional testimony, Securities and Exchange Commission Chairman John S. R. Shad stated publicly that the growth in insider trading cases was due to the rash of corporate takeovers that created the opportunities for windfall profits. Post-Reagan politicians and Wall Streeters are thus left to wrestle with some of the most profound quandaries that a capitalist society can face: business ethics, corporate concentration, and the size and powers of financial institutions. But any solutions were complicated by the increasingly impersonal and international nature of the modern financial world.

The solution to insider trading seems simple. As Senate Banking Committee Chairman William Proxmire (D.-Wisconsin) has said, "Those who abuse their positions of trust should be put in the slammer." Others have suggested punishing firms by revoking or suspending broker-dealer's licenses, ending their ability to operate. But if, as SEC Chairman Shad has suggested, the increased potential for enormous profit has increased the likelihood of insider trading, then the reform movement may have to delve deeper into the executive character. One place to start was obviously in the business schools that give these young people the skills and credentials to gain such power, and it has become fashionable for executives and firms to give money to business schools to pay for ethics courses. Only a small percentage of business school students have expressed interest taking such classes, but even if they do their education may have to start earlier. I sat in on several sessions of the ethics class at the Harvard Business School a few years ago and noted that most members of the class were Jews, women, or foreign students. There were only a few of the presumably Christian, American males who make up the vast majority of business school students. When those few did participate in class discussion, they seemed remarkably unable to formulate an argument on any of these questions. Discussions of ethical behavior require an ethical framework, and I could not help but wonder if the young boys who are raised in Greenwich, Scarsdale, Short Hills, and other executive suburbs around the country had been given any moral lessons.

On the issue of corporate concentration, the question is whether there are ways to at least cut down on the number of mergers without destroying the market's ability to discipline poor management. Congress has already considered legislation to force individuals and institutions which have bought 5 percent of a company's stock to report their purchase to the Securities and Exchange Commission earlier than the 10 days currently required. Other proposals would prohibit "greenmail," tax junk bonds, and somehow make golden parachutes illegal.

This spectacle also muddied the debate over the future of both investment banking houses and commercial banks. Faced with the stiffest international competition since they began to dominate world finance during World War I, the commercial banks have been pressuring Congress to allow them to sell stocks, underwrite municipal revenue bonds, and offer other financial services—activities forbidden to the banks since the 1933 Glass-Steagall Act separated commercial banking and investment banking to prevent a repeat of conditions that had led to the 1929 stock market crash. The bankers have argued with some justification that these restrictions are keeping them from competing with banks in other countries which can offer their customers a broader range of services. As evidence, they cite the fact that several of the biggest banks in the world are now outside the United States.

The brokerage houses are fearful that the questions about their integrity will encourage Congress to permit the banks to compete with them. The investment bankers have tried to save themselves from competition by their increasing donations to political campaigns. The commercial banks' own integrity problems stem from the enormous, ill-considered loans they made to Third World countries during the early 1970s when they were awash with deposits from oil-producing countries. As Martin Mayer, author of *The Bankers*, has written of the Bank of America, "In organizations of a certain size unforeseen problems seem to become unrecognized difficulties and then unmanageable losses. Perhaps the populists (of both parties) are right, and the time has come to resume the crusade against bigness."

Ultimately the issues of both corporate structure and financial regulation seem headed for the political arena. Considering Americans' historic distrust of concentrated financial and economic power, and the anger over loss of corporate headquarters and jobs in some parts of the country, the restructuring of corporate America in the eighties has proceeded with remarkably little public outcry. Two factors softened the public's nervousness about this situation: the profits that investors made in the fantastically buoyant stock market of the eighties and the plain good luck that none of these mergers or trading scandals resulted in an economic disaster producing thousands of angry stockholders or unemployed workers. But the business world's deregulated days of delight do seem to be numbered. Americans of all economic classes and in all regions have ended up furious over the delays and increased accidents since airline deregulation. Even before the October 1987 crash, the Democrats could already smell a perfect issue if they could manage to get a handle on it. Democratic pollster Tom Kiley suggested that Democrats "are going to have to turn big businessmen into the welfare queens of the late 1980s." It won't be that simple. As in so many areas of late-twentieth-century American life, any action that we take will depend on international competition, and most other countries do not have the tradition of decentralized power that Americans revere. But with enough financial anguish and scandal, the reregulation of Wall Street and American business could be the biggest theme of American public life in the 1990s.

BIG CITIES, BIG PROBLEMS:
THE HOMELESS, THE UNDERCLASS, AND THE CORRUPT

The cities of the New York–Washington axis represent the greatest concentration of highly developed urban civilizations in the United States. They are birthplaces and centers of business and financial institutions, labor unions, universities, foundations, and cultural institutions. Yet several times in the 1980s the biggest news from these cities was of violence. In Philadelphia in 1985, police burned down an entire neighborhood and killed 11 people when they used water cannons, gunfire, and finally a bomb dropped from a helicopter to rout a black radical organization called MOVE. In New York, four blacks were shot by a white New Yorker, Bernhard Goetz, after they tried to extract money from him on a subway, and in a separate incident in the Howard Beach section of Queens, three white teenagers forced a young black man to run onto a highway where he was killed by a passing car. All three incidents revealed how strained life can become in these huge cities with their populations of every racial and ethnic group in the world. But for the average New Yorker, Philadelphian, or Newark resident who rarely encountered violence, there were still the omnipresent problems of poverty and corruption.

The homeless became a constant presence. We have all seen them homesteading on heating grates in cold weather, roosting on park benches during warmer times, sifting through trash cans looking for bottles and cans, collecting shopping carts full of old blankets, pots, and other trash. As members of Congress from rich suburbs and rural areas have learned, the homeless are now everywhere in the United States.

There are somewhere between 300,000 and three million Americans with no permanent place to live. The greatest concentration of them, as of most things American, is in the huge metropolises of the northeast. In New York City alone, some 8,300 people crowd into city shelters on particularly cold winter nights. But most of the time, they wander the streets begging for money, stretching out their hands from behind their cardboard signs reading "Homeless and Hungry." Some are old, dressed in tattered clothes—winter overcoats, crushed felt hats, checkered shirts, pants draped over red canvas and laceless high-top shoes. Some are younger, dressed in olive army jackets and jeans. Many are drunk or emotionally disturbed and terribly intimidating. Some are almost aloof, but menacing, protecting their piece of the sidewalk like a fox protecting its den.

The homeless are the urban phenomenon of the eighties, the cities' symbol of the decade just as surely as civil rights marches and inner-city riots were in the sixties. The problem is known to have started out of a very progressive concern for the mentally ill. After decades in which it was considered humane to take mentally and emotionally disturbed people out of society, social activists began to argue that too many people had been locked up against their will. With modern drugs and halfway houses, they argued, these people did not have to be institutionalized. Eventually some doctors and judges agreed, and the courts released thousands of people. The theory was that the former patients would return to their families or go to halfway houses, which would care for those not fully able to handle the world. But

there was no corresponding construction of halfway houses or arrangements for the former patients to live with dignity, and they took to
the streets. In recent years, they have been joined by poor families and
elderly people who were pushed out of apartment buildings when they
were fixed up and sold as condos to the wealthy. Public housing did
not expand to meet the need. Many of New York's homeless once
lived in the residential hotels and rooming houses that have since been
demolished in the city's renaissance. And now there is evidence that
as many as one-third of the homeless are Vietnam veterans who have
been unable to find a place in society.

The earliest defense of the homeless came from the inner-city
churches and synagogues to whom the homeless turned when the city
governments had nothing to offer them. The cause of the homeless,
in fact, proved that even in our modern welfare state these religious
institutions could be out front and play a crucial role. In New York's
Greenwich Village, for example, two church laymen started a shelter
in 1981 and out of that experience founded the Partnership for the
Homeless, which eventually attracted 12,000 volunteers from 300
churches and synagogues, operating 100 shelters throughout the city.

These activists first recognized the breadth of the homeless problem.
"You'll find every type here. We even have ministers, college professors and nurses," said the Reverend Steadman Bent, head of the
Coffee Pot Community Center, a drop-in center for the homeless at
Manhattan's First Moravian Church. "It's by the Grace of God that
you and I are not homeless. It's just a thread that separates us from
being where they are."

Even New York City, with the most proactive of city governments,
at first resisted helping the homeless. New York did spend $81 million
on shelters in 1986, but it was not until after advocates for the homeless sued to require the city to offer shelter to all who needed it. The
problems—both financial and logistical—remained enormous. New
York, used to poverty on a large scale, warehoused the homeless in
mass shelters where dozens of beds were crammed into rooms and
alcoholic or psychotic people ranted and raved. To provide a more
humane level of assistance, Congress, against all fiscal odds, passed the
1987 Stewart B. McKinney Emergency Homeless Act, providing close
to $1 billion for food, shelter, and health programs for the homeless
over a two-year period. The bill could not have been enacted without

the recognition that the homeless had become a national problem, but credit for the bill's development must go to the well-established Mid-Atlantic tradition of activist government.

The campaign to pass the national legislation was organized by Maria Foscarinis, a young New York attorney who defied the yuppie trend by leaving her $70,000 job with a Wall Street firm to open a Washington office of the New York–based National Coalition for the Homeless at a salary of $10,000 per year.* Even better known nationally was Mitch Snyder, the Washington, D.C., activist whose commitment to the homeless had inspired a television docudrama starring Martin Sheen. While Snyder and his Community for Creative Nonviolence held an outdoor vigil, Foscarinis was aided by the well-connected law firm of Covington & Burling, which donated the lobbying talents of partner Roderick A. DeArment, who had been chief of staff for former Senate Majority Leader Bob Dole. A network of social service organizations ranging from the National Mental Health Association to the National Low Income Housing Coalition and the Association of Junior Leagues pitched in with lobbying aid. President Reagan, who had maintained that the homeless were the responsibility of private philanthropy and state and local government, finally included a request for the homeless in his 1988 budget, though it was for only $100 million. Crucial Republican support on Capitol Hill came from Senator Pete Domenici of New Mexico, who is usually known as a budget cutter, but who had a long-standing interest in the mentally ill. "It's a bit of an embarrassment for those of us who know this is a very prosperous country," Domenici said. "We'd been hiding our heads in the sand under the guise of fiscal responsibility." He might have added that without the social activists between New York and Washington they still might be.

Even this assistance for the homeless found its critics, however, people who noted—perhaps correctly—that the homeless were getting disproportionate help because they were so visible. To these social critics the biggest urban issue in this country and especially in the Mid-Atlantic cities remained the huge underclass of people who seemed more deeply than ever outside the American system—such as

*I am indebted for the detailed coverage of these events to my *National Journal* colleague, Julie Kosterlitz.

long-term welfare recipients, violent street criminals, hustlers, the socially detached such as hobos and the de-institutionalized, and poor
whites from Appalachia. With federal aid to cities cut from $55.8
billion in 1979 to $25.6 billion in 1986, according to the National
League of Cities, there seemed no denying that these unorganized
people have borne the worst brunt of the Reagan ideology.

Perhaps even more disturbing was that New York, Philadelphia,
and Washington, D.C., were all ending the eighties with major City
Hall scandals. The problems were first seen in New York City when
Donald Manes, a Queens Democratic leader, committed suicide in
1986 amid charges that he had masterminded a bribery and kickback
scheme that had turned New York's parking violations bureau into
a fiefdom of corruption. The only mayor personally under investigation appeared to be Washington's Marion Barry. The other mayors
claimed to be unaware of what was happening, and there seemed to
be some truth to their contentions that their only mistake had been
unwise appointments and decisions.

"I am embarrassed, chagrined and mortified that this kind of corruption could have existed and I did not know of it," said New York's
Ed Koch as a string of his associates or appointees came under investigation and were indicted or convicted and resigned or retired to protect their pensions. The scandals that made the biggest headlines
involved Queens borough president Manes and Bess Myerson, commissioner of cultural affairs and former Miss America, who was indicted for giving a job to a judge's daughter in exchange for a
reduction in the alimony payments of Myerson's lover, Carl Capasso.
Capasso, in turn, was awarded $150 million in city sewer contracts
before he began serving a term in federal prison for income-tax eva-
sion. These celebrities were only the most famous of dozens of city
officials in trouble. So many retired under a cloud that the New York
Daily News ran a list headlined "The Check is in the Jail."

Corruption, of course, is legendary in these big eastern cities in
which politics became a way for poor—and not so poor—people to
get ahead. But there are new circumstances in the eighties, according
to John Parr, executive director of the New York–based National
Civic League, a good-government group born in the 1890s to fight the
corruption of that era. In their attempt to maintain services in the face
of federal aid cuts and union-bargained high wages for public em-

ployees, cities often contracted with private concerns to do many jobs city employees used to perform. Businesses that wanted jobs such as collecting unpaid parking tickets took to offering bribes to the city officials in charge of awarding the contracts.

Union leaders said all along that "contracting out," as this system is called, would end in corruption, but city officials were not so willing to give it up. Private contractors managed to collect millions of dollars in parking tickets in New York, Washington, and other cities, officials pointed out. Philadelphia zoo director William Donaldson, former city manager of Cincinnati and of Scottsdale, Arizona, said it would be a shame to throw the system out because contracting is the only way to get an idea of whether the city's bureaucracy is competitive.

Finally, the pro-business climate of cities and the rise of costly television-based mayoral campaigns may also have encouraged an ethically loose atmosphere. New York went full cycle from its municipal socialism and fiscal imprudence of the early seventies to pared-back budgets and a pro-business stance, offering many tax giveaways and zoning concessions.

Manhattan's boom proved the policy worked. But excessive concessions to developers were part of the package. Even the opulent Trump Tower got a tax break. Developers, real estate brokers, brokerage houses, and other special interests poured $7 million into Koch's 1985 re-election campaign. And as cities became professional economic developers, their specialists often passed through a revolving door to highly paid private-sector jobs—a transition that has been strictly legal.

Blacks and some white liberals said the Reagan administration's Justice Department was carrying out a vendetta against officials from big Democratic cities where the Republicans got few votes. That may be true, but what citizen would be angry over having the truth revealed?

The extent of municipal corruption became clear in the summer of 1987 when a sting operation led by Rudolph W. Giuliani, U.S. Attorney for the Southern District of New York, found that 105 of 106 officials in 40 towns in 15 of New York's 62 counties were willing to take bribes. The 106th official refused the bribe because it was too small! The big cities could find some consolation that the reputation for sleaze was spreading to smaller, supposedly cleaner, more conservative places, but it only made the situation more depressing for residents of the rest of New York state and raised questions in the minds of people living in the other Mid-Atlantic states.

Throughout this disgusting display, only one big city, Baltimore, showed a proud face to the nation. Baltimore—indeed the entire state of Maryland right up to former Governor and Vice-President Spiro Agnew—had a reputation for bribes and payoffs, but in the eighties remained relatively free of corruption charges. Baltimore also gained another distinction in 1987 after its mayor, William Donald Schaefer, became governor of Maryland, and Robert Embry, a former U.S. Housing and Development official and local politician, declined to run for mayor because he discerned a city-wide consensus that it was time for the 55 percent black city to elect a black mayor. In a race between two blacks, Clarence "Du" Burns, an old pol who was city council chairman, and Kurt Schmoke, a Harvard-educated city prose-cutor in his 30s, Schmoke won. Schmoke inherited a city not as shiny as its much-heralded downtown development would indicate—its eth-nic and black neighborhoods have plenty of dilapidated houses and unemployed people—but when it comes to civic leadership, no other city in the Mid-Atlantic region can beat it.

The New Northeast

In the 1920s, F. Scott Fitzgerald described Princeton, New Jersey's pre-eminent university town, as "rising, a green phoenix, out of the ugliest country in the world." If Fitzgerald were to return today, he would find even that one small trustworthy piece of America had betrayed him. The town itself remains remarkably true to its college-town traditions, its architecture and scale in keeping with its colonial heritage. But at the city's very edge begins an explosion of offices, industrial parks, and housing developments that is making Princeton and its environs leaders in a nationwide architectural and planning disaster.

Along a single, two-lane highway, U.S. Route One, eight million square feet of office space—the size of New York's World Trade Center towers—have been built in less than a decade. Such biggies as Exxon, Xerox, and Siemens have joined the Princeton office crush.

By 1992 that highway agglomeration, spread through 14 towns on a road that Barbara Boggs Sigmund, the mayor of Princeton, calls a "rinky-dink old highway," will equal downtown Milwaukee's office space; by century's end it will be the largest "city" in all of New Jersey. At rush hour, traffic along Route One slows to a crawl; sewers, schools, and police, firefighting, and other emergency services are all overburdened. Housing growth has not kept up with job growth. The prices of modest houses have risen to stratospheric levels, and those who can afford to pay the prices of new condominiums and single-family homes have taken to camping out *overnight* in front of newly opened sales offices.

Princeton has a special cachet because its university is internationally renowned, but its story was repeated up and down the Mid-Atlantic coast from New York to suburban Washington. The basic appeal to developers and corporations is always the same: access to major cities and airports (in Princeton's case, both New York City and Philadelphia), lower land costs and taxes, and the country's best educated, most highly skilled—and predominantly white—workers.

The resurgence of the Northeast in the 1980s has brought on the greatest tidal wave of suburban development since the post–World War II migration out of the cities. While generous federal programs to house World War II veterans helped propel that first suburban movement, this time housing is only a small part of the picture. In the eighties businesses—from high-tech manufacturers to Wall Street brokerage houses—have led the charge. The suburbs are being transformed from bedrooms to boardrooms, from grassy refuges to roaring traffic arteries. Huge office and industrial complexes are sprouting up along the super-roads and local highways that circle and radiate far out from our great cities. This evolution has dramatically transformed the feel, the shape, and the look of the New York, Philadelphia, Wilmington, Baltimore, and Washington metropolitan areas, all but remaking economic and political balances of power between central cities and suburbs in less than a decade.

Amidst the greatest Manhattan building boom in history, there are signs aplenty the suburban phenomenon is overtaking even New York City. The city's share of office space in the metropolitan area slipped from 75 percent in 1982 to 60 percent in 1986. While every Midtown street corner seemed to sport a new construction site or office tower, three times as much office space was taking shape in the New York suburbs. Sometime in the 1990s, the amount of office space in the North Jersey suburbs—places as disparate as Morristown, Paramus, and Secaucus—will surpass the total office space in midtown Manhattan.

Similar super-concentrations of homes and offices are sprouting on the sod fields, potato farms, and wooded areas of Pennsylvania, Maryland, and the counties of northern Virginia outside Washington, D.C. These are the new extensions of Mid-Atlantic urban America. The metropolitan Philadelphia economy, according to recent studies, is no longer driven by center city businesses, but by "superburbs" such as King of Prussia and former villages such as Blue Bell. Along Washington's 66-mile-long Beltway, the first half of the decade brought $832 million worth of commercial construction as major American corporations gravitated to the city's outskirts hoping to capture a slice of the federal contracting pie. Were the Washington Beltway a city, its commercial construction would rank alongside the totals for Milwaukee, Birmingham, Baton Rouge, and Honolulu combined. More than 60 percent of the work force that lives in Montgomery County, Maryland, now works in the county, never commuting to Capitol Hill or Pennsylvania Avenue.

Not by accident have offices and industries moved to occupy once tranquil suburbia. As the U.S. economy moves from manufacturing to service and management-oriented activity, the green spaces of suburbia, often only minutes from major metropolises, have become the ideal home to the engines of the "information age." The suburbs are where the most skilled American workers—from fast-moving high techers to highly educated housewives—live. Rapid advances in telecommunications have made far-flung corporate outposts practical. "We have come to an era in which technology is allowing firms like ours to make the most cost-effective real-estate choices," says Michael Woodford, a Merrill Lynch vice-president who is directing the financial services firm's moves to two New Jersey locations.

King of Prussia, which started out in the 1950s as a lonely corporate outpost for General Electric, is a good example of the other type of growth that is transforming Mid-Atlantic America: the massive office-hotel-shopping center complex. These megacenters, or "urban villages"—to use a friendlier phrase—are places where "people can work, live, shop and play in close proximity, thereby enjoying many advantages of urban density but avoiding its high costs and problems," according to Los Angeles–based consultant Christopher Leinberger. Most incorporate huge office buildings, shopping centers, hotels, restaurants, bars, and movie theaters—everything you could hope for, say the developers—all in one package.

King of Prussia is part of the belt of high-tech-driven hot growth on suburban Route 202 that threatens to remake the verdant, rolling hills of rural Chester County into nonstop industrial-office-strip development. Today, boasts a developer responsible for some of the area's biggest projects, "Philadelphia has more to gain by being linked [to such suburban agglomerations as King of Prussia] than the suburbs gain by being linked to Philadelphia." There's more than boosterism to such claims. By the end of the decade, sales at the sprawling shopping malls that form King of Prussia's "downtown" will eclipse those in downtown Philadelphia. Traffic surveys have found more rush-hour commuters headed for King of Prussia and Route 202 in the morning—and, creating, of course, heavier traffic congestion—than traveling towards downtown.

Urban advocates view the suburban workplace boom with alarm. They see it as a movement for and by the affluent, resegregating America, as jobs and opportunity move farther and farther from inner cities, away from the minorities who lack either the transportation or the money to make it to the new work sites. Throughout the Mid Atlantic, study upon study substantiates that the region's poorest people can neither afford transportation nor commute for hours to take minimum wage jobs located in the new suburban prosperity. From 1967 to 1982, employment in the booming Washington, D.C., metro area grew by just over one-third. The beneficiaries of the growth were by and large the residents of three suburban counties—Maryland's Montgomery and Prince Georges and Virginia's Fairfax— which together accounted for more than 80 percent of the job gains. With suburban counties reporting unemployment rates among the nation's very lowest, the District of Columbia's jobless rate remained stuck near 10 percent.

Those serious societal consequences aside, the growth wave has precipitated a revolt among the suburbanites themselves, who are wondering what is happening to the quiet havens they treasure as a respite from the city and the working world. Up and down the East Coast, candidates for city and county government started running on antigrowth or slow-growth platforms, major newspapers featured front-page series detailing the discontent, and even some politicians who championed growth were worried that their communities would choke on the traffic and congestion.

The issue has become bipartisan. Princeton mayor Sigmund, a Democrat and the politically skilled daughter of Louisiana representative Lindy Boggs, sued other municipalities in the Princeton corridor to stop approvals for projects that could affect the way of life in neighboring communities. She was joined in the suit by Bill Mathesius, the elected Republican Mercer County executive, on the grounds that the county had the authority to intervene when one community takes action that has a negative impact on another community. Princeton and Mercer County lost in the lower New Jersey courts, but Sigmund and Mathesius won many followers in their quest for a moratorium on building permits while officials draw up an inventory of infrastructure needs.

Poor architectural quality is not so much an issue as it was in the fifties and sixties when soulless glass and concrete shells ruled the day. As construction has moved to the suburbs, so have the finest design firms, creating postmodernist corporate headquarters with magnificent landscaping. But the designers still must conform to suburban zoning and architectural principles that are relatively unchanged since the suburbs were built as strictly controlled residential communities. And developers must surround the new buildings with vast seas of parking, which is only the ugliest symptom of the real horror of suburban life in the eighties: traffic. Even the simplest excursion from one of these buildings to another requires a lengthy automotive ordeal.

Massive traffic gridlocks, former U.S. transportation official C. Kenneth Orski predicted, "will be the major suburban issue of the late '80s and the '90s, displacing housing, crime or air pollution." Gone is the temporary respite from ever-expanding auto use provided by the energy crises of the seventies. Many highway corridors that flowed smoothly in 1980 are now hopelessly clogged. "Getting stuck in traffic jams, once the dubious privilege of the downtown commuter, now affects everyone," said Orski.

Suburban governments do not seem up to the challenge of guiding and controlling this explosion. There has been little, if any, constituency for serious long-term planning, and few localities have put serious dollars into it. Mid-Atlantic suburbanites often distrust their local councils, and not without reason, because developers contribute the biggest campaign dollars. The confusing tangle of small suburban governments just makes things worse. Only a handful of counties have proven that they are serious about future planning.

Sometimes what localities actually do makes things worse. Local zoning often requires more square feet for a worker's parking place than for his work location. It is a prime reason, noted Leinberger, "for these huge, inhuman parking lots out in suburbia" that contribute to abysmal site design and for the solo auto culture in which people drive instead of walk from office to shop to restaurant.

Suburban citizen groups are hardly innocent either. Witnessing concentrated development in a suburban center, they blame it for the road congestion and fight to "downzone"—to permit less and less concentrated building. But it is self-defeating for citizens to fight dense development centers, said Thomas Black of the Urban Land Institute: the alternative is spread-out development, which simply intensifies automobile use and precludes the use of mass transit that might relieve the jamups.

Sadly, where there is room for state leadership in making growth control a matter of law, no Mid-Atlantic state has evolved as far as Oregon and Florida, which have passed tough statewide growth guidelines. None have followed the lead of Massachusetts in making it a matter of official state policy to steer new businesses and offices away from super-heated corridors and towards inner-city neighborhoods and depressed towns. Some local governments in the region are showing signs of having the political willpower to take steps to try and put the lid on sprawl or megacenters before it's too late.

The suburban growth explosion is physical proof of the Mid-Atlantic region's reassured prosperity. Some expansion in these suburbs was probably inevitable to accommodate economic growth and to house the now-adult baby-boom generation. But the uncritical, anarchic, and mindless fashion in which it is now proceeding is a reminder of a previous experiment in American land development: urban renewal. Across the nation, tens of thousands of historic buildings were torn down before the famed little old ladies in tennis shoes threw themselves in front of bulldozers to gain public attention to the problem. Slowly, but surely, the recognition is dawning that this growth is equally destructive and must be managed. The only real question is how.

The Larger Picture

The eighties have reaffirmed the Mid Atlantic as the most prosperous, stable, and diversified region in the country, but that did not mean these states sailed blithely through the decade. As they have through most of the twentieth century, the Mid-Atlantic states continued to watch the South and West diversify and offer products and services that once could be obtained only from the East. While the region retained its pre-eminence as the national center of business decision making, the Mid-Atlantic states did lose *Fortune* 500 corporate headquarters, as they have for several decades. Small business thrived, a sure sign of economic regeneration, but this development also produced its own chaos since small firms do not offer the same employment stability and high benefits of old, established companies. And while the central cities did better in economic development than in the sixties and seventies, the majority of the new businesses grew up in the suburbs. Big corporations, meanwhile, continued to move their headquarters to suburban locations.

New York was the first of the Mid-Atlantic states to go through the economic transition from manufacturing to finance and high tech. Partial credit must go to Hugh L. Carey, the Democrat elected to two terms as governor starting in 1974. When Carey took office, both New York City and the state were headed toward a financial abyss, the city through its well-publicized near-bankruptcy, the state through the borrowing it had undertaken to finance the public generosity of four-term Governor Nelson A. Rockefeller, Carey's Republican predecessor. Carey decreed strict state guidance and fiscal control for teetering New York City as well as Yonkers and Buffalo. Budget cuts were made across virtually all state programs. With spending reined in, Carey cut taxes to stimulate the state economy. New York reduced its maximum personal income tax from 15 to 10 percent and eliminated various business taxes. It also enacted the nation's most generous investment tax credit—up to 15 percent on business equipment, with the biggest benefits reserved for new businesses adding employees and for research and development firms. Start-up businesses, waiting for their first profits, could even get cash refunds for the investment tax credits due them. The plan worked despite the fact that, even after reductions, New York's state and local taxes remained the country's highest. Governor Mario Cuomo, Carey's Democratic successor, continued the pattern by again cutting business taxes and promoting business more than most liberals realized.

While New York City's Manhattan Island was booming, so were the high-tech, defense-laden suburbs from Long Island, home of Grumman Aircraft, up through Westchester County north of the city. The boom also leapt to Rochester, home of Eastman Kodak. Cuomo's little publicized fight for Fort Drum in depressed upstate New York demonstrates, however, the Mid-Atlantic's soft underbelly: the arc from Buffalo through western Pennsylvania that resembles the industrially troubled Great Lakes more than the power centers along the Atlantic Ocean. In 1984, when the Army decided to create a new division, Cuomo pulled out all the stops to win this military plum for New York. The stakes were high. The economic fallout from the new 10,000-soldier-strong 10th Light Infantry Division amounted to more than $400 million annually, providing several thousand new jobs and at least $1 billion in new construction. In an uncharacteristic move for a politician, Cuomo came to Washington for an unpublicized meeting with Army Secretary John O. Marsh, Jr., and promised to smooth over personally any obstacles the Army might encounter. In their talk, Cuomo used the usual Northeast argument that the region does not get its fair share of military bases, but dwelled also on the Army's historic roots at the U.S. Military Academy at West Point, N.Y. "Marsh was surprised to hear that from what he perceived as a liberal governor," said Brad C. Johnson, director of the state of New York's Washington lobbying office. But the effort worked, and New York beat out Alaska, California, Georgia, Kentucky, New Jersey, Virginia, and Washington even though the construction and other development costs of the base in New York were higher than in other states.

Pennsylvania continued to be the most troubled Mid-Atlantic state, but there was actually a lot of economic success in the state in the eightics. Its rarely noted cluster of high-tech and growth-oriented industries along Route 202 in Chester and Montgomery Counties near Philadelphia finally came into their own. After a survey of 46 such medical-service, computer, robotics, and biotechnology firms in the Delaware Valley revealed that only a minuscule amount of their venture capital came from rich Philadelphians, city and state civic leaders began to break out of their lethargy. Under Republican governor Dick L. Thornburgh, Pennsylvania started a "Ben Franklin Partnership" with business to encourage advanced technology centers focusing on transferring high-tech innovations in the universities to steel, coal, and other existing industries. But an indication of the state's strong partisanship was the decision of Thornburgh's successor, Democratic governor Robert Casey, to declare the Franklin partnership unsuccessful and start his own.

Pittsburgh has received much publicity for its growing number of yuppie jobs in companies such as PPG Industries, the now-diversified glass giant which had Philip Johnson and John Burgee design a cathedral-like glass headquarters in the early 1980s during a downtown Pittsburgh building boom. Yuppie jobs there are in Pittsburgh, but not enough to make up for western Pennsylvania's loss of jobs in the steel industry or those lost by the merger of corporate headquarters. During the eighties, Pittsburgh suffered a severe loss of corporate headquarters, down from 19 in 1983 to 14 in 1987. Pennsylvania, it must be concluded, did better than most states in the 1980s, with a per capita income of $13,944, 96 percent of the national average and 21st among the states. But its population, which was 11,865,000 in 1980, grew to only 11,889,000 in 1986, a sure sign that hundreds of thousands of talented young Pennsylvanians were looking for jobs elsewhere.

Tiny Delaware, by contrast, was the only one of the Mid-Atlantic states to grow faster than the national average, its population rising in the eighties from 594,000 to 633,000 or 6.5 percent. Delaware has been undergoing an economic resurgence and diversification from chemicals, auto parts, and agriculture. In 1980 it capitalized on eastern banks' distress about state interest rate ceilings in New York and other states by eliminating its ceiling and allowing banks to charge market-level fees on credit cards. As people all over the country know from the credit card applications they receive in the mail, banks from New York, Pennsylvania, and Maryland and eventually other states established operations in Delaware. The banks, by law, were required to create at least 100 jobs per institution. Business was also helped by tax cuts urged by former Governor Pierre S. (Pete) du Pont after it became clear that the state some still call a feudal empire of the du Ponts had developed an anti-business reputation.

Maryland, straddling the old industrial North and the Sunbelt, also boomed in the eighties. As in other places, Baltimore's heavy industries—steel production, automobile manufacturing, and ship repairing—were hit very hard in the recession of the early eighties, but Bethlehem Steel and General Motors both modernized their plants and the city was sustained by its harbor, one of the busiest in the United States. Downtown Baltimore was revived by the popular Inner Harbor development, including the National Aquarium and Harborplace, a highly successful festival market place filled with tourist shops and restaurants. The Reagan administration's cutbacks in federal domestic spending and opposition to salary increases for federal government employees might have been expected to hurt Maryland (and Marylanders certainly were, in individual cases), but Maryland also has its own high-tech industries and ranks 15th in defense spending so it seems to benefit whether the government is spending money on people or on weapons.

Washington, D.C., with its special status as the nation's capital and its special semiautonomous government, continued to thrive as more and more office buildings went up. Washington is indeed an odd place. Its per capita income is higher than any state ($18,900, more than $4,000 above the national average). Seventy percent of the city's population is black, a combination of one of the largest black middle classes in the country and others living in abject poverty. But as market analysts frequently point out, the rich are hard to find in Washington since the income figures depend on federal salaries, which are never very low, but never reach the stratosphere of Wall Street either. This may be changing. The Washington metropolitan area is now so popular as a site for corporate headquarters and so many people work outside the government that economists have pointed out the region is no longer protected from national business cycles.

Politics State by State

It is not possible to speak of Mid-Atlantic politics in the same way that one thinks of Southern, Mountain, or even New England regional politics. These populous and powerful states have enjoyed such prominence that they have spent most of their histories competing with each other rather than worrying about competing with other parts of the country. In politics too, each Mid-Atlantic state goes its own way.

The prominent Mid-Atlantic states remain prizes for every presidential candidate, and political consultants say that no Democrat could win the White House today without New York, Pennsylvania, and Maryland. But the stagnation of the Mid-Atlantic's population growth is most visible in the decreasing size of its U.S. House delegation. The Mid-Atlantic states lost eight seats after the post–1980 census redistricting. The delegation is still huge—80 members (47 Democrats, 33 Republicans in the 1987–88 Congress) from the five states plus the nonvoting delegate from the District of Columbia—but New York and Pennsylvania are expected to lose two seats each after the 1990 census.

City machines, some Republican, but most Democratic, once dominated the politics of these very urban industrial states but as the central cities have lost population and the suburbs have gained, all these states except Maryland have become competitive for both parties. Every Mid-Atlantic state's roster of statewide leaders and House members is a combination of Republicans and Democrats. And as hard as it has been for the old timers to accept, California-inspired media politics are now just as important here as anywhere else in the country. In fact, every candidate's most pressing problem is to raise enough money to buy television commercial time in some of the most expensive media markets in the country.

New York, long considered a bastion of liberal Republican and Democratic politics, still has a Democratic governor, Mario Cuomo, and Democratic senator Daniel Patrick Moynihan, but only 20 of its 34 members of Congress are Democrats, and its other senator is Alfonse D'Amato, a conservative Republican elected on the 1980 Reagan bandwagon. In typical New York fashion, however, D'Amato comes out of Long Island patronage politics, and he has shown an unusual interest in getting federal grants for New York state.

New Jersey is represented by two Democratic senators, Bill Bradley and Frank Lautenberg, but its very popular governor is Republican Thomas Kean, and six of its 14 House members are Republicans. Pennsylvania, traditionally the most Republican of the Mid-Atlantic states, still has two Republican senators, John Heinz and Arlen Specter, but while the Republicans were gaining governorships in many other states, they lost Pennsylvania in 1986 when Dick Thornburgh retired, and Pennsylvanians chose Democrat Robert Casey over Lieutenant Governor William Scranton, the son of a former governor.

Maryland remains the most Democratic of the Mid-Atlantic states, with a Democratic governor, former Baltimore Mayor William Donald Schaefer and six Democratic members of Congress to two Republicans. The Maryland delegation became even more Democratic in 1986 when its liberal Republican senator Charles Mathias retired, and Marylanders chose Baltimore Democratic representative Barbara Mikulski to join Democrat Paul Sarbanes in the Senate.

As the Reagan era came to a close, Delaware's statewide offices were evenly split between Democrats and Republicans. In the Senate were Republican William V. Roth, Jr., and Democrat Joseph R. Biden, Jr. In the U.S. House, the state's sole statewide representative was Democrat Thomas R. Carper, and in the governor's mansion was Republican Michael N. Castle who had been lieutenant governor under Pierre S. du Pont.

In Washington, the Mid-Atlantic delegation holds remarkably little committee power compared with its other frequent displays of domination over the rest of American society. Only two Mid-Atlantic Republicans had enough seniority to win committee chairmanships—and they were relatively minor ones—when the GOP took control of the Senate in 1980: Roth on Governmental Affairs and Mathias on Rules and Administration. When the Democrats came back into power, Biden took over as chairman of the Judiciary Committee, but none of the others had enough seniority to win a position. On the House side, Peter W. Rodino of New Jersey, who first gained fame in the Watergate era, remained chairman of the Judiciary Committee while James J. Howard of New Jersey presided over Public Works and Transportation and John J. LaFalce of New York took over Small

Business. But the most powerful congressman from the Mid-Atlantic region during the eighties was William H. Gray III, the Philadelphia Democrat who rose to chair the House Budget Committee. The Budget Committee chairmanship is rotated so Gray's power is not permanent like the other chairmen, but he has proved that a black politician can run a major committee and command the respect of the other members.

Presidential Contenders and Other Politicians of Stature

It has been a long time since the Mid-Atlantic produced an American president. The last Mid-Atlantic vice-president was former New York governor Nelson A. Rockefeller, appointed by Gerald Ford in the wake of Watergate and abandoned when Ford sought election in his own right and the conservatives in the Republican party objected to Rockefeller's liberalism.

As the South and West continue to grow and the nation seems to trust candidates with a more middle or western American experience, the Mid-Atlantic still keeps trying to produce a winning candidate. For 1988, each party has produced two candidates—the Republicans former Delaware governor Pierre S. (Pete) du Pont and New York representative Jack Kemp and the Democrats Delaware senator Joseph R. Biden, Jr. and New York governor Mario Cuomo. Both Cuomo and Biden bowed out of the race early in the campaign season, though for very different reasons.

Cuomo has been the great mysterious hope of the Democratic party ever since his riveting speech before the 1984 Democratic convention in San Francisco, where he eloquently defended the party's commitment to using government to improve the lives of common people. Democratic liberals and minorities felt they had found their voice of the eighties. Activists and the press, already resigned to a Mondale defeat in 1984, quickly began talking of Cuomo as a candidate in 1988 and were sorely disappointed in early 1987 when he casually announced on a radio call-in program that he would not be a candidate this time around. His announcement came before Gary Hart's departure from the race, and journalists, faced with a set of little-known candidates they called "the seven dwarfs," hounded Cuomo until he reiterated that he would not rule out being drafted by a divided convention to be the party's candidate.

There are many accomplishments in the Cuomo record: a start in politics as the successful mediator between advocates and opponents of a low-income housing project in the middle-income Forest Hills section of the New York City borough of Queens; a leading role in keeping state and local taxes deductible during the tax-reform movement of the eighties; the achievement of raising New York's drinking age from 18 to 21 to combat teenage auto fatalities; principled judicial appointments; and unusual sensitivity, for a liberal, to the need for business growth and a tax structure to encourage it. Cuomo said he was unwilling to run for president because there were already good candidates in the field. Some political observers have noted that Cuomo has responded in prickly fashion to comments about his Italian-American background—at one point he even said that the Mafia does not exist—and they believe he may not wish to go through the agony experienced by former New York representative and 1984 Democratic vice-presidential candidate Geraldine Ferraro and her husband John Zaccaro over their finances and business dealings.

Cuomo's oratorical abilities and governmental accomplishments are unquestioned, but there is ample evidence that Cuomo still has some broadening to do before he seeks national office. Liberals liked it when Cuomo told the Catholic hierarchy that Catholic politicians in a pluralistic society had to consider more than church positions on abortion and gay rights. But his degree of involvement in the internal issues of his church created an image of a man who was highly principled, but dangerously parochial for a politician with national aspirations. When Cuomo visited Hispanics in San Antonio, Texas, for example, his foray out of New York was hailed as the eighties equivalent of John Kennedy's coming to Texas during his presidential campaign. Kennedy's mission, everyone seemed to forget, had been to reach out to Baptists. Perhaps most troubling was the frequency with which New Yorkers would declare that up close they were not impressed with Cuomo or his reliance on his son as an aide above all others. As one college administrator who had lobbied the governor's office told me, "Cuomo is more interested in politics and philosophy than policy."

Cuomo's departure from the 1988 race heightened the position of Delaware's Biden, who declared his intentions to run in mid-1987. Biden had been a boy wonder of national politics since he won a Senate seat in 1972 at age 29. Two facts about Biden were best known: his wife and daughter died in an auto accident right after the election, and as a senator he made it a policy to take the train home every night to be with his children and (with remarriage) his second wife. Biden was hoping that the hearings on the nomination of Robert H. Bork to the Supreme Court would catapult him to the head of the pack, but his campaign came to an abrupt halt when videotapes (supplied by John Sasso, campaign manager for Governor Michael Dukakis of Massachusetts) revealed that Biden had adopted British Labor Party leader Neil Kinnock's speeches practically verbatim. The "attack video" snafu resulted in revelations that Biden had misled people about his law school record and other matters, and he dropped out of the race. Biden promised to return to presidential politics one day, but even if he can get over the character issue, his theories about the future of American politics are questionable. In his campaign, he contended that the baby-boom generation (of which he, born in 1942, is technically four years too old to be a part) was looking for a Kennedy-style mandate to "Ask what you can do for your country." But Kennedy had asked the question at a time when the baby boomers had youth to give, not children to raise and homes to finance.

On the Republican side, the story of Representative Jack Kemp of New York is one of the most fascinating in American politics today. Kemp grew up in California, first came to Buffalo as a football player for the Buffalo Bills, and stayed on to be elected to Congress in 1970 from a district that is now totally suburban. As he viewed the serious economic problems in his district, Kemp came to believe that productive people—business owners who created jobs—were being taxed too much and he promoted "supply-side economics," which contended that reducing taxes would improve the economy. He became a leader of the tax cut and reform movements which led to the 1986 Tax Reform Act.

On the surface, Kemp looks like the perfect example of the conservatism that has arisen within the New York Republican party since the death of Nelson Rockefeller, whose liberalism and money dominated it for a generation. But Kemp is not as worried about the deficit or opposed to government programs as it would appear, and even supports unions, affirmative action, and sanctions against South Africa while opposing cuts in social security. He also sponsored a bill to establish urban enterprise zones, a plan to encourage business in the worst areas of cities around the country by reducing or eliminating taxes there. Enterprise zones were derided by liberals as ineffective, but for conservatives they marked an unprecedented signal of interest in the problems of the poor. Kemp does support a return to the gold standard, which conservatives love, but that was not enough to keep his 1988 campaign for the presidency on the fast track. Kemp has been unapologetic in his stands. "To bash government as the sole cause of all our problems is to lose sight of the fact that some people look to government to help them," he said. With positions like that Kemp may sound too much like an old-fashioned conservative Democrat to get a Republican presidential nomination, but he seems destined to remain an influential thinker within his own party.

The long shot for the Republican nomination in 1988 was Delaware's du Pont. A member of the family whose chemical company dominates the state, du Pont developed a reputation as a moderate mainstream Republican both in the U.S. House of Representatives and in his eight years as governor. Under his direction, Delaware modernized and cut its taxes and enjoyed good economic times. But as a presidential candidate, du Pont has chosen to play the intellectual gadfly, coming up with radical changes in social security, welfare, and farm programs. All were interesting to conservative intellectuals, but seemed like political death in presidential primaries.

A roundup of Mid-Atlantic politicians would be incorrectly skewed if the entire focus were on those with presidential inclinations. Three of the most interesting senators in the Mid-Atlantic region are not among the presidential contenders: New York's Daniel Patrick Moynihan, New Jersey's Bill Bradley, and Maryland's Barbara Mikulski.

Moynihan has the résumé of a George Bush—Harvard professor, aide to Averill Harriman when he was governor of New York, assistant secretary of Labor under Kennedy and Johnson, chief domestic advisor and ambassador to India under Nixon, and ambassador to the United Nations under Ford—with Irish-American, Oklahoma roots. Moynihan is the most forward-thinking and courageous politician in America today. It was Moynihan who was warning, back in the Nixon presidency, of the repercussions of the breakup of black families and the possible role the welfare system played in that development. He was shunned by both blacks and liberals at the time, but they have come to recognize his wisdom in raising the issue. In the late eighties, charging that while the United States had largely dealt with the problem of poverty among the elderly, it was still doing far too little for poor children, Moynihan led a battle for welfare reform. As U.N. ambassador, he also refused to sit back quietly as Third World countries criticized the United States and voted with the Soviet Union. Moynihan has long been identified with the conservative Democratic foreign-policy camp and has been a supporter of tuition tax credits for school children, but he resisted invitations to join the neoconservative jump to the Republican ship.

Among Washington economists and political thinkers, Rhodes scholar and onetime basketball player for the New York Knicks, Senator Bill Bradley of New Jersey, is a hero. As a Democratic senator, he managed to move beyond traditional party thinking but avoid falling into the Reagan camp in developing the 1986 Tax Reform Act. Bradley first displayed his interest in taking a fresh look at tax policy by voting for Reagan's budget cuts but against his tax cuts. It was Bradley who decided that reducing the 11 tax brackets to 3, eliminating most deductions, and cutting rates was the way to reform the tax system. Bradley's intellectual and political leadership are so revered that he has been promoted as a presidential candidate. If the new tax code proves popular, Bradley's hero status could extend beyond the intellectual community. But if Bradley really has presidential ambitions, he will have to find issues more exciting to the average American than the confusing and annoying issue of tax policy.

Maryland's Barbara Mikulski, elected to the Senate in 1986, has yet to prove herself as a serious player in the world's most exclusive debating society, but her election itself is as inspiring a tale as one will find in American politics of this or any other generation. Polish-American in origin, the daughter of a bakery owner, and a social worker by profession, Mikulski had started out in Baltimore politics opposing a highway, winning a seat on the city council, and winning a respectable 43 percent of the vote against veteran Charles Mathias in a 1974 Senate race before winning a House seat in 1976. While in the House, Mikulski developed a reputation as a loud, angry, impatient woman; associates said her style was rooted in her 4'11" height and her lifelong need to fight to be seen. Many of her colleagues saw Mikulski as the embodiment of the ethnic politician most concerned with what government benefits she could bring to her district. Mikulski did spend a considerable amount of time on district issues, but in fact since her opposition to highway construction she had been bucking the system rather than supporting it. A Roman Catholic from a Catholic district, she took a pro-choice stand on abortion and also developed an interest in foreign policy.

When Mikulski announced she would run for the Senate in 1986, many people thought she was foolish since she had to oppose fellow Democrats Michael Barnes, the highly regarded congressman from the Washington, D.C., suburbs, and Governor Harry Hughes. The Washington intellectuals and other people with a national perspective went for Barnes, and the Democratic money men divided between Barnes and Hughes. But Mikulski turned out to be the most modern politician of the lot. Her public-opinion polls showed that Hughes had been hurt by a savings and loan scandal in which people could not gain access to their money, and that Baltimore—the state's most populous area—knew little of Barnes. Mikulski took her polls to unions and Democratic fatcats, and eventually they were convinced they should go with a winner. The money was used to finance a series of superb television commercials which depicted the 50-year-old Mikulski as both concerned about the future of Maryland's baby boomers and knowledgeable about foreign policy since polls showed that suburban voters were worried about an ethnic woman politician on both those issues. Mikulski won the primary, and in the general election defeated Linda Chavez, a union activist turned Reagan White House aide and affirmative action opponent, who had moved into Maryland to oppose Mikulski.

In the campaign, Mikulski appeared on television wearing pearls and acting like a lady in the best sense of that word. In the Senate, Mikulski surprised her peers with her new relaxed demeanor—some said she had finally risen to the status to which she thought she was entitled—but her male colleagues appeared less mature. In the winter of 1987, word leaked out that Senator Pete Domenici of New Mexico, described by the *Washington Post* as "normally a bland Republican," got up to deliver the speech of a presidential candidate at the annual party of an all-male institution of politicians and big businessmen called the Alfalfa Club. "I'm blessed with the talent of . . . whipping the electorate to a frenzy." Domenici proclaimed. "Just like the singer Tom Jones, women often throw their panties at me when I speak. It happened again just yesterday. I just don't know what got into Senator Mikulski." Months later Mikulski admitted, "I was livid. Livid." But at the time, Mikulski had followed her best political instincts and got the last word. "I think it's outrageous and I find it insulting," she said. "I have other responses, but that's the one for public dissemination."

Glory Days: New Jersey in the Eighties

While riding high in the 1984 primary season, Gary Hart made the first major blunder of his political career in New Jersey. Why, he asked, was he campaigning amidst toxic waste dumps while his wife was in Beverly Hills?

New Jerseyans turned down Hart's 1984 bid, teaching him what people from other Mid-Atlantic states had learned: that New Jersey, the state which had always lived in the shadows between New York and Pennsylvania, was finally coming into its own, and that its people were gaining a pride and self-confidence they had never known before.

In the eighties, every Mid-Atlantic state prospered, but it was New Jersey that shone above the rest. Not all of the New Jersey story is positive. The New Jersey suburbs experienced so much growth that their way of life was threatened. The rejuvenation of Atlantic City through casino gambling was far from a complete transformation.*

---

*The "success" of Atlantic City's casino gambling appears to be as filled with smoke and mirrors as the casinos themselves. The popularity of gambling in the tired old boardwalk city so close to the population centers of the East cannot be denied. In less than six years after its approval by voters in 1976, Atlantic City was attracting twice as many visitors as Las Vegas, Nevada. Atlantic City has had a massive increase in taxable property wealth. The casinos have paid more than $35 million per year in property taxes to the city, and more than $100 million in a gross winnings tax to the state government.

New Jersey's biggest city, Newark, saw signs of hope while the overall picture looked dreary. But overriding all these problems was the prosperous, increasingly independent economy and high-quality political leadership. For the first time since the American Revolution, New Jersey has achieved a stature of its own.

Bruce Springsteen's haunting odes on the demise of working-class life were the first signal that there is more to New Jersey than boring suburbs and polluting industry. In 1981, the state elected a Republican governor, Thomas Kean, and in the process got itself a new image. Up and down the East Coast, Americans saw television travel commercials of a New Jersey they had forgotten—or never knew—existed. "New Jersey and You—Perfect Together," the ads said.

While Springsteen's lament was true, New Jersey was moving fast into the high-tech and professional economy. In the eighties, New Jersey saw its per capita income climb to the nation's second highest and its unemployment rate fall to the second lowest among all industrial states (only Massachusetts had a lower rate of joblessness in 1987). The state added more than a million jobs between 1970 and 1987, and state planners expected that by 2010, New Jersey would gain 212 million square feet of office space plus another 750,000 jobs. The development wave has become so intense that along the shore of the Hudson River, old industrial towns such as Jersey City and Hoboken are being transformed into back-office and residential havens for Manhattan. Why? New Jersey's large service industries, stable pharmaceutical companies, growing high-technology and telecommunications sector, and—one must add—defense contractors were the growth industries of the eighties. New Jersey's largest employer is American Telephone & Telegraph Company, and even after the divestiture of its regional companies, its Jersey employment rolls expanded because of the continued presence of Bell's long-distance

---

But the price paid for those "gains" has been very real. Instead of the housing and community development promised when gambling was approved, a "hurricane of land speculation" forced many of Atlantic City's poor and elderly to move, according to "Atlantic City Gamble," a major independent study by Rutgers University professors George Sternlieb and James Hughes. Many renters saw their homes burned, allegedly by landlords hoping to profit from the rampant speculation, Sternlieb and Hughes wrote. And, of course, gambling brought with it a prodigious increase in the crime rate and in prostitution, and encouraged a significant Mafia presence eager to lay its hands on the vast amounts of cash that change hands. But perhaps most troubling, the authors found that Atlantic City's new prosperity was a sitting duck for competition from any other East Coast city that got its state legislature to allow gambling.

operations and Bell Laboratories. More importantly, New Jersey seems to offer the keys to corporate America's future: an educated population, plenty of space, and nearness to two real metropolises—New York and Philadelphia—and their airports.

Kean's election was the shock of at least the quarter-century. The Democrats had held the office for 24 of the past 28 years, and Governor Brendan Byrne had won praise for the first serious efforts in cleaning up the state's reputation for corruption dating from Prohibition days. Kean, a bonafide aristocrat whose family was prominent before the Revolution, won by only 1,700 votes. Kean did not turn out to be a Reagan conservative. Instead, he acted like a classic northeastern liberal Republican; he defended capitalism and cut taxes, but also signed a law establishing a low and moderate income housing obligation for every municipality in the state. Kean went out of his way to build ties with the black community. Under his leadership, New Jersey became the first state in the nation to divest itself of holdings in South Africa. But Kean's greatest surprise was changing state educational policy: to take over from localities schools with poor educational records and replace school boards, superintendents, and other key administrators. In the 1985 election, Kean had picked off so many Democratic issues that he won 43 percent of registered Democrats, two-thirds of all union households, and an astounding 60 percent of the black vote. He won 70 percent of the total vote, and talk began of a vice-presidential spot on the Republican ticket.

While the state prospered Kean still had plenty of urban problems to address. A 1987 tally by Rutgers University's Center for Urban Policy Research found close to half of the Garden State's jobs are now located in just nine suburban growth corridors. Newark and Jersey's other older cities faced, by contrast, a decimated job base. Camden, Elizabeth, Jersey City, Newark, Paterson, and Trenton have lost one-fourth of their jobs in two decades. In 1967, Newark had 200,000 jobs, about 74,000 of them industrial; by 1981, the figure had dwindled to 126,600. Manufacturing employment fell to 37,000.

"We can't live as a state where three-quarters are doing well and the other one-quarter are not," Kean said. "If we can solve our urban problems then the future is totally bright. If we can't, then those problems will creep out to people who think they've gotten away from them." Asked what New Jersey was actually doing for its troubled cities, Kean quickly cites the list of Garden State programs: an urban enterprise zone program that has yielded $312 million in investments and 5,000 jobs in Newark alone; a Local Development Financing Fund that makes low-interest business loans; targeting of industrial development bonds to cities; an Urban Development Corporation capitalized with $30 million; for-profit neighborhood development corporations, with neighborhood residents as shareholders, that will receive state financing for development projects.

Kean has supported an alternative to New Jersey's Mt. Laurel court decision, which requires wealthy suburbs to build low-income housing. The new policy allows suburbs to trade off their obligations—and the money to build the homes—to cities around the state. Although the move has been criticized as a circumvention of the Mt. Laurel decision that will exacerbate suburban racial segregation, the arrangement has been embraced in the cities where most of the poor live. Newark, for example, has agreements with several suburbs to receive $4 million for the construction of 234 homes. Kean also fought for Jersey's cities in the legislature. He has sought unsuccessfully to repeal a state property tax deduction and use part of the money for an $80 million "distressed cities fund." In 1987 he vetoed a $30 million special appropriation for New Jersey's cities because "it was a small and unsatisfactory amount of money," he said. "The cities need more from state government done according to need and on a long-range basis."

But the biggest test of Kean's and New Jersey's commitments will come in Newark, which suffered from brutal rioting in 1967 that claimed 26 lives and left $15 million of property in ruins. Twenty years later Newark's Central Ward was still a sullen and desolate place. Teenagers huddled in the doorways of the Hayes Homes, the graffiti-scarred high-rise housing project where the six days of violence began. A jungle of weeds flourished on thousands of vacant lots piled high with trash and littered with the remnants of abandoned, stripped cars. Most streets were unmarked, the signs torn down long ago by vandals and never replaced.

Since the riots of July 12 through 17, 1967, so many people have fled Newark that the city's population is below its 1910 level. Most of those left behind are black or Hispanic, and most are poor. Three-fourths of Newark's 314,000 residents are minorities. One-third live below the poverty line, the highest percentage of any U.S. city. Unemployment is double the Garden State average; among black teenagers it reaches 40 percent. An estimated 8,000 homeless people walk the streets. The crime rate is close to New Jersey's worst; property taxes are the nation's highest. The value of Newark's assessed property has fallen by a crippling two-thirds since 1960. The school system is a shambles. Half the residents are under 20, it's hard to find a movie theatre, bowling alley, or skating rink.

And while New Jerseyans have profited handsomely from the suburban office campuses that dot the state, most of the new jobs are only a distant dream for Newark residents. "Newarkers are cut off in at least three ways from the new jobs: skills, training and transportation," said Robert Curvin, dean of the Graduate School of Management and Urban Professions at the New School for Social Research in New York. "It's not all that easy to get to a job in the Meadowlands or a suburban shopping mall or to some of the new offices where the jobs might be."

But there are signs the nation's premier bust town may be emerging from its long decline. In 1987 alone, 47 commercial projects, totalling nearly a half billion dollars in investment, were proposed or developed. Prudential Insurance completed the fourth of six planned office towers in its fully leased 2.2-million-square-foot Gateway project. And there's much that downtown Newark never lost and seems in no danger of losing now: the headquarters of The Prudential Insurance Company of America, Mutual Benefit Life Insurance Company, and Public Service Electric & Gas Company, among others.

Real estate values are on the increase and Newark's auctions of city-owned property—an inventory approaching $85 million—have sold out. While the median sale price of a home in the city is still well below the going prices of $150,000 to $200,000 elsewhere in northern New Jersey, the figure increased from $34,000 in 1980 to $45,000 in 1986.

"Newark is going to realize its potential," said Mayor Sharpe James, a behavioral sciences professor at Essex County Community College who was elected to the City Council in 1970 and defeated four-term incumbent Kenneth A. Gibson in 1986. "People expected us to roll over, well, we're not dead yet."

In Newark's run-down City Hall, James has tried to take a Mr.

Fix-It approach to running a city government that, by all accounts, is reeling from decades of rule by ethnic machine politicians and their successors. By the time Gibson ousted Hugh J. Addonizio in 1970, Newark's reputation for "administration by grand jury" and tales of political corruption—both petty and grand—had become legendary. In addition to the scores of city administrators and councilmen jailed on corruption charges, Addonizio was eventually convicted of conspiracy and extortion and sentenced to 10 years in prison. The long trail of indictments and convictions continued under Gibson (who was himself indicted, but later acquitted, on charges of conspiracy to create a no-show job for a city councilman).

James commissioned a management review from Coopers & Lybrand. Among the deficiencies uncovered: $45 million in unpaid property, water, and sewer taxes; an 80 percent property tax collection rate (lagging behind most major U.S. cities); a backlog of 10,000 warrants waiting to be entered on police computers; and one-third of the parking meters in the city broken. The study, observed the *New Jersey Monthly*, revealed both "organizational dry rot" and "carnival bureaucracy," adding: "The sobering message derived from reading the entrails is that cronyism and complacency can undermine the best intentions of black politicians as well as whites."

Adding to the administrative nightmares, Newark's budgetary woes have deepened since federal aid has been cut in half since 1981. Increased state assistance hasn't come close to filling the gap. Democrats contend that Kean's efforts are not enough, that his administration has devoted precious few dollars to its cities, even though the state has run a half billion dollar surplus for several years. "New Jersey has the dollars," said James, "but we're the victims of state priorities."

Some New Jerseyans still think Newark will never recover. But citing the booming state economy, the city's abundant and inexpensive vacant land, its colleges, and a location that combines the New York metropolitan area's busiest airport, the nation's largest container port, eight major highways, and a ten-minute rail commute to Lower Manhattan, Saul Fenster, president of the New Jersey Institute of Technology and chairman of the Newark Collaboration Group, said "Newark is inevitable." Fenster may be an optimist, but for Newark—and New Jersey, which lived so long in the shadows—a little leap of faith is allowed.

NEW
ENGLAND:
The Resilient Society

T he image is so strong it has been fixed in the American consciousness: Lowell, Massachusetts, an old mill town with boarded-up storefronts and near 15 percent unemployment, is transformed into a high-tech boom town with unemployment below 3 percent. Relaxed and happy city leaders turn their attention to projects like rebuilding the network of stone-walled canals that lace the city and drumming up funds for outdoor sculpture.

The situation looks so good that the governors of other states and even Britain's Prince Charles troop in for walks past the grimy brick mills that now house fledgling computer firms, asking "If you can do it, can't we?" The hero-governor of Massachusetts, Michael Dukakis, sees it from a different angle as he begins his presidential campaign. "The first question I'm asked everywhere I go is, 'We know what you've done in Massachusetts. Can you do it for us here?' And my answer is, 'Yes, we can.'"

After traveling to so many troubled farm states and manufacturing cities, there is a measure of relief in visiting New England. There are still plenty of desolate mill towns (Lowell is an exceptional case), but on Route 128, the circular highway around Boston, the high-tech concentration is as visibly real as it is in western New Hampshire, southern Maine, Vermont, Connecticut, and Rhode Island. The enthusiastic, informal high-tech executives make the visitor feel excited about the future of American business and relations between management and labor. The products themselves—state-of-the-art computers, lifesaving medical devices, and other exotic new machines—are fascinating. Here seem to be the answers to our declining standard of living and our ability to compete with other countries and proof that we can still be technologically superior.

By the late 1980s, no other region of the United States could come near New England's economic well-being. In 1986, the unemployment rate for the six-state region—Massachusetts, Connecticut, New Hampshire, Rhode Island, Vermont, and Maine—was 3.9 percent, barely half the national average. Massachusetts's jobless rate was the lowest among the industrial states and New Hampshire's of all the states. New England's regional per capita income was also the highest in the country and had increased at the fastest rate of all the regions during the eighties.

But I finally came to believe that the economy in New England today—and the local people's enthusiasm for it—is so white hot that it is better viewed from a distance. New England in the eighties is like Texas in the seventies: it's easy to believe the good times will last forever even though every historical trend tells you the opposite. Today's New England is alluring but dangerous. Certainly there is much to learn from New England's commitments to education and entrepreneurship, and from its ability to transform its economy and respond to changing times. But New England's economy is too special, too small, and too unlike most of the country to offer lessons for every region.

A detailed look at New England reveals some characteristics that other states may not long for. The region is not subject to the ups and downs of world commodity prices, but that is because it doesn't have many commodities. Its lack of energy and minerals was a major problem in the 1970s when their prices were high, and the region was dependent on expensive imports. New England agriculture is so small and specialized—amounting to a mere one-half of one percent of the

gross regional product, and producing only a small percentage of the
regional food supply—that some New Englanders have become obsessed with the notion of food self-sufficiency. New England has not
had to cope with the decline of heavy industry because it never had
very much compared with the Great Lakes and Mid-Atlantic states.
Perhaps most significant of all, the high-tech prosperity is much more
dependent on the Reagan defense buildup than New England's liberal, peace-minded people want to admit.

These reservations about New England as an economic model do
not mean that the rest of the country should ignore it. New England's
high-tech revolution does offer more economic lessons for the rest of
the United States than any other single region. The New Englanders'
high level of interest in politics and government is a model for all
Americans. And most important of all, through its monuments and
history as the starting place of American society, New England exists
to remind us of the values of individualism and democracy on which
our culture is based.

THE ROLLERCOASTER ECONOMY

Viewed from the perspective of history, New England's current prominence in high technology is the latest high point of an economic
rollercoaster that the region has ridden through the centuries.

Religious independence could be described as New England's first
"growth industry," the one that induced its initial settlement and the
development of hundreds of towns. The early settlers found a rocky
landscape that was more exciting to the eye than susceptible to the
plow, but they pressed into the forests and onto the open lands once
tilled by the Indians to create a strong agricultural base that enjoyed
its heyday between 1830 and 1880. Then came an immense family
farming depression as the opening of the Erie Canal, and more particularly the advent of the railroads, propelled New England farmers to
forsake the region and move onto the broad and fertile fields of the
Midwest.

This pattern of rise and decline was to be repeated again and again.
New England grew into a great maritime power, only to be eclipsed

by New York City and later by Baltimore. The birth of the American insurance and banking industry in Boston and Hartford was later overshadowed, at least in part, by activity in New York. And the momentous New England industrial boom in textiles and shoes lost out, after decades of prosperity, to cheaper production in the American South and overseas.

New England's rise after each reversal, like a phoenix from the ashes, has been traced to pluck, luck, the China trade and clipper ships, cheap immigrant labor, tariffs, smart financing, technological innovation, and the momentum gained from the region's head start in the Industrial Revolution. The residue of each wave of innovation left an invaluable base in finance, skilled labor, cheap but reusable old buildings and, most critically, the educational institutions created with money donated by the magnates of earlier industries.

The gatekeepers of New England's vast pools of capital in its banks and insurance companies have often been criticized for being too cautious and conservative, but they also showed flashes of brilliance and risk-taking that allowed the modern high-tech economy to develop. In 1946, Ralph Flanders, a Vermont industrialist and later U.S. senator who was head of the Federal Reserve Bank of Boston during World War II, organized American Research and Development, the first venture-capital firm to finance aspiring high-technology companies founded by scientists who had graduated from MIT and other New England institutions. The firm invested in companies such as Tracerlab and Digital Equipment Corporation, the first of the thousands of high-tech companies that were born in Massachusetts and later in neighboring New Hampshire, Vermont, and southern Maine.

By the mid-1970s, however, New England had the earmarks of a historic relic—the birthplace, to be sure, of American university life, shipping, banking, insurance and manufacturing, but hard pressed to hold its own in the harshly competitive world of the twentieth century. New England textiles, shoes, and heavy industry were continuing their long decline, and the region's early high-technology industries had, it turned out, become dangerously dependent on Vietnam-era defense contracts. Bereft of its own energy sources and heavily dependent on imported petroleum, the region was hit harder than any other by the 1973 Arab oil embargo and escalating energy prices. In the 1975 recession, New England had the highest unemployment rate of all major regions.

But through its great educational institutions, led by Harvard University and the Massachusetts Institute of Technology, New England maintained a pre-eminence in the nation. During this very period, New England capitalists, tapping the talents of the graduates of the region's universities, were expanding old firms or opening new ones to exploit what they saw as an exploding market for business and personal computers in the 1980s. The role of New England's great educational institutions cannot be overstated. MIT, especially, proved crucial. Seventy percent of the companies located on the famed Route 128 around Boston trace their origins to the university, according to Ray Stata, president of Analog Devices, Inc., a Norwood, Massachusetts, semiconductor manufacturer. Indeed, 8 of every 10 engineers with doctoral degrees in Massachusetts are MIT graduates; with the 9th hailing from Harvard. "If we didn't have 120 colleges and universities, including some of the best in the world," Dukakis has said, "I could be standing on my head and we wouldn't have the conditions for economic success and innovation and new products and new businesses."

New England's Dirty Little Secret and the Slow-Growth Society

There is no question that New England has the most "high-teched" regional economy in the United States. About 10 percent of New England jobs are due directly to high-tech design and production. More importantly, economists figure that for each high-tech manufacturing job, another one-and-one-half to two jobs are created in establishments ranging from consulting and software design firms to banks, construction companies, and shopping malls. In all, high tech is directly or indirectly responsible for one-fourth of all the jobs in the region.

New England's economy in the eighties thus looks like the United States at the very top of its form in the modern world: an ad-

vanced, highly educated society inventing, financing, and manufacturing products people want and need all over the world. But the
behind-the-scenes details of the high-tech revolution and the state-
by-state differences reveal a less exemplary portrait. Many new
companies and new jobs were created in the late 1970s, but it took
the Reagan defense buildup, with its emphasis on high-tech weapons research, to produce the incredibly low unemployment levels
and new wealth for which New England has been admired in the
eighties.

New England won 15 percent of prime defense contracts—three
times its population share—awarded from 1981 to 1984. That money
accounted for 10 to 15 percent of the region's 1981–85 job growth,
according to estimates by Gary L. Ciminero, senior vice-president of
Providence's Fleet National Bank and chief economist as well as
president of the New England Economic Project, a venture backed by
businesses, universities, and state governments.

The defense receipts and dependence of all the New England
states are astonishing when you think of how weak this region's
defense image is compared with the West Coast. Massachusetts
ranked 9th in the country in defense receipts in 1985, receiving
$14.4 billion, and Connecticut 12th, with $10.7 billion. A full 10.7
percent of Connecticut's economy was defense-related, nearly a
full percentage point higher than California's and the third highest percentage of all in the nation. Defense was responsible for 8.3
percent of the Massachusetts economy, making it the eighth most
defense-dependent state. The other New England states receive relatively small amounts of money compared with Massachusetts and
Connecticut, but they are still among the most defense-dependent.
On a per capita basis, the New England states rank second after the Pacific states, receiving an average of $2,496 per capita.
Connecticut's per capita share of 1985 defense spending led all
states.

Even with these fantastic levels of defense spending for such small
states, New England's income and unemployment statistics are not so
impressive when its six states are examined individually. Connecticut
has the highest per capita income in the nation ($19,208 in 1986,
almost $5,000 above the national average). But high tech is only a
part of its affluence; for several generations New York executives have

been attracted to Fairfield County because Connecticut has no income tax, and in the last two decades have been resettling corporate headquarters close to their residences.

Massachusetts, the center of high-tech research and development, ranked fourth in per capita income in 1986 at $17,516. But Massachusetts also has one of the highest costs of living in the United States. The Boston area's housing is the nation's most expensive and its housing industry is geared to the construction of individual homes, not cheap mass-produced Sunbelt-style subdivisions. Statistics also show that the rate of job creation in Massachusetts has not been much greater than the national average.

"The economic miracle per se wasn't exactly a miracle," contends David L. Birch, director of the program on neighborhood and regional change at the Massachusetts Institute of Technology. "Relative to our situation in 1974–75, it was quite nice, but our employment growth rate for any period you want to pick has been right about the national average. From 1982 to the present, employment in Massachusetts grew at 12.2 percent; New England, at 13.1 percent, and the United States was at 11.9 percent. From 1975 through 1985, Massachusetts was 29 percent, New England was 31 percent and the U.S. was 27 percent. So we are consistently a point or two below the New England average and a point or two above the national average."

Of the smaller New England states, New Hampshire, the only state in the nation without either an income tax or a sales tax, is by far the star in income and growth. With income at $15,922 per capita in 1986, New Hampshire ranked 8th among the states. But Rhode Island ranks only 16th, and Vermont and Maine are almost $2,000 *below* the national average, ranking 33rd and 34th, respectively. Rural Vermont, and especially northern Maine and New Hampshire, all know rural poverty that is sometimes as severe as the South's.*

---

*New England dairy farmers have found themselves in difficult straits just like those in other parts of the country. So many dairy farmers took advantage of the Reagan-era program to kill off their overproductive dairy herds that a minor "Buttergate" scandal occurred in Vermont when it was discovered that dairies were selling butter from "foreign" Massachusetts, New York, and Wisconsin.

The population and growth statistics for the New England states also reveal how few people have benefited from the region's high-tech revolution. All together, the six New England states are home to only five percent of the American people and do not grow nearly as fast as the South and the West. "The only reason we look to be booming is because the unemployment rate is low, and the only reason the unemployment rate is so low is that no one moves to Massachusetts," Birch said. Birch is certainly right about Massachusetts, which *lost* 28,000 people more than moved in between 1980 and 1986 and which grew only 1.7 percent or by 95,000 people because babies were born. But it wouldn't seem true of New Hampshire, which grew by 11.5 percent, until you realize that the state's population is so small that it took only 106,000 new residents to produce that number and bring the state just over the million mark. The growth figures in the other New England states are smaller yet: Connecticut, 81,000; Maine, 49,000; Vermont, 29,000; Rhode Island, 28,000. Contrast those figures with the growth in the Sunbelt in the same period: Florida, 1.9 million; Texas, 2.4 million; Georgia, 641,000; California, 3.3 million. Illinois in the Rustbelt grew by 126,000 people in the first six years of the eighties.

Finally, the high-tech economy remains subject to the vagaries of both defense spending and worldwide competition. The high-tech peak of the eighties has already passed in New England. The computer industry, faced with a saturated market, and declining domestic capital spending for new equipment, has gone into a cyclical downturn. Wang Laboratories, Lowell's leading employer, laid off 3,000 people in 1985 and 1986, and by late 1986 New England high-tech employment had actually decreased 4 percent from two years before. No one was predicting a bust, and many still believed Dukakis's view that "knowledge has become a lot more important in the economic equation. I don't think there's anything very cyclical about what's happening here." But less boosterish New Englanders, seeing overseas competition in both design and production, remind themselves that the region's welfare depends on producing innovations that people want. "To the extent the world continues to need our brains, we will continue to prosper," Birch said. "To the extent it doesn't, we won't."

Boston: Paradise Unregained

Boston, America's first great city and still the capital of Massachusetts and the cultural center of all New England, has not been richer or more internationally influential in many decades. By the 1990s, it should look great, too, as the Central Artery along the waterfront, the ugliest elevated highway in the urban United States, is buried—at a fantastic price, of course. Boston's population profile, like those of Washington, D.C., San Francisco, and Manhattan, reflects the new high-tech service economy. From 1970 to 1980, Boston lost 12 percent of its population, but the number of people 25 to 34 years old increased by one-third. The number of college graduates doubled so that one in five Bostonians has a college degree, and the number of people with professional, managerial, or technical jobs rose from 22 to 30 percent. The 1980 census found that 42 percent of Bostonians were born outside Massachusetts. At the same time, the number of voters with Irish surnames dropped to less than one-third; it was one-half in the 1950s.

While ethnic Bostonians were leaving the city and the yuppies were arriving, black Bostonians stayed, and theirs is not an easy story to tell. Boston was one of the centers of the pre–Civil War abolitionist movement, but relations between working-class whites and blacks have always been tough. Boston's race relations are peaceful today compared with the 1970s when the courts forced the integration of the public schools in the city's Irish and other working-class neighborhoods and incidents of violence were common. After Raymond Flynn was elected mayor in 1982, one of his first acts was to hand over personally an $843,498 settlement check to the widow of a black man shot nine years before by two white police officers. Flynn's actions were considered particularly important because he was one of the leading opponents of busing in his native South Boston. About the same time, in a carefully planned operation, black families began moving into the Bunker Hill public housing project in Charlestown, another largely white, working-class section. Black Bostonians have also been making small advances in politics, electing two city council members. Four of the 13 Boston School Committee members are now minorities. And 40 percent of the city workers Flynn has hired have been minorities.

The high-tech boom has doubtlessly trickled down a little bit to the black community since there are a few high-tech plants in the city. But overall the sense of frustration among blacks has only gotten worse as they see whites prosper. "Overall during the past 10 years," said School Committee member Juanita Wade, "I don't want to say things have gotten worse. I'd say things have been stagnant." The statistics make Wade's viewpoint look pollyannish. In 1980, black Bostonians were about twice as likely to be unemployed as white Bostonians. But by 1985, according to the Boston Redevelopment Authority, the unemployment rate among whites in Boston had fallen from 5 to 3 percent while the rate among blacks rose from 9 to 12 percent. While median household income for whites rose from $13,701 in 1979 to $22,500 in 1984, blacks' incomes rose from $10,277 to only $13,800. While blacks were moving into suburbs in other parts of the country, in Boston they still did not dare look for housing in many sections of the city—West Roxbury, South Boston, and parts of Dorchester, Hyde Park, Roslindale, and Charlestown.

The frustrations of this black community so outside the mainstream reached a kind of intellectual fever pitch in 1986 with a referendum for the secession of 25 percent of Boston's land area—Roxbury and Mattapan along with parts of Dorchester, the South End, Jamaica Plain, Columbia Point, and the Fenway—and 22 percent of its people. The new municipality would have been called Mandela, after the South African civil rights leader, and 90 percent minority. The measure was rejected three to one, and not just because the city establishment poured money into a campaign to oppose it. With the city population already 38 percent minority, more mainstream black leaders foresaw the day when they would have control over all of Boston, not just its poorest fourth. But in the meantime, the only thing black Boston seemed to attract was a few more welfare dollars. "The Mandela campaign opened a door on black Boston and revealed it to be a community in a state of political disarray," wrote Charles Kenney in the *Boston Globe Magazine.* "It is a community with an embryonic leadership class that lacks any real measure of political clout." Some blame the lack of cohesion on the differences between Boston's old black community and more recent southern migrants. But it is also true the problems in Boston are tremendously difficult to solve.

An example is the compact the Boston business community pioneered with the school system to guarantee inner-city public-school graduates a first shot at entry-level jobs if the city school system would commit itself to improved academic performance, starting with increased student attendance. Some 300 corporations now offer jobs under the compact, and the idea has spawned copies in big cities across the nation. But the compact has yet to crack the tragedy that half of Boston's students drop out before they graduate from high school. William Edgerly of the State Street Bank, chairman and "father" of the compact, has said he wants to reach these students. But the astounding fact is that 80 percent of parents with children in the Boston schools are either jobless, on welfare, or underemployed; and the business community is now attacking this grim statistic by running a literacy and vocational training program for the parents.

THE HIGH-TECHERS: NEW ENGLAND'S NEW ELITE

The battles between the Protestant, capitalist Yankees and the mostly Catholic Irish and Southern European immigrants are the stuff of history. The Irish and the other ethnic groups first were exploited and then through their numbers gained political power. The Yankees, however, had their own "liberal" tradition stemming from the abolitionist movement against slavery, and over time the Yankees and the ethnic groups combined to form a pro-government political tradition rivaled only by New York and California. By the 1970s, this had translated into a cozy relationship between management and labor, with high levels of regulation and government spending in every New England state except New Hampshire. In Massachusetts, the system was seen in its boldest relief.

Into this scene in the 1970s came the equivalent of barbarians: a bunch of high-tech executives claiming that young engineers were unwilling to move to Massachusetts or stay there because of the state's reputation for high taxes, free government spending, and politics marked by liberalism and corruption. This "critical raw material" of their industry, the executives said, did not care a whit about Boston's high culture. They liked Massachusetts for three reasons—its proximity to high-quality engineering schools where they could keep abreast of the latest scientific developments, the variety of jobs, and good schools for their children. But there were limits, and they preferred a warm climate, a suburban or rural setting, a variety of recreational opportunities—and low taxes.

When the Massachusetts establishment proved totally unwilling to confront their issues the high techers formed their own Massachusetts High Technology Council which went on to cause a near-revolution in Massachusetts political life. In 1978, the high techers joined with other business leaders to back conservative Democrat Edward J. King in his successful primary challenge to Governor Dukakis. Then, in 1980, following the passage of Proposition 13 in California the high techers promoted a citizens' initiative, Proposition 2½, which promised eventually to limit property taxes to 2.5 percent of assessed valuation. The initiative was ostensibly sponsored by Citizens for Limited Taxation, a grass-roots group, but it is generally acknowledged that the high-tech council provided much of the organizational muscle as well as a $250,000 campaign chest. Government and union leaders opposed Proposition 2½ and most business groups either opposed it or remained neutral. But the initiative appealed to the electorate, and the high techers learned that Massachusetts was ready to put its old elite out on its ear. Seven years later, only the staunchest liberals were complaining about its effects. And in 1986, the council helped conservatives pass a referendum to put a cap on state revenues.

Their views on government are only the beginning of how different the high techers are from the traditional powers in Massachusetts and the rest of New England. First of all, they were not necessarily born in New England. Second, they are aggressively modern and unimpressed by tradition. Third, they are nouveau riche.

In their companies, the high techers are vigorously anti-union, considering it a matter of personal honor to create working conditions that are so favorable that their employees won't seek assistance from union organizers. Like their counterparts in California, the New England high techers have gained a reputation for such innovations as campus-like workplaces, gyms and other recreational facilities, stock options, flexitime, and sabbatical leaves. Some union-oriented critics have charged that this informality is limited to the upper rungs while their production workers are paid low wages and have no job security or opportunities for advancement.

Peter M. Senge of the Sloan School of Management at MIT told me that while "it's difficult to make generalizations," the new high-tech companies and some other fast-growing firms are trying to create "non-hierarchical, decentralized organizations that are profitable but have a sense of purpose that goes beyond profitability and the rate of growth." The origins of the new management form may lie in the necessity "to get and keep the best," Senge said, but the high techers also have a strong distaste for corporate politics.

No one is certain where the high-tech management approach originated. Senge believes the origins lie in the engineering training of the high-tech entrepreneurs, which encourages them to place a higher emphasis on management systems than the finance-minded graduates of business schools. California-based high techers have claimed that firms around the country are following the lead of early California companies that operated in the relaxed, less hierarchical fashion typical of that state. Such California chauvinism is rejected by Analog Devices chairman Ray Stata, who contends that the entrepreneurs behind many high-tech firms have rejected "the whole authority syndrome" of western culture in favor of eastern cultural values and a "more holistic, organic concept" of management.

In that revolutionary spirit, Stata has charged that Massachusetts has too many liberal arts programs and too few for engineers. "Massachusetts suffers from what you might call intellectual snobbery, looking at educational value as being primarily related to the intellectual development of the individual. There's a certain amount of disdain for the concept that career-oriented, professional education is quite legitimate. A lot of graduates from universities are not prepared to take jobs where they're available."

In politics, the high techers are notoriously independent in a party-conscious region. "The hard-line right is just as evil as the hard-line left," Stata said. "The hard-line right argument ends up with the situation where the funds aren't available to support the worthiest of causes, education. On the left, it's a question of tax policy—ultimately soaking the rich and egalitarianism."

To make matters worse in Massachusetts, the high techers have tried to keep their pure, modern image by refusing to buy tickets for political dinners. With thinking like that, it's not a surprise that Howard Foley, president of the high-tech council, described high tech's relations with other industries in the early eighties as "uncomfortable," an analysis that James M. Howell, chief economist of the First National Bank of Boston, called an "understatement." Relations have improved since—but only some.

EDUCATION AND ENERGY:
NEW ENGLAND CONUNDRUMS

New England is more than high-tech and defense spending. Tourism, forestry, and fisheries—the last revived in recent years by federal restrictions on foreign fishing within 200 miles of U.S. shorelines—are also significant sectors of the economy. But more significantly in the fast-changing, research-minded eighties, Boston has grown ever-more important as an international center in medicine and research, law, business consulting, international trade, architecture, and engineering. Hartford, Connecticut, is one of the world's great insurance centers. And the area around Stamford, Connecticut, becomes more powerful each year as a headquarters of *Fortune* 500 companies.

The "industry" basic to all this activity, however, is the "noble" endeavor of education itself. New England is home to our oldest educational institutions, and it has maintained a pre-eminence in education far beyond its size and wealth. Tradition and a head start are elements, of course, but as anyone who has visited a New England campus in October, November or March, April, and even May suspects, the long cold season must play a role in keeping students indoors studying while their counterparts in California and Florida are being tempted by the beaches.

New England's intellectual reputation is not based solely on the glamorous and famous intellectuals at Harvard, MIT, and Yale. The region has some 800,000 students (about a fourth from outside New England) enrolled in some 260 colleges and universities. And New Englanders are better educated than people in every other region in the country except the Pacific states. In 1980, fully 19.3 percent of New England residents 25 years or older held a college or advanced degree compared with 16.3 percent nationwide. Connecticut and Massachusetts, with 21.2 and 20 percent of their residents college-educated, are near the very top of the national scale. Only 15.3 percent of New Englanders 25 years or older had less than an eighth-grade education, well below the 18.4 percent level for the entire nation and the 23.9 percent level for the Southeast.

But for all its reputation for excellence, New England's educational establishment is understandably worried about its future. Many of the region's colleges and universities were beefed up to educate the massive baby-boom generation, and as the number of college-age people declined, these schools now worry about their ability to maintain their programs or even survive. In addition, the high cost of private New England educational institutions makes students think twice about attending them, especially since many public universities around the country have improved their offerings. By the late 1980s, the New England Board of Higher Education had started issuing press releases to inform the world that there was still room in the region's colleges and universities. In May 1987, the board announced there were still some 27,000 freshman openings available in 175 New England educational institutions for the coming fall, a 13 percent increase over the year before. Education officials predicted that the real test of their institutions' strength will come between 1989 and 1994 when the number of high school graduates declines dramatically. The fears are understandable. The New England birth rate is the lowest in the country (13.2 births per 1,000 persons compared with 15.6 per 1,000 nationally and 19.5 per 1,000 in the youthful Rocky Mountain states).

With these birth rates, New England institutions must continue to attract students from outside the region. New Englanders worry that any decline in enrollment would imperil their economy in two ways: first, by diminishing the economic benefits of the education industry itself, and, second, by reducing the number of the "best and brightest" graduates who stay on to give the region's industries their absolutely vital shots of talent and ingenuity.

While its education-based, "thinking economy" flourishes, New England has a long-term worry that will not go away: energy. In 1973, oil—all imported from outside the region—was used to satisfy 85 percent of New England's total energy needs. By the early 1980s, that figure was down to 72.9 percent. With implementation of rigorous conservation policies, New England's energy consumption, as measured by average use per home, per vehicle, or per unit of production, dropped 35 percent between 1973 and 1980, compared with a 20 percent reduction nationwide. By the late 1980s only 30 percent of New England electricity was still oil-produced. In their attempt to control energy costs, the New England states agreed to import substantial amounts of hydropower from Quebec, though some business leaders fear that might provide a new, undesirable form of dependence on outside energy sources. The New England states have also tried to avoid building more plants by buying power from private producers.

But in another of its many political-economic contradictions, peace and safety-minded New England derives 26 percent of its power from nuclear energy. The biggest political football in the region is the nuclear power plant at Seabrook on New Hampshire's 18-mile window to the sea. Seabrook has been stalled for years by law suits, civil disobedience, and even violent demonstrations. Massachusetts governor Dukakis delayed Seabrook's start-up by refusing to draw up a plan for the evacuation of his state's people should there be a nuclear accident. The low-priced energy of the eighties has meant the best of times for New England. But there are fears the region will have a hard time coming up with increased energy (or new conservation measures) to meet economic growth and survival in the nineties. For New England, energy is the problem that just won't go away.

THE DUKE

One man emerged as the political powerhouse of New England in the eighties: Michael Dukakis, the governor of Massachusetts. It is a bit ironic that Dukakis should end up as the region's political star, but he did not start out that way. A Greek-American by heritage and a state legislator who fathered the nation's first "no fault" insurance law, Dukakis was elected governor in 1974 as a conventional politician in the Massachusetts liberal reform mode. In other words, he liked using big government to help people, but eschewed old-style political tradeoffs and preferred ideas that emerged from thorough research and detailed intellectual debate. In his first term as governor, Dukakis ran into the worst situation for a liberal. State government spending had gotten so high and the economy was so bad that he had to both cut programs and raise taxes. To make matters worse, Dukakis suffered from the usual bad traits of the intellectual politician: he was often cold when dealing with the public and didn't like having to convince people that his ideas were sound. A classic story was told of him riding the Boston subway to work to set an example of saving energy, but not talking to anyone on the trip.

Dukakis also ran head-first into the conservative decade. In 1978, the same year that California passed Proposition 13, the Democratic primary voters of Massachusetts threw Dukakis out in favor of Edward J. King, an old-style Democrat who was anti-abortion, anti–gun control, and pro–capital punishment. These stands would have seemed to offend Massachusetts liberals, but they were so upset about Duka-kis's budget cuts that many stayed home. The chastened Dukakis spent the next four years at Harvard's Kennedy School of Government and in 1982 returned to beat King—who ran into ethical trouble—in the primary and easily win the general election. Dukakis was over-whelmingly re-elected in 1986, and in 1987, on the crest of his state's fantastic economic performance, he announced he would run for president in 1988.

Dukakis certainly had the reputation to make a presidential race. He had become nationally known in his first term for his courageous stand against the "scatterization" of jobs and development to su-burbia. "We were being engulfed by spread city while the people who needed jobs the most were left behind in declining urban neighbor-hoods," Dukakis said. His solution was to focus all the state's existing regulatory powers and public investment programs on the old cities in a single-minded fashion in order to keep activity in the old town centers. The state shifted sewer assistance programs to favor densely settled areas, diverted state and federal highway funds from new pro-jects in the open countryside to bricking sidewalks and improving city roads. After a heated battle with the Massachusetts education bu-reaucracy, the state began putting its money in the rehabilitation of old school buildings rather than building new ones on the edge of town. He successfully opposed a new shopping mall in western Massachusetts by signalling that there would be no access to a nearby highway.

Dukakis's record in his second and third terms remained creative. He instituted a program of tax amnesty and a tough tax collection policy which has netted the state more than $900 million since 1983. And he has won national praise for his Employment and Training Choices (ET) program for welfare recipients. The program combines the usual elements of job-training programs, but the state pays for day care. Some critics have noted that Massachusetts welfare recipients are better educated than most, but Judith M. Gueron, president of the New York–based Manpower Demonstration Research Corporation, which evaluates state welfare programs, has said, "They have done an unusual job in focusing on getting people out of poverty. That is very impressive to people who see how moribund these bureaucracies usually are."

After winning back the governor's office, Dukakis dissipated business opposition. John Gould, senior vice-president of the Shawmut Corporation, one of Boston's major banks, said "He's matured. He's recognized that social needs are best met when the economic engine is running well. . . . There's a social contract in effect." But his very acceptance by the business community produced criticism that Dukakis had turned from a lone crusader to a consensus-building politician not in order to be a better governor, but to make sure that he stayed in office. Some political activists believe the differences are so great that they discuss his governorships as "Michael I" and "Michael II." Welfare advocates contend that he has not raised benefits as much as the state could afford—or the recipients need—in the affluent high-tech, high-cost age. The legislature and Dukakis did approve increases of 39 percent between 1983 and 1988, but the benefits are still only 81.5 percent of the poverty level and below those of nine other states—a sad record to Massachusetts liberals. Dukakis has maintained it is more important to keep the ET experiment going (it takes about 15 percent of the welfare budget) than to increase benefits even further. Dukakis has also thrilled environmentalists with his outspoken opposition to the Seabrook, N.H., nuclear power plant, but they criticize him for failing to clean up Boston Harbor and slowness in cleaning up toxic waste dumps. The severest liberal critics claim that the improvements in social programs under Dukakis are due entirely to the growth in the economy and resultant tax receipts and wonder if Dukakis would ever fight hard for any cause that might threaten his political standing.

When one considers the performance of his peers, Dukakis has been by all standards—except those of the political extremes—a superb governor. One could also argue that a Dukakis is the best that liberals can expect in this conservative age. But it is something of a tragedy that in beginning his presidential campaign, Dukakis began taking more credit for his state's economic performance than he could possibly deserve and making promises to the nation that he could not possibly keep. "If there is one unique strength I bring to this race," he told *National Journal*, "it is a knowledge of economic issues . . . and a record on economic issues. I believe that what has worked in Massachusetts can work in every state in the nation."*

During his later administrations, Dukakis has continued to encourage economic development in the old towns and other impoverished areas of the state. State financing agencies have provided capital for new businesses and job training, made investments in roads, sewers, and other basic infrastructure, and also provided partial public financing for business-academic research partnerships in such fields as biotechnology and photovoltaics.

But despite this record Ronald F. Ferguson, a Harvard economist, and Helen F. Ladd, a professor at Duke University, contended in a thorough study of the Massachusetts economy that "the state's policy has affected the geographic distribution of economic activity at least marginally, but not the overall level of economic activity. Neither the scope nor the timing of recent policy initiatives in Massachusetts supports the view that they were an important catalyst to the remarkable economic turnaround of the past decade."

This question has come up so often that Ferguson has taken to pointing out that he does not think that Dukakis's activities were a waste of time, just that they have not produced the results that have been claimed for them. Herman B. (Dutch) Leonard, another Har-

*For detailed reporting on the New England scene, I am indebted to coverage by my *National Journal* colleagues Neal Peirce, Ron Brownstein, and Burt Solomon.

vard professor, said Massachusetts' development model is preferable
to other states' because it adapts and fosters economic change, rather
than trying to "lean against the wind;" it "uses government to foster
communication among economic decision-makers, rather than pouring in a lot of dollars."

Dukakis also chooses to emphasize the forms of economic activity
that are popular with liberals. In his 1986 State of the State address,
Dukakis described his visits to plants and offices throughout the state
in which men and women of the commonwealth were "thinking,
creating, investing, producing, pushing into the frontiers of the future,
working together to create the 21st century here and now." He told
of visiting textile manufacturers in Fall River who are applying new
machinery and technology, state-of-the-art egg producers at a farm in
Westminster, the Artificial Intelligence Laboratory at MIT, and the
Falmouth inventors of undersea technology that was used to find the
Titanic. But he ignored the crucial role of military spending in his
state's growing affluence.

As a presidential candidate from high-tech Massachusetts, Dukakis
immediately became the strongest free trader of the 1988 Democratic
crop. In a reflection of his region's dependence on imported oil, he also
viewed an import fee as an extension of industrial protectionism. But
his New England orientation is also a reminder that a candidate so
regional must be subjected to intense scrutiny before he wins public
acceptance. In October 1987, the American public learned that it was
John Sasso, Dukakis's campaign manager, who had anonymously
supplied to newspapers and television networks tapes comparing the
speeches of another presidential contender, Senator Joe Biden, and
British Labor Party leader Neil Kinnock. The speeches showed that
Biden had been copying from Kinnock. Dukakis had said he would
be "astonished" to find out that such an act had been performed by
his campaign, and there is every evidence that he was telling the truth.
Dukakis at first said he would not accept Sasso's resignation, but
within a few hours both Sasso and another aide, Paul Tully, who had
lied to the press about the matter, were out of the campaign. Informing the press of a competitor's questionable actions is part of politics,
but the underhanded way in which the Dukakis aides handled the
matter and their eagerness to damage the already-weak Biden campaign severely damaged the Duke's reputation.

BEYOND DUKAKIS: POLITICS AND POLS

The most extraordinary New England political event of the 1980s was the Massachusetts vote for Ronald Reagan in both 1980 and 1984. If ever there was a signal that President Carter and Walter Mondale had disappointed the nation it was this vote by the state that had supported George McGovern in 1972 while everywhere else except the District of Columbia voted for Richard Nixon.

The Massachusetts vote for Reagan was also an indication that Reagan's power was in his personality rather than his conservative ideology. Reagan's election seemed to follow perfectly on the heels of the rejection of the liberal Michael Dukakis in favor of the conserva- tive Democrat Edward J. King in 1978 and the passage of Proposition 2½ in 1980, but the conservative "revolution" never found very deep roots here. In 1978, Massachusetts had also thrown out its liberal Republican senator, Edward J. Brooke, the only black in the U.S. Senate, in favor of Democrat Paul Tsongas. And in 1982, when Duka- kis was re-elected, voters in suburban Boston were forced by Massa- chusetts's loss of one congressional district to faster-growing parts of the country after the 1980 census to choose between a liberal Republi- can congresswoman, Margaret Heckler, and an even more liberal Democrat, Barney Frank. They chose Frank.* After Heckler's defeat, the only Massachusetts Republican left in the House was veteran Silvio Conte from the western part of the state, and the delegation has remained 10 to 1 Democratic. In 1984, after Tsongas announced that

---

*In 1987, in the wake of the intense scrutiny of politicians' personal lives following the demise of former Colorado senator Gary Hart's presidential campaign, Frank became the second Massachusetts House member to reveal that he is gay. The first was Representative Gerry E. Studds, who was censured by the House in 1983 after revelations that he had sexual relations years before with a young man who was serving as a congressional page. Neither Studds nor Frank appeared to have chosen to discuss their sexuality in public, but it appears that New England's libertarian views on personal morality will prevent these revelations from becoming the political suicide they would be in some other parts of the country. Studds, who sits on the House Merchant Marine and Fisheries Committee and has been in office since 1972, was re-elected by 56 percent in 1984 and 65 percent in 1986. Frank's district is believed to be equally safe. The homosexuality of a third New England congressman, Connecticut's Stewart B. McKinney, was sadly revealed in 1987 when he died of acquired immune deficiency syndrome. A classic liberal Republican congressman beloved in his Fairfield County district and known in Washington for his serious interest in the governing of the nation's capital city, McKinney was accorded a funeral appropriate to his 16 years in the U.S. House.

he had a slow-developing form of cancer and would not run again, Massachusetts replaced him with another Democrat, Lieutenant Governor John F. Kerry, who had risen to national prominence as one of the organizers of Vietnam Veterans Against the War.

Massachusetts's historic liberalism is not the only reason the Democrats have continued to win so many elections. The Republican party, once the bastion of Yankee Protestant liberalism, has become dominated by the right wing. The Republican senatorial candidate in both 1982 (against Edward M. Kennedy) and in 1984 (against Kerry) was Ray Shamie, a self-made millionaire who had once been involved with the John Birch Society. In 1984, Shamie won the primary against Elliott Richardson, the symbol of the old Republican establishment and holder of multiple U.S. cabinet positions. In 1986, the Republicans had a terrible time recruiting a candidate for governor. One man lied about his record in Vietnam, and another was found nude twice in his office. The party finally turned to George Kariotis, a King cabinet officer, who failed miserably.

All together, the New England delegation in 1987–88 added up to 15 Democrats and 8 Republicans in the House and 6 Republican and 6 Democratic senators. Democratic domination of populous Massachusetts hid how well the Republicans have done in the other New England states. But the Reaganites cannot claim much credit for these Republican successes—nor would they want to considering how often New England Republicans have been a thorn in their sides in legislative battles. Connecticut sends three Democrats and three Republicans to the U.S. House and a senator from each party, Democrat Christopher J. Dodd and Republican Lowell P. Weicker, Jr., who vigorously opposes anti-abortion and pro–school prayer legislation. Rhode Island and Maine are perfectly matched politically, each sending one Democrat and one Republican to the U.S. House and also a senator from each party. The Republican House members from these states are both women—Rhode Island's Claudine Schneider and Maine's Olympia Snowe—and among the most liberal Republicans in the House. Rhode Island's senators are Democrat Claiborne Pell, who must pay the price of his aristocratic roots by bearing the nicknames of "well-born" and "still-born," and Republican John H. Chafee. In 1987, when the Democrats won back control of the Senate, Pell rose to chair the Senate Foreign Relations Committee. A former foreign service officer, Pell opposed aid to the Nicaraguan Contras. Rhode Island is also home to the only House chairman from New England, Fernand J. St Germain, chairman of the House Banking, Finance and Urban Affairs Committee and described by *The Almanac of American Politics* as "one of the politically sharpest but ethically most dubious members of the House of Representatives." St Germain has no trouble raising campaign money from banking and savings and loan executives and can campaign in French and Ukrainian, but he has declined to release his income-tax returns and is continually subject to charges—unproven—that he is somehow using his chairmanship to enrich himself through stock deals.

From Maine comes Republican William S. Cohen, who beat an incumbent in 1978 at the start of the conservative decade. (Aside from his political work, Cohen is a writer of poetry who wrote a spy novel with former Colorado senator Gary Hart.) The junior Maine senator is Democrat George Mitchell, the successor to Edmund S. Muskie and chairman of the Democratic Senatorial Campaign Committee in 1986 when the Democrats recaptured control of the Senate.

Republicans continue to dominate Vermont, sending James M. Jeffords, the state's only U.S. representative, and one senator, Robert T. Stafford, to Washington. But both Jeffords and Stafford have been much too liberal and critical of the administration by Reagan standards. When the Republicans controlled the Senate, Stafford, who has been in office since 1971, finally got a chance to chair the Environment and Public Works Committee, but it was little comfort to the White House since he opposed the administration's attempt to gut the Clean Air Act and fought for an acid rain bill. The other senator from Vermont is Patrick J. Leahy, elected in 1974 and still the only Democratic senator in the state's history. In 1987, when the Democrats took control of the Senate again, Leahy had enough seniority to become chairman of the Senate Agriculture Committee. Leahy's agricultural background is all dairy, and his coming from a region of the country so far from places where diversified agriculture is dominant put off some people; but he seems interested in the welfare of farmers and properly concerned about the effect of agricultural subsidies on international trade and the deficit.

The only real center of Reagan Republicanism in New England is

New Hampshire, which by the end of the Reagan era could claim to be even more Republican than Utah or Idaho since its governor, two senators, and two congressmen were all Republicans. It was logical for the Reaganites to build a strong base in New Hampshire since the state's politics have always been dominated by French-Canadian (now sometimes called Franco-American) workers once Democrats, but above all tax haters. New Hampshire is the only state without either an income tax or a sales tax, and its high growth reflects the allure of a cheaper cost of living and doing business. In the midst of the high-tech boom and low unemployment, its new residents only intensified the anti-tax conservative atmosphere. Both New Hampshire Republican senators defeated sitting Democrats, Gordon J. Humphrey winning against Thomas J. McIntyre in 1978 and Warren Rudman winning against John A. Durkin in 1980. Both were beloved by the Reagan White House. But Rudman, one of the authors of the Gramm-Rudman-Hollings budget law, surprised everyone including the White House staff when he turned out to be one of the toughest questioners on the Iran-Contra investigating panel and one of the senators angriest about how the White House had ignored the Congress and the Constitution on foreign-policy issues.

The Republicans made real progress in New England governorships during the Reagan era, rising from only one in 1980 to three in 1987. At the beginning of the Reagan presidency, the only New England Republican residing in a governor's mansion was Vermont's Richard Snelling, whose frustrating lot it became to try to make the Reagan White House live up to its rhetorical promise to return power to the states. Most of the time he found that what the Reaganites wanted was not government closer to the people, but less government altogether. When Snelling retired in 1984, he was succeeded by Democrat Madeleine Kunin. Massachusetts continued to elect Democrat Dukakis and Connecticut to elect William A. O'Neill, the lieutenant governor who had assumed the office upon the death of Ella Grasso, but New Hampshire, Rhode Island, and Maine all switched to Republicans. New Hampshire had thrown out the very conservative Republican Meldrim Thomson, Jr., in 1978 over his support for electricity rate increases to pay for the Seabrook nuclear plant, but by 1982 they were ready for a Republican again, this time John H. Sununu. When

Rhode Island Democratic governor Joseph Garrahy retired in 1984, he was succeeded in this most traditionally Democratic of states by Republican Edward diPrete who reduced taxes, including a 16 percent cut in the state income tax, and got the state legislature to repeal a notorious law allowing strikers to get unemployment benefits.* Maine solidified the Republican statehouse gains in 1986 when it elected Republican John McKernan to succeed Democrat Joseph Brennan, who retired and won a seat in Congress.

The Tarnished Kennedys

Senator Edward M. Kennedy of Massachusetts remains New England's most prominent politician, the keeper of his brothers' flame, and the everlasting presidential hope of those liberals who believe that the only problem with Lyndon Johnson's Great Society was that not enough money was spent on the poor. Kennedy's position in the Massachusetts political firmament seems secure; it was considered a comedown in 1982 when his election percentage dropped to 61 percent. Kennedy also remains a ray of hope to people all over the world who see his family's rise from poor Irish roots to wealth and the White House as a symbol of the upward mobility that is possible in the United States. But in the rest of the United States, Kennedy's star has definitely been tarnished. The reasons are obvious: his failed 1980 bid to wrest the Democratic presidential nomination away from Jimmy Carter, his divorce after campaigning with his wife, the constant pouring forth of books attacking the Kennedy family's once-royal image, and most of all the never-ending fascination with the Chappaquiddick affair. Kennedy stalwarts point out that in the campaign

---

*The changes in "Little Rhody's" state laws may be the surest signal in the entire nation that the era of ever-increasing big government has ended. For most of the twentieth century, Rhode Island has been a Catholic, working-class state in which unions and high taxes have been dominant and educational institutions (except for Brown University) less important. When the educationally based high-tech good times did not show up in Rhode Island, Garrahy and civic leaders offered the voters in 1984 a typical big-government solution—a "Greenhouse Compact," which would have used $250 million in state funds to help companies modernize the economy. But the people of Rhode Island apparently had little faith that their state government so notorious for corruption and deal making could help business and rejected the proposal 80 percent to 20 percent. Instead, Rhode Island got itself a Republican governor and reduced both taxes and the power of unions.

year 2000 Kennedy would be only 68 years old, younger than Ronald Reagan when he took office, but if he has any hopes left for the White House his only salvation would seem to lie in a public that has learned so much about the foibles of all its politicians it no longer judges them on this basis. Even if that happened, the fact that a young woman died in questionable circumstances on Chappaquiddick may still prove an insurmountable obstacle to winning the White House.

Edward Kennedy has, in fact, established a stronger legislative record than either of his brothers, John or Robert, perhaps because he has been in the Senate longer than they were. He has begun to move away—or perhaps beyond—automatic liberal positions, voting for the 1985 Gramm-Rudman amendment opposed by the Democratic leadership. In 1986, he chose to become chairman of the Labor and Human Resources Committee rather than Judiciary, which he chaired through 1980. In his new committee position, he abandoned his long-term goal of a full-scale government-run national health insurance scheme in favor of a campaign to require all businesses in America to offer health insurance to their employees and dependents. His chairmanship of Labor and Human Resources should also allow Kennedy to do what he does best: act as the nation's most eloquent defender of justice and fairness for poor people. Kennedy may have proven himself incapable of defending his own personal life in television interviews, but when speaking for others he can still be the best orator in the land.

A measure of the difference between the press corps' relationship with the Kennedys in the sixties and the eighties was the national scrutiny given to Joe Kennedy, son of Bobby, in his election to the Cambridge seat of retiring House Speaker Thomas P. (Tip) O'Neill. Young Kennedy's nonprofit company that bought wholesale oil and redistributed it to poor people was "more hype than heat," *The New Republic* commented, and his campaign "a repackaged legend for a third-generation Kennedy . . . a vast publicity machine . . . very big on the cult of personality." Kennedy's campaign appeared to be a throwback to the personal politics of his machine-style great grandfather, Honey Fitz, and steered away from the intellectual. A string of ideological candidates were prepared for Cambridge-style philosophical debates over peace, socialism, Jesse Jackson's Rainbow Coalition, gay rights, and the antinuclear movement, but once Kennedy was in the race the voters didn't seem to care. As liberals often forget, the Eighth District that encompasses Cambridge also contains thousands of blue-collar workers and widows and they elected Joe Kennedy by a landslide.

THE SPIRIT LIVES:
A NEW ENGLAND POSTSCRIPT

New England may be too small, too specialized, and too remote a corner of the United States to offer the nation a model of economic development or politics. But in matters of the spirit, Mother New England is still, more than any other place, the physical repository of American values. It is not that other parts of the United States are less democratic or less worthy, but in our frenzied, modern age of material ease, it is often easy to forget how hard it was for the Puritans to set out for these uncharted shores, light their moral flame, and sustain it. In New England, the Puritans' Plymouth Rock, the churches, and the revolutionary battlegrounds are there to remind us.

As twentieth-century Americans, we often joke about our Puritan background and have wisely abandoned much of their thinking, especially in personal behavior. But the early New Englanders also left us a positive legacy that has managed to become the very core of our ever-more-pluralistic society: self-reliance, hard work, and the belief, as Henry David Thoreau wrote, that the individual's first duty was "to live his life as his principles demand." The tradition of individualism and nonconformity that had given the culture its birth lived on, too—a perverse independence of mind that still makes American values admired the world over and attracts refugees and immigrants with the possibilities of freedom and economic opportunity. This independence would fan the flames of the American Revolution (starting with Massachusetts' famed Committee of Correspondence) and lead the Abolitionist cause in the years preceding the Civil War. The same spirit has evidenced itself in myriad forms straight down to the firm rejection of McCarthyism by New England senators like Margaret Chase Smith and Ralph Flanders, to the region's status as a center of the most vocal opposition to the Vietnam War, to Elliott

Richardson, the attorney general, who resigned his office rather than break his word and discharge Special Watergate Prosecutor Archibald Cox (another Massachusetts man).

In the Reagan eighties too there has been a New Englander who, as Ralph Waldo Emerson counseled, remained "a minority unconvinced." His name is Edward P. Boland, and he is the congressman from Springfield, Massachusetts who wrote the Boland Amendment, really a series of measures, that gave Congress the authority to investigate the Reagan administration's questionable dealings in Nicaragua and Iran. Boland was for 24 years the roommate of Representative and later Speaker Thomas P. (Tip) O'Neill. O'Neill made him his emissary to the Central Intelligence Agency, and it was his idea to create the congressional intelligence committees to oversee the spy agencies. Unlike many younger members of Congress, who have gone through the Vietnam War years, Boland was not easily moved to confront the administration on its Nicaraguan policies, but became outraged when he discovered in 1984 that the CIA had mined Nicaragua's harbors without informing either the House or Senate intelligence committees. Congress then decreed that no funds could be spent on the Contra war without its approval. The administration went forward with its private war, ultimately precipitating the crisis that threatened to ruin the last years of the Reagan presidency. To Boland, the question ultimately became whether the president and the National Security Council had to follow the law. Legal experts disagreed on whether the Boland Amendment could or should stand a constitutional test, but even if it did not, the spirit would.

In these same years, there has been the city council of Lowell, Massachusetts, which chose to build a memorial to Jack Kerouac, the Lowell native who rejected his New England Catholic working-class roots and the responsible life of the 1950s for marathon drives around the United States and trips by ship to foreign ports. Kerouac captured the imagination of his Eisenhower generation when he wrote, in *On the Road*, "The only ones for me are the mad ones, the ones who are mad to live, mad to talk, mad to be saved, desirous of everything at the same time, the ones who never yawn or say a commonplace thing, but burn, burn, burn like fabulous yellow roman candles exploding like spiders across the stars and in the middle you see the blue centerlight pop and everybody goes, 'Awww!' "

Kerouac was a tortured man who is rarely considered a New England writer in the tradition of the Protestant Yankees. It does seem a big stretch from Emerson and Thoreau, Transcendentalism, and the Abolitionist movement, and even Edward Boland, to Kerouac. But the connection is there. Kerouac is the product of a later generation after hundreds of thousands of immigrants and their children had threatened the homogeneity of Yankee culture but ended up unintentionally absorbing some of the Yankees' best and worst characteristics. Kerouac's writing is pure Americana, imbued with the Puritan independence of mind and the prospect of a full and open continent in front of him. And in his own way, Kerouac was a reformer like Emerson, Thoreau, and Harriet Beecher Stowe. As his biographer Charles Jarvis has said, "you've got to remember in the 1950s the country had fallen asleep and was snoring. The beats were like a breath of fresh air. They said this country had to move on now." Norman Podhoretz, the staunch Reaganite and editor of *Commentary*, tried to start a national campaign to oppose the memorial on the grounds that Kerouac had tried to undermine the very middle-class values for which Lowell stood. With only one city council member in opposition, the Lowell city council went ahead with its plans.

Except for those fans who think Kerouac would never have wanted such a symbol of acceptance by the establishment, the memorial will be welcomed by the hundreds of people who visit Lowell every year looking for Kerouac's grave and the homes where he lived. They come from all over the world, and to them Kerouac represents the freedom, possibility, and adventure of America.

Kerouac's writing and the actions of the Lowell City Council remind us that, as George Wilson Pierson has written, "The New England independence of mind is not dead. Nor is the New England conscience. . . . Just as the philosophy of the Greeks, or the laws laid down by the Romans, the moral attitudes of the New England culture persist, though the people who gave them birth have long since passed away." As the United States continues its southern and western development and grows ever more pluralistic, Lowell in the eighties is a good reminder that the best of the Puritan spirit still lives.

Index